ALSO BY JO SGAMMATO

Keepin' It Country: The George Strait Story

Dream Come True: The LeAnn Rimes Story

For the Music: The Vince Gill Story

Country's Greatest Duo: The Brooks & Dunn Story

American Thunder

American Thunder

THE GARTH BROOKS STORY

Jo Sgammato

BALLANTINE BOOKS
NEW YORK

A Ballantine Book
Published by The Ballantine Publishing Group

Copyright © 1999 by Jo Sgammato

http://www.randomhouse.com/BB/

Library of Congress Cataloging-in-Publication Data
Sgammato, Jo.
American thunder : the Garth Brooks story / Jo Sgammato. — 1st ed.
p. cm.
ISBN 0-345-43107-3 (hc : alk. paper)
1. Brooks, Garth. 2. Country musicians–United States Biography.
I. Title.
ML420.B7796S47   1999
782.421642'092—dc21
[B]   99-31747
CIP

Text design by BTDnyc

Manufactured in the United States of America

First Edition: July 1999
10 9 8 7 6 5 4 3 2 1

For Bubba—

he knows why

CONTENTS

AUTHOR'S NOTE

I have met Garth Brooks on a number of occasions and am always awed by his intensity and courtesy. Listening to his music and attending his live shows have given me hours of pleasure and excitement. Therefore, I was surprised, when doing the research for this bio, to read three separate books about the country music business, published in the past two years, with Garth's name or face on the cover, that were most unflattering to Garth. I think those books are part of the reason Garth's organization wouldn't let me interview him for this one.

I am a fan of Garth Brooks. I started out that way and, after researching him and talking to many other people who know him, I ended up respecting him even more. So if you're looking for another slam at one of the most phenomenal entertainers of all time, you're in the wrong book.

Garth Brooks is the reason I came to Nashville in the first place. My husband, Ira Fraitag, was asked to become vice president of a record label started by one of Garth's managers. Through that connection, I was privileged to meet Larry Jones and discover his great organization, Feed the Children, and to become friends with Garth's booking agent, Joe Harris.

I am grateful to all the people who sat down and shared their Garth Brooks stories and memories with me, including Pam Lewis, Allen Reynolds, J. D. Haas, Dewayne Blackwell, Shirley Harris, Joe Harris, Jr., Robert Metzgar, Ira Fraitag, Alan Mayor, Andrew Francis, Taya Branton, and Chuck and Rose Wheeler.

Garth is lucky to have friends in so many places, and music fans are lucky to have Garth.

ARTIST OF THE DECADE

*I*t happens only once every ten years.

The Academy of Country Music selects the artist deemed by its fifty-three-member board of directors to have been "most outstanding and successful and having best exemplified, through appearances and recordings, the image of country music during the decade."

In the 1960s, it was Marty Robbins. In the 1970s, it was Loretta Lynn. In the 1980s, it was Alabama.

In the Shrine Auditorium on May 5, 1999, the Academy of Country Music selected for this incredibly high honor a man most people hadn't even heard of ten years ago.

The thousands of industry insiders in the auditorium and the millions of fans watching the show at home weren't the least bit surprised when the 1990s Artist of the Decade award was announced.

Who else could it have been but Garth Brooks?

American Thunder

CHAPTER ONE

THE BOY

In February of 1962, according to the Census Bureau, 318,090 people were born in the United States. These babies entered the world with the potential to be or do anything. In America, a land of limitless opportunity where citizens were encouraged to reach for the sky, no dream was too big, no ambition unattainable.

Troyal Garth Brooks was born on the seventh day of February 1962, at St. John Medical Center in Tulsa, Oklahoma. In America's heartland, wheat grew tall, cowboys stood taller, and proud Native Americans kept the country's true history alive. Giant oil rigs gushed black gold, fueling the prosperity and peace that made dreaming possible.

Two weeks after Garth's birth, John Glenn safely orbited the earth three times and President John F. Kennedy traveled to NASA headquarters in Florida to personally welcome him home. Meanwhile, back in Washington, First Lady Jacqueline Kennedy was conducting the first nationally televised tour of the White House. From suburban New Jersey to rural Arkansas, the talk was of desegregation, as Martin Luther King, Jr., was spreading his dream. Overseas, the United States was expanding its military role in a country called Vietnam. And a "crisis of abundance," a surplus of agricultural products, including milk, led the government to pay farmers to produce less.

The proud parents on that seventh day of February 1962, Colleen Carroll Brooks and Troyal Raymond Brooks, had begun their lives together with a family that consisted of three of Colleen's children and one of Troyal's. Together they had been blessed with one son, Kelly, and now, eighteen months later, they completed their family with the birth of their last child. Two loving parents and six lucky children formed a household where the words *stepchildren, half brother,* and *half sister* were never used.

Tulsa was a town that loved music. Cain's Ballroom, over on Fourth and Main, was known as Western Swing's own Alamo. Cain's had been christened by the sounds of Bob Wills and His Texas Playboys, the swingin'est band in the West, which played there almost every Thursday and Saturday night from 1935 to 1943.

Bob Wills's unique style—a mix of everything from the blues to cowboy music, from Mexican mariachi to German polka, and from Dixieland jazz to pure bluegrass—did more than transform American music forever. It drew everyone at Cain's Ballroom to the curly maplewood dance floor mounted on sets of Dodge truck springs. Another attraction at Cain's in the 1930s and '40s was the availability of bootleg whiskey—Prohibition wasn't repealed in Oklahoma until 1957. Dancing and booze made for some wild times. When things got too rowdy, Bob Wills tapped the microphone with his fiddle bow and played a church hymn.

Colleen Brooks, Garth's mother, loved music herself. As Colleen Carroll, she'd been a featured singer on "Red Foley's Ozark Jubilee," the pioneering radio and television show. Her black curly hair draping down to her shoulders, a ribbon tied sweetly at the neckline of her fringed shirt, Colleen sang her heart out. Her strong, sweet, clear voice captured the attention of the folks at Capitol Records, where she recorded four singles in the mid-1950s. Her talent might have led to fame and fortune, but it was hard to be a female singer back then, and even harder if you were married and had children. Colleen loved music, but she loved family life even more.

Troyal Brooks, called Raymond by everyone who knew him, was a former U.S. marine. He worked as an engineer and draftsman for one of Tulsa's many oil companies, Union of California (Union 76).

The big city of Tulsa was exciting, but Colleen and Raymond wanted a quieter life for their family. In 1966 they moved to Yukon, a town of 10,000 residents about fifteen miles southeast of Oklahoma City. The ride from Tulsa to Oklahoma City was along America's most famous highway, a road of legend, music, and dreams—Route 66. Woody Guthrie's folk music, John Steinbeck's classic novels, and Jack Kerouac's amazing book *On the Road* all memorialized the lives that were spent, enjoyed, endured, and sometimes lost on Route 66. What a fitting backdrop for a future American hero.

Yukon sits squarely on the famous Chisholm Trail. Less than a mile from the Brookses' new home was a remnant of the trail where, in the late 1800s, more than a million longhorn cattle traveled from San Marcos, Texas, to railroad loading yards at Abilene, Kansas. This was cowboy country, pure and simple. It is also flat country with sweltering summers, frequent tornadoes, and winters that see fierce blizzards.

Over on Main Street in a town where kids could roam freely as long as they came home in time for supper, two-story brick and cinder-block buildings housed the town's businesses and stores. The MFC Farmers Co-op and Yukon's Best Flour Mill across the street were the tallest structures in town. Several blocks south of Main Street, at 408 Yukon Avenue, was the white split-level house where Garth Brooks grew up. From the street, the Brooks home looked like any other pleasant, quiet suburban home in 1960s America.

Inside was a different story. How quiet could it be with six kids running around, feeling free to play, laugh, enjoy life, and listen to music? As Garth would later say about the home he grew up in, it was "just totally cool. You could live in the house. You could try things, stretch your imagination." Like other households where the kids were encouraged to dream and allowed the freedom to falter, it was, he said, "a house you could make mistakes in."

Colleen and Raymond were serious about raising their children right. When the kids asked permission for something, the answers were clear: "yes" or "no." "Maybe" was not an option and "We'll see" generally meant no. Garth wasn't allowed to go out of his yard unless he asked his mom or dad. With all those older brothers and a big sister, who he says was tougher than any of the boys, Garth was surrounded by lots of love and plenty of protection.

The Brookses didn't have much money to spend on their children, but they gave them something more valuable—time and attention. Many evenings would find the whole bunch of them sitting around telling jokes. Raymond Brooks enjoyed picking the guitar and singing as a hobby. Jerry, Mike, and Betsy played the guitar too. Colleen still loved to sing songs like "Kansas City," "Lo Siento Mucho," and "Too-Ra-Loo-Ra-Loo-Ral" for this audience of her biggest fans. With Jim on harmonica and Garth and Kelly playing the waxpaper comb kazoo, the happy sounds of music filled the house.

But the most fun on those Brooks family "funny nights," as they were called, came when each kid took center stage to tell more jokes, do some solo singing, or devise a skit. Colleen says it was always Garth who would "come up with some of the darnedest stuff you ever heard in your life." Even at the age of two, Betsy said, Garth would "capture your attention." As the youngest of the six children, he got plenty of it.

If the game involved Kelly pretending to "shoot" Garth, Garth would take as long as he could to "die." As long as he could hold the attention of the family, he'd try to keep it.

Maybe that's why he was bold enough to repeat the words he'd often heard his dad say. Colleen says that Garth's first complete sentence was "I'm the boss around here." This from a man still in diapers.

Decades after he was in diapers, and long after he'd become one of the biggest stars in the history of American entertainment, Garth Brooks surprised everyone by putting on a baseball jersey and joining the 1999 spring training camp of the San Diego Padres. Snorting doubters all over America wondered what made Garth think he could play baseball. Well, his love for all sports started in Yukon, first in the backyard, where Raymond taught his sons about football, baseball, and being team players. Garth learned about competition—particularly competition with himself. He played on the Little League teams his dad coached. Right back then, he began developing the competitive instincts and belief in his own talents that would sustain him when it looked as if he'd never achieve his dream of a career in music.

Garth credits his mother with giving him permission to have unlimited dreams and his father with giving him frequent doses of reality. Raymond set standards of perfection, and Colleen said, "Hey, a mistake is okay if you tried your best."

At Central Elementary School on Oak Avenue and Seventh Street, Garth learned to read and write. In second grade, he became friends with a guy named Mickey Weber.

Garth's third-grade teacher, Pearl Kinsey, said, "I never had a discipline problem with Garth. He was a very good boy. The only problem I had was I couldn't keep all the little girls away from Garth." LaDawna Urton, his fourth-grade teacher, said that after he participated in a school talent show she knew he was destined for stardom.

"Anyone who can pat their head, rub their tummy, dance, and sing a jingle about a Fig Newton will make it far in the entertainment world," Urton said. Perhaps one of the things those Oklahoma schoolgirls loved about the young Garth Brooks was his unabashed love of music and his delight in sharing that love with anyone who would listen.

People listened to all kinds of music at the Brooks home, where dozens of kids came to the scores of parties the family loved to host for Halloween, Christmas, birthdays, and often for no reason at all. Garth's mom loved Harry Belafonte's captivating Caribbean rhythms. Raymond had Johnny Horton's *Greatest Hits* album, Merle Haggard's *Swinging Doors,* and *The Best of George Jones.* The age range in the household—Garth's oldest brother was fifteen years his senior—meant that Garth was exposed to music of many eras. He heard Peter Paul and Mary, Tom Rush, and Arlo Guthrie. His sister Betsy loved Rita Coolidge and Janis Joplin and Janis Ian. Of course, the family often tuned in to the Grand Ole Opry broadcasts from Nashville's famed Ryman Auditorium and later from Opryland.

When Garth was about ten years old, one of his older brothers bought a James Taylor album. Garth probably didn't actually put the record on the turntable, but James Taylor's music entered his ears on an almost daily basis. Years later, he and the world would discover just how strong a connection had been made from the soul of James Taylor to the heart of Garth Brooks.

That heart was touched in another way on December 31, 1972, when he heard the tragic news that baseball player

Roberto Clemente had been killed in a plane crash while flying to Nicaragua to deliver supplies and humanitarian aid to earthquake victims. Clemente, born in Carolina, Puerto Rico, in 1934, had been a star right fielder for eighteen years with the Pittsburgh Pirates. He led the league in batting four times during the 1960s. A few months after his death, Clemente became the first Latin American player to be elected into the Major League Baseball Hall of Fame.

Roberto Clemente Sports City was established a few years later in Puerto Rico, with a museum dedicated to Clemente, facilities for a variety of sports, and many counseling and rehabilitation programs. The facility serves as a recreational area, but it is really a launching pad to a better life for many Latin Americans.

It's easy to see why Clemente became a hero to the young Garth Brooks—and fueled Garth's own dream to excel, to help people in need, and to leave his mark on the world.

At Yukon High School, Garth's passion was sports. "I really stunk at sports," he said, "but that's what I wanted to do."

Garth played for the Millers, Yukon High's football team. He was a distance runner on the track team. Raymond and Colleen attended almost every one of their kids' games and other school events, Raymond taking time off from work for what mattered most to him.

As Garth was growing up, the farming town of Yukon was becoming more suburban, like thousands of small towns across America. The mom-and-pop businesses were being replaced by national chains. But Rick's Donuts, a coffee shop on Main Street just across from the bowling alley, stayed in business. Garth loved to walk over to Rick's for the delicious, fresh-baked sweet rolls.

In the ninth grade, Garth played a lot of music with his friends. His first acoustic guitar was a Gibson, which he played at first with only three strings, adding strings as he learned to play better "to keep from killing my fingers." Then he got an electric guitar and an amplifier. For his sixteenth birthday, Garth was given a banjo. That got him interested in bluegrass, so he formed a bluegrass band. In his senior year, he sang in one of the school's vocal clubs. He started another band called The Nyle with his good friend Mickey Weber, but as Weber's mother Jacque said later, the other kids in the band gave up. Garth, however, began to say music was something he was going to put his mind to.

Garth appreciated the pure country sounds of Merle Haggard and George Jones. He especially loved Billy Joel and Elton John. He was a huge fan of Dan Fogelberg. Disco was hot, the Eagles were soaring, and the lines between country, pop, and rock were blurring every day. Even with all of the rock music dominating the airwaves, it was kind of hip to be square and to like country music. Groups like Poco, Pure Prairie League, and the Byrds were combining southern rock with traditional country. In the seventies, rock and roll radio played a huge variety of music—some of which would surely be called country today. The hard-rock groups KISS and Queen could often be heard blasting from Garth's stereo, and when he went to a Queen concert for the first time in Oklahoma City (he's still got the ticket stub), he noticed how great it felt when Freddie Mercury seemed to look straight at him from the stage.

When Garth first heard Don McLean's epic "American Pie," he was hooked on the song, which told of a generation's journey through the worlds of politics and music.

Raymond Brooks brought Garth a poem called "The Man in the Glass" and hung it in Garth and Kelly's bedroom. It was an amazing bit of foresight on his part—telling his son that you're not a success until the man in the glass looks at you and says you are. Be true to yourself, Raymond was telling Garth, and the rest will fall into place.

Garth was popular in high school. He enjoyed being the center of attention. He didn't date until he was sixteen, and then, he says, he "went from one girl to another." He was vice president of his freshman class and senior homecoming king. Can't you just see Garth Brooks escorting the homecoming queen into the prom? He even had the guts to do something most teenage boys wouldn't want to be caught dead doing.

The Future Homemakers of America club had begun a campaign to convince young men to take home economics courses. Garth accompanied Yukon High's home-ec teacher, Pam Sheldon, to some speaking engagements. "Garth said, 'Guys, it's okay to be in home ec and to be in FHA chapters,'" Pam Sheldon says, adding that Garth was always easygoing and well mannered, one of those guys who got along with everyone.

Yukon High football coach Milt Bassett reluctantly asked Garth to give up his position as starting quarterback on the Millers in his senior year. The coach wanted a junior to take that spot and have time to develop into a stronger player. Garth agreed. Bassett thought it "took a lot for a young man to give up the starting quarterback position and still play for the team."

Even with the time he spent on music and sports—and on his part-time job reading water meters for the city of Yukon—Garth got good grades in high school. Education was important to the Brookses, and all of Garth's brothers had gone to college. (His sister Betsy went to college for one day and didn't like it.) Garth was accepted into Oklahoma State University in Stillwater (remember that name) before he graduated from high school in the spring of 1980. His brother Kelly was already there on a track scholarship. Garth got a sports scholarship as well, a nice break for a family with two kids in college at the same time. No doubt it was also nice for the Brookses that OSU was only an hour and a half's drive from Yukon.

Music filled the corridors of Iba Hall, the athletic dormitory at Oklahoma State University where Garth roomed with his brother Kelly. The hauntingly rich and beautiful voice that has now enthralled millions around the world grew and developed in that dorm as he jammed with his fellow students, playing whatever songs captured his musical imagination. All of that singing and playing paid off when Garth was elected to represent Iba Hall in a talent show at the Student Union's Little Theatre in April of his sophomore year. For playing a few songs by Dan Fogelberg, Garth walked away with the $50 first prize.

Garth became a regular player at the OSU Student Union on Friday nights during the "Aunt Molly's Rent-Free Music Emporium." With his friend Dale Pierce, who loved bluegrass and folk music, and another pal, Jim Kelley, a graduate-assistant hurdler coach at OSU, Garth would perform in the children's ward at Stillwater Medical Center.

With Dale and Jim, Garth formed a group called Dakota Blue. The three musicians were great together—writing songs and playing constantly in Iba Hall and anywhere else they could—and it seemed they might have a shot at something big. Then something happened that nearly crushed Garth: Jim Kelley was killed when a small plane in which he was a passenger crashed near Stillwater Airport.

Another person Garth met and played music with at OSU was Ty England, a guitar player. Ty and Garth played really well together—and promised each other that whoever got a break first would bring the other one along for the ride.

Garth was working on his guitar playing—with great results—and writing songs as well. His performances at and around OSU had the same effect on girls as Garth had in high school: they loved him! The fact that Garth didn't have a steady girlfriend at the time only made the college girls more enamored of his charms onstage.

Most performers will tell you that at a certain point the response of listeners to their music becomes as vital to the experience as the playing itself—perhaps more so. As fans, we know the rush we get while watching and hearing music, feeling it move our bodies and touch our hearts. The energy that gets stirred up in us reflects back onto the performer, who becomes enveloped in the love and joy of whatever number of people he's reaching with his song. If it's a thrilling experience for fans, imagine what it must feel like for the performer up on the stage.

There at Aunt Molly's or at the many campus parties where he was often asked to play, Garth Brooks got a taste of the power of his music to move people, to bring out their emotions. The more of that feedback he experienced, the more he strived to make his music stronger, more direct, a deeper call to the hearts of his listeners.

A call came into Garth's own heart in the summer of 1981. As he was driving to the store with his father, the radio was playing a song called "Unwound" by a singer Garth—and most everyone else, for that matter—had never heard of. His name was George Strait.

Throughout the late 1970s, while Garth Brooks was in high school discovering rock and pop and heavy-metal music, George Strait was struggling to get Nashville—the center of country music—to give him a record deal. Strait had grown up in Pearsall, Texas, south of San Antonio in the brush country where the land is flat and dry and the sky is vast and blue. The longhorn cattle that were brought up the Chisholm Trail through Oklahoma had been brought to Strait's South Texas ranch country a century earlier.

George Strait was a genuine cowboy. As he put it, "About the time most young men were playing Little League baseball, I was learning to rope and ride." Strait discovered his love for playing and singing genuine American country music—notably the songs of Bob Wills and His Texas Playboys—while in the army, stationed in Hawaii in the early 1970s. He returned home to attend Southwest Texas State University in San Marcos and with some fellow college musicians formed the Ace in the Hole Band. These guys tore up every country music bar in the area.

Guys loved George Strait because he was a tall, cool cowboy. Girls loved George because he was so good-looking and charming. Music fans loved what he was playing. But Nashville didn't love him at all when he first came to town seeking a record deal. Here was a great singer with a great band playing real country music—and Music City in the late 1970s dismissed him as being "too country." It wasn't that people didn't think he was good, it was just that Nashville was going through a time when pop music's influence on country was strong.

Finally, in 1979, when Strait was about ready to quit music and take a job with a cattle pen outfit in Uvalde, Texas, MCA Records gave him the kind of deal cautious record companies were trying in those days—a deal for a single. If the single became a hit, MCA would agree to release a George Strait album.

That single was "Unwound." The song became a hit for George Strait, which is something all country music fans are grateful for. One fan is even more grateful. Garth turned up the radio in his daddy's car and listened intently to the song.

"All of a sudden, it hit me," Garth says. "It was like, 'My God, I love this sound. That's it! That's what I'm gonna do!'"

By this time, music was center stage in the life of Garth Brooks. He continued to run track, but with his heart and his interests elsewhere, he didn't particularly distinguish himself there. He became a javelin thrower, hurling the light metal spear distances that never much exceeded two hundred feet. In later interviews, Garth would refer to himself as more of a javelin catcher than a thrower. He did win a medal at the Kansas Relays.

"Athletics was a way to keep my interest in school," he says. It became clear to those who knew him that Garth's music was the passion that drove him. Sports fans might wish their favorite teams had someone with Garth Brooks's drive and passion, but it wasn't to be. Music fans, needless to say, are thrilled Garth turned his attention from sports to his other passion.

From Aunt Molly's and campus parties, Garth moved to his first real paying gig as a musician: Shotgun Sam's Pizza Parlor in Oklahoma City near an air force base. He played there four nights a week for five or six hours a night in 1982, earning $175 a week—and still had to pay for his own pizza. Still, doing that solo gig with his guitar and banjo gave him experience playing to a live audience that we all appreciate today.

The crowd was a little restless in Willie's Saloon. But they quieted down when a young man wearing sweatpants, a T-shirt, and a baseball cap took the stage. Many of them had already heard about this musician who was wowing folks wherever he had the chance to play.

Willie's Saloon, with its redbrick and wood-plank exterior, is on the section of Washington Street known in Stillwater as "The Strip." All the usual college-town businesses are there—restaurants, clothing stores, and bookstores. Bars with names like Coney Island and the Turning Point—and even one called Nuevo Wavo—were quieter now that the state of Oklahoma had raised the drinking age to twenty-one, but they were still busy enough to have live music. Dollye and Bill Bloodworth ran Willie's and paid the young singer $100 for a four-hour set. The folks sitting at the bar had a bird's-eye view of the small stage around the corner from the entrance and just past the two pool tables.

With a mustache, a full beard, and shoulder-length hair, Garth Brooks played a set that couldn't be characterized as any one type of music. He went from a Willie Nelson tune to a Neil Young song. He paid homage to his musical heroes, James Taylor, Dan Fogelberg, and Billy Joel. Someone requested a song he'd heard only a few times, so he improvised it. Someone else called out the name of a song he'd never heard, and he tried to play it anyway. As the evening wore on and the beer kept flowing, people came up onstage and sang with him. Like every musician trying to please a crowd while still furthering his own musical dreams, between cover songs he snuck in a few he'd written himself. Willie's wasn't exactly a major musical venue, but it was a good place to start. And from the start, Garth Brooks took the stage seriously.

He was going to lots of concerts, seeing everyone from Kansas, Queen, and Styx to his country idol, George Strait, and observing what made each concert memorable. Elaborate stage settings, sound, and lights appealed to him. But so did the way George Strait simply stood at a microphone, making his own voice the star, backed by the great Ace in the Hole Band.

Garth ended his show with one of the songs he loved best. The audience sang "American Pie" along with him.

It was nice to be paid a hundred bucks to play music. In addition to Willie's, Garth played at any Stillwater nightspots that would have him. "Every club was a different type of music," he says. "I had a repertoire of three hundred and fifty songs—everything from Slim Whitman to Elton John."

But the gigs weren't regular, and even when he played a few nights a week it still was tough to make ends meet. So in addition to trying to keep up with his college courses, Garth needed a job.

DuPree's Sports Equipment store, across the street from Willie's, was owned by Eddie Watkins. Watkins and his wife, Ann, had taken a liking to Garth's music and loved his shows. Eddie Watkins realized Garth was struggling, so he offered him a job in the store.

Garth was majoring in advertising in college (he thought he'd learn about writing jingles as a way to make money with music). He had a great way with people, re-membered their names, gave customers extra service, and was an asset to Watkins's business. Working at DuPree's gave Garth a chance to hone his people skills—skills that would become considerably greater as the years wore on. As for re-calling people's names, maybe learning the lyrics to all the songs he sang onstage had something to do with Garth's su-perior memorization skills.

He wasn't afraid to work hard, and his energy seemed to have no limits. That's why Garth Brooks took yet another job during his senior year at OSU—as a bouncer at the Tumble-weed Ballroom, about seven miles west of town on Country Club Road.

It was here that Garth, who had never been a drinker to begin with, developed his disgust for alcohol. There's nothing like the smell of a bar where patrons have been drink-ing—and you-know-what-elsing—all night. Working as a bouncer in clubs—and cleaning up when the night was through—Garth came to hate that smell.

But the job was cool—he got to hang out with his friends and listen to a lot of music. Most of the customers wanted to pick on the bigger guys (Garth is six feet one, but in Okla-homa there are plenty of guys bigger than that), so he didn't get into too many fights. He danced a lot, played pool, and had fun.

When passing through Oklahoma, many national acts stopped in to play for the folks at the Tumbleweed. The lo-cals who loved to get out and hear some good music filled the large metal building on Friday and Saturday nights. Plenty of OSU students also made their way to the Tumble-weed, including Sandy Mahl.

Sandy Gail Mahl was born in 1965 in the same hospital where Garth Brooks had been born almost three years earlier. She grew up in Owasso, Oklahoma, a city half the size of Yukon just north of Tulsa. Sandy's parents, John and Pat Mahl, had raised her and her older sister, Debbie, to do their chores—which included taking care of all the family's animals—and to go to church each Sunday. Growing up, Sandy loved the outdoors. In high school she ran track, was a cheerleader, and played basketball, activities that took a lot of discipline and commitment. Sandy promised her mother she would go to college and made good on that promise, arriving at OSU in the fall of 1983. Like so many other young girls experi-encing their first real freedom away from home, she spent her freshman year of college partying.

Sandy Mahl had noticed the new bouncer at the Tum-bleweed. She'd seen him surrounded by all the girls who loved to flirt with him. The young musician was a charmer, but he didn't have a steady girl—he was pretty single-minded about his music.

As a bouncer, there was no telling what scuffles Garth might have to deal with on any given night. Still, he had to be surprised one evening in 1984 when he was asked to straighten out a situation going on in, of all places, the ladies' room.

Sandy Mahl and another girl had gotten into a pretty heated argument concerning—what else?—a guy. The argument escalated and Sandy warned the other girl she might have to hurt her, but the girl would not back off. So Sandy hauled off, prepared to throw a punch, and instead stuck her fist through the wood-paneled wall of the rest room in the Tumbleweed Ballroom.

As if that weren't bad enough, she couldn't pull her hand back out.

And that is the way Sandy Mahl looked the first time Garth Brooks laid eyes on her. In her tight black jeans, black shirt, and a black cowboy hat, with her blond hair tousled from all the excitement, she looked good to Garth. So good, in fact, that after he delicately removed her arm from the wall, he told her the club's policy was that they couldn't let her leave by herself, since she'd had a few drinks. He convinced her to wait for him until he finished his night's work. He said he would see her home.

"I don't believe in love at first sight," Garth said, "but there was something there."

Garth drove Sandy back to campus. When he discovered they lived in neighboring dorms, Garth told Sandy his roommate was away and asked her to come up to his room. She told him to drop dead after calling him a few choice words. Garth took Sandy to the elevator at her own dormitory, and the two said good night. Garth thought she was pretty cool.

He called her the next morning, and they spent the day together. At first their dates consisted of walking around the beautiful OSU campus holding hands. Some time later, they started going to the movies together. The first movie they saw was *Starman*.

When Garth failed to qualify for the Big Eight track and field finals that year, he realized he hadn't been putting his all into sports. He was lying in the pole vault pit when a coach walked by and said the words that changed his life: "Now you can get to doing what you're supposed to do." Garth knew he was supposed to do music. And he knew with music he could say, "Maybe I'm not a loser." It was at that moment that Garth knew what he'd be putting his all into.

Garth decided to create a demo tape of some of his songs. The demo tape is the ticket inside any doors in the music business—if you're lucky enough to get any of those doors to open. Music business executives—and anyone remotely connected to them or working in any part of the business—are always handed new demos to listen to, songs by aspiring singers or songwriters who dream of the big break that will turn them into stars. For managers, agents, and A & R (artist and repertoire) people, all the nice talk, sold-out local club dates, appealing head shots, and giant plans don't amount to a hill of beans next to what really counts—the music. Garth knew that short of getting a powerful music business executive to come hear him live, a great demo tape was the only way he could prove he had talent.

To create his first demo, Garth managed to get himself into a real recording studio in Stillwater. He assembled several musicians from a country band in Claremore, Okla-

homa, and a few female backup vocalists. They spent an entire weekend creating a tape with some of his original songs,
the ones Garth considered his best.

In the summer of 1984, representatives from the Opryland Hotel in Nashville held open auditions in Oklahoma
to find musicians to sing in the various theaters and attractions in their amusement park just east of downtown
Nashville. After the folks from Music City heard Garth sing,
they offered him a job singing popular country standards at
Opryland. Garth had only one semester of college left. He
told his parents he wanted to move to Nashville and pursue
his dream of making it as a country singer. Colleen begged
him not to go. She said she wanted her son to get a "real
job." Raymond insisted that Garth finish college. Garth
turned down the job and finished school. Nashville would
have to wait a little longer.

By December of 1984, Garth Brooks and Sandy Mahl
were a couple and Garth had finished up all of the credits he
needed to get his bachelor of science degree in advertising
from the Oklahoma State University School of Journalism.
He gave his mother his graduation tassel, as his older brothers had done, and asked for her blessing to pursue a career
in music. She withheld it but promised to pray for him, remembering how hard the entertainment business had been
on her.

Garth wasn't thinking of how hard it would be to become
a big country music star. Maybe he should have been: after
all, when he graduated from college the number-one song in
America was "Like a Virgin" by Madonna.

In the summer of 1985, Garth Brooks packed all of his
stuff into his Honda Accord and took his dream east on Interstate 40. It was a twelve-hour drive straight to the heart of
the country music business: Nashville, Tennessee.

His local audiences thought he had a chance. Folks at the shows in Stillwater had passed the hat to give Garth a few extra bucks for his journey. He told everyone he was going to Nashville to become a star in the country music business. He gave up his apartment in Stillwater and quit his job at DuPree's.

Garth would admit later he was even ready to walk away from his relationship with Sandy. He figured he'd go to Nashville and become a swinging bachelor with tons of bucks. Nothing mattered except making it in Nashville. He drove nonstop to Music City, listening to tapes of James Taylor and Chris LeDoux, listening to the beating of his own excited heart.

"*I* came to Nashville thinking that opportunity just hung on trees," Garth said, "and that all I had to do was take out my guitar and strum and sing."

He wasn't the first guy to arrive in Music City with a heart full of dreams and a head full of illusions. The highways into Nashville are jammed with talented singers, songwriters, and players hoping their moment has come. It hadn't occurred to Garth that music was a business. After all, he hadn't exactly been making a fortune—or even a living, for that matter—playing music.

Garth did have an advantage when he came to town— an appointment with Merlin Littlefield, who was the director of ASCAP, the American Society of Composers, Authors and Publishers.

Littlefield listened to Garth's demo tape. You know how lucky he was to get someone of Littlefield's stature to even listen to his tape?

Garth was waiting to hear the words every artist spent hours dreaming about, the words he'd no doubt prayed for on the whole ride from Stillwater to Nashville.

Instead he heard Littlefield say, "You've got a choice. You either starve as a songwriter or get five people and starve as a band." Garth sat there and listened to Littlefield talk about the realities of the country music business. The words "you've got a deal" were nowhere to be heard.

While Garth was in Littlefield's office, Littlefield received a call. He hung up the phone and said, "You're going to see one of the greatest writers in Nashville." Then the guy—a songwriter Garth had actually heard of—came into the office and said he was having trouble paying off a $500 loan.

Now Garth was really stunned. "I make more than that in a week back home."

"Go back home," Littlefield replied.

Garth went back to the Holiday Inn near Music Row. He left Nashville within twenty-three hours of his arrival, feeling, he said later, like a whipped pup. He stopped in Arkansas and called Sandy and told her, "I'm coming home." She was as confused as Garth by what had happened, but glad he was coming back. But Garth didn't go straight to Stillwater, where all his friends and well-wishers would no doubt have been as disappointed as he was. Instead he went home to Yukon, where Colleen did her best to comfort him. "It wasn't failure," she said about Garth's disappointing experience in Nashville. "He just didn't know the ins and outs." What a great mom—and one who knew better than most moms how tough the music business was.

"I pulled into Nashville expecting to see my name on every water tower around the place," Garth said. "I thought the world was waiting for me, but there's nothing colder than reality."

In June of 1985, the world was rumbling. There were hostilities between Iran and Iraq, unrest in Nicaragua and San Salvador, tensions between the United States and Israel over how to deal with the hijacking of a TWA flight from Athens by Lebanese terrorists, and controversy in Washington over military spending for such items as a $432 hammer. Tornadoes and earthquakes were shaking the country—hitting in such unlikely places as New York and Pennsylvania, and causing significant damage.

Madonna and Bruce Springsteen, along with the artist then called Prince, were at the top of the musical charts. But another event taking place in 1985 would play a major role in Garth Brooks's future.

Sam Walton decided to change the cash registers in his Wal-Mart stores from old-fashioned ones to computerized ones. When he did that, he discovered that his previous estimates of how well country music was selling in his stores had been way off. To make a long story short, the formula retailers use to calculate the profitability of merchandise showed country music was doing three times as well as Walton had previously believed. Rock music, on the other hand, was less profitable than he'd thought it was. With that discovery, Walton upped the amount of country music offered in the stores and lowered the amount of rock.

Garth was miserable. But his mood didn't stay that way for too long. He returned to Stillwater after a few weeks of licking his wounds in Yukon and found out his old place was still available for rent. He got his job back at DuPree's Sports. The crowd at Willie's Saloon was thrilled to have Garth's great music back for themselves. His friends were just as happy to see him as if he had made it big in Nashville. That helped ease the pain. And though it took a little coaxing, he even won back the heart of the woman he loved, Sandy Mahl.

It was okay. He played lots of music and had a good time. But the dream of bigger stardom wouldn't die. Ed and Ann Watkins over at DuPree's even had T-shirts made up that said "Garth Brooks World Tour." Garth was taking orders and selling the shirts, learning early on about merchandise and music.

"I've always felt that success is how you deal with failure," he said later. His energy, optimism, and determination were bigger than his disappointment.

Garth's home was a typical college apartment in a house just a few blocks away from the OSU campus. The floor was crooked, the ceiling was cracked, and the kitchen faucet leaked. Garth hung a picture of John Wayne on the wall. Songbooks from everyone from George Strait to Bob Seger were all over the living room.

But it was from this old house at the young age of twenty-four that Garth Brooks launched his plan to get the experience he needed to conquer the music business and achieve his dream.

That dream was of more than a career in music. He wanted to connect with people in a special way. He'd seen firsthand from the small stage at Willie's what effect his music could have—not just on a crowd but on each person in that crowd. The feeling he gave was tremendous. What he got back was just plain addictive.

To play a lot of music, Garth needed a good band. Tom Skinner, who had grown up in Bristow, Oklahoma, was a bass player who had formed a group with his brothers. The Skinner Brothers Band had recorded nine original songs in Tulsa but hadn't landed a record deal. By August of 1983, Tom was married and he and his wife Jeri had a child. Tom and his brother, Mike, both got jobs in the Stillwater post office and continued performing on the Strip in Stillwater, where Garth often sat in with them.

When Garth decided to form his own band he convinced Tom to join him, promising him they wouldn't go on the road so Tom could be home with his family.

Then he recruited Jed Lindsay, who hailed from Bartlesville, Oklahoma, to join the band as lead guitarist. Jed had formed a rock group called Bliss and taken the band to Tulsa, opening for the big acts that came through to play at Cain's Ballroom. Later, Jed played with Rocking Horse, featuring Ronnie Dunn, who would later become half of country's greatest duo, Brooks & Dunn. He also performed at the Cornucopia Club in West Tulsa, where Betsy Smittle, Garth's sister, was a singer and bass player.

Couldn't have a band without a drummer. Matt O'Meilia lived just a few doors down from Garth. He was surprised when Garth knocked on his door one day and invited him to join the band. O'Meilia considered himself a rock and roll purist. Playing in a country music band—which was what he thought Garth was asking him to do—was not in his plans. But when Garth explained that the band would be playing all kinds of music, covering artists from James Taylor to Bob Seger to George Strait, Matt decided he'd give it a try.

On a Friday night in April 1986, Bink's was hopping. Mac Overholt had opened Bink's after running two other successful clubs in Stillwater. Bandalero's—where a bathtub full of salty peanuts kept the crowd thirsty—was followed by Cattle Country, where Garth sometimes played solo gigs. When Mac decided, along with Edmund "Bink" Simank, to open a bigger club closer to downtown and away from the Strip, he needed some entertainment to draw the college crowd. So he told Garth he could have the gig as house band. By that Friday night in April the band—which Garth called Santa Fe for no reason that anyone could figure out—was ready to make its world premiere.

The stage was about ten times as big as the one at Willie's. And the dance floor, surrounded by a wooden fence, was huge. As soon as Santa Fe started playing, the floor filled up with two-steppin' couples who, like those in most dance bars, were more interested in each other than in the music. Like the music coming from the stage, the audience was of a mixture of ages and backgrounds—sorority and fraternity members, cowboys, older couples. Garth's pals from DuPree's Sports were there, as was his new fiancée, Sandy Mahl.

Garth played his round-backed Ovation guitar while harmonizing with Tom. Jed played lead in his uniquely exciting style. Matt on drums was a little tentative at first but got into it as the night wore on. To give some variety to the show, Tom Skinner took the microphone with a couple of songs by popular singer/songwriter Rodney Crowell, while Garth stood behind playing the bass. It wasn't a bad first gig. It was a great display of Garth's range. Rock, pop, and even "The Tennessee Waltz" rang through the big new club.

Tom Skinner remembers that Garth "wanted to be an entertainer and a hero to people and music was the way to get there."

Matt O'Meilia later wrote a book about his experiences playing with Garth's first band, called *The Road Out of Santa Fe*. It's a wonderful story of all the ups and downs and often hilarious adventures of young musicians playing their hearts out and actually making enough of a living to survive in a college town in the mid-1980s. O'Meilia describes seeing Garth perform onstage close up from his seat behind the drums and being amazed by the intensity and wonder that Garth seemed to feel.

"His face and his entire body were in perpetual motion," O'Meilia writes. "He walked, he jogged, he strutted with mock heavy-metal bravado . . . his every emotion naked."

That evening was the beginning of more shows just like it. Bluegrass, gospel, Gene Autry classics—whatever the crowd wanted to hear, Santa Fe would play. In the process, Garth Brooks was developing that amazing voice, a voice that could sound like anyone else, a voice that always sounded distinctive as well.

It was at Bink's that Garth and Santa Fe played the only original song they ever played in their sets full of covers—one that Garth had written with a friend, rodeo rider Randy Taylor. The song was called "Much Too Young (To Feel This Damn Old)."

The lyrics refer to "a worn-out tape of Chris LeDoux." On his twelve-hour ride from Stillwater to Nashville for his one-day lesson in the harsh realities of the music business, Garth had almost worn out his own Chris LeDoux tape. It's easy to see why Garth was so enamored of LeDoux—a great musician whose first big accomplishment was winning the horseback-riding championship (and being runner-up in the bull-riding competition) at the national finals of the Little Britches Rodeo when he was just fourteen. That set him on the path to becoming famous on the rodeo circuit. As a junior in college, he joined the Professional Rodeo Championship Association.

Being born in Biloxi, Mississippi, and raised in Austin, Texas, gave LeDoux his love of music. He wrote rodeo songs in college, making his first records in a basement studio, then went on to record twenty-two albums over twenty years as an independent artist. These albums included every old cowboy song he could find as well as more than a hundred songs he wrote himself. His concerts were incredibly popular. His stage performance was wild and free.

Soon after that first gig at Bink's, Garth convinced Tom Skinner's brother Mike to join the group. Mike was a great fiddle player who had honed his chops down in Lake Charles, Louisiana, not with a group but playing alone in his apartment after working all day as a pipe fitter. Mike's great voice harmonized with Garth's, and his fiddle playing lent a distinctive country accent to whatever the band was playing.

The band was playing a lot. But on May 24, 1986, Santa Fe's founder and lead singer was busy, so they took the weekend off. In a small ceremony in Owasso, Oklahoma, Sandy Mahl and Garth Brooks were married as their happy families looked on. If the newlyweds took a honeymoon it was a short one, because Santa Fe was back on the Bink's stage the following Saturday night.

Sandy and Garth's house on South Duck Street—the same house Matt O'Meilia had been living in when Garth invited him to be his drummer—was painted bright yellow with white trim and had a small but inviting front porch. O'Meilia reports that in the winter the house's old heating system made the upstairs sweltering hot and the downstairs freezing cold. But the young couple was happy there, finding among the many things they had in common a love for breakfast cereal and sweets, especially Coca-Cola.

The band hadn't been together a month when Garth got them booked on a local morning show, *A.M. Oklahoma.* Few are the musicians who appreciate having to be up at the crack of dawn for any reason, but this TV appearance could only help Santa Fe, as the already savvy Garth Brooks well knew. In addition to the show's regular audience, all of the band's friends and family tuned in to watch.

They couldn't help but be delighted by what they saw. First of all, the folks from DuPree's Sports saw Garth wearing a ball cap with their logo on it. Nice touch, Garth! Santa Fe began their morning set with Charlie Daniels's "Drinking My Baby Goodbye." After some chitchat with the host—in which

Garth managed to sneak in another plug for DuPree's—Santa Fe played a great rendition of George Strait's "Nobody in His Right Mind."

The appearance on *A.M. Oklahoma* only made Santa Fe more popular. Even better, Bink's was booking some of the biggest acts in country music during the summer of 1986, people like Steve Earle, Johnny Paycheck, and the New Grass Revival, among others. Santa Fe got to open for all of them. Like many new bands, they hoped to outplay the headliners. Whether they did or not, the idea made them stretch their talents and strive even harder to be great.

One of the big acts that Santa Fe opened for was Dwight Yoakam. Yoakam was a dozen years older than Garth and was headlining around the country in small clubs and medium-size venues after the release of his first album, *A Town South of Bakersfield,* and his highly acclaimed 1986 *Guitars, Cadillacs, Etc. Etc.* Born in the coal-mining area of Kentucky, Yoakam had started to write music at the age of eight.

Yoakam spent a few years in Nashville in the mid-seventies, but it wasn't until he went to California in 1977 that he found the inspiration that would make him stand out from the pack. The Bakersfield sound, made famous by Buck Owens, got a new interpretation from the young Yoakam and the emerging audience for the fusion of country and rock.

After seeing the excitement Yoakam could generate with his show, Garth looked at Santa Fe and said, "There it is. There's our show." From that moment, he knew he could combine the best of a rockin' show with a country music feel.

Santa Fe also played at the Tumbleweed Ballroom—where Garth had once been a bouncer and was now the headliner—and the Cimarron Country Ballroom. At the Cimarron, seven miles south of Stillwater, an older crowd of ranchers and businessmen was getting hooked on the sounds of Garth Brooks and Santa Fe. Garth tailored the song selections to the age and apparent interests of the crowd, creating the show as he went along, pulling from the seemingly endless list of songs whose lyrics he knew by heart.

Even with all of this work, Garth still played at Willie's at least one night a week, as a solo act.

Local bands play local clubs and honky-tonks all the time throughout America. Maybe some of them are just happy to be there, playing their music, making a small living, having a good time, being part of a constant party. Maybe some of the guys in Santa Fe felt the same way. But not all of them. Garth Brooks was having a ball, to be sure, but he still was looking east with reverence all the time, planning his return to the promised land of Nashville. Between sets he went out and mingled with the audience. While the other guys in the band were out in the parking lot taking a break, Garth would be in the middle of the crowd, shaking hands and talking to people. Between gigs all he wanted to do was play some more.

And all the while in those little clubs, he dreamed about playing in the big arenas like his rock and roll heroes.

Tulsa City Limits! If it isn't the best country music and dance club in America, it's sure up there with the best. And it was definitely the hot place to play in Tulsa. For its first year, it was a rock club—until country music became cooler than rock and the club became a boot-scootin' funfest. Gary Bentley and his wife, Delaney, run it with sass and class.

Santa Fe was booked at the club on the perfect weekend in mid-September of 1986: OSU's football team was playing the University of Tulsa. For two nights, the band showed Tulsa—and all the Yukon and Oklahoma City and Stillwater folks who'd come to the show—a great time. Garth's sister Betsy, who was then playing in a hot local band with Gus

Hardin, joined Santa Fe onstage, as did Ty England, Garth's friend from the OSU dorms.

In October, Santa Fe competed in the Marlboro Talent Roundup semifinals in Tuttle, Oklahoma. Inaugurated in 1983, the Marlboro Talent Roundup rounded up local bands in cities across America in a contest for a cash prize and the opportunity to be the opening act for the company's concert tour. Garth and Santa Fe—like all the bands doing their best that day—were eager to open for Merle Haggard, Ricky Skaggs, and The Judds when they came to Oklahoma City's Myriad Convention Center later in the month. The grand prize was the real attraction: a trip to Nashville and a recording session in a major studio with a top producer and recording engineer. Everyone wanted to win that!

The judges had lots of bands to listen to, so each band was really careful not to risk breaking the many rules—including being disqualified on the spot if their set went over ten minutes.

With their local fans cheering them on, Santa Fe performed "Unwound," the George Strait hit that had knocked Garth's socks off when he first heard it, followed by a Randy Travis tune, "Diggin' Up Bones," and finished with Tom Skinner singing and doing lead guitar on "Guitar Town" while Garth played bass. They didn't win the contest, but they came in third. Not bad. It got Garth thinking that the band should test whether they were really any good—or whether it was hometown spirit that gave them so many fans in Oklahoma.

So in late October, Santa Fe headed south to—where else?—New Mexico, the Land of Enchantment, to play a show at New Mexico State University in Las Cruces. Before they left, Colleen and Raymond made them a feast at their house in Yukon. With Jed, Tom, and Matt in Jed's SuperCab and Garth and Mike Skinner in Garth's GMC Jimmy, Santa Fe was going on the road.

The first show the band played in front of the Student Union didn't enchant anyone. But the following evening in the main Student Union auditorium, at a show for the alumni, Santa Fe blew the roof off. The crowd was dancing, the music was flowing, and Garth got the answer to his question: he and Santa Fe were able to make believers out of strangers as well as friends.

Toward the end of 1986, Garth was ready to make his move— or at least to start planning it. He'd formed Santa Fe for the purpose of having a band, playing constantly and getting ready for his next assault on Music City. That goal had been achieved.

He talked to the band members. Tom Skinner and his wife were ready to pack up their family and go. Mike Skinner agreed he'd like to see what Nashville was all about. Jed Lindsay was thrilled to say yes. But Matt O'Meilia decided to stay behind. He had just gotten his teaching certificate, and though he was ready to leave Stillwater, he didn't want to go to Nashville. He agreed to stay with Santa Fe until they found a new drummer who was willing to travel along the road Garth had mapped out.

Randy Taylor and Garth wrote another song together, called "Oklahoma Christmas." They recorded it on a very low budget and added some live crowd sounds. Garth sent it to several Oklahoma radio stations and got a story about the song in the *Stillwater NewsPress*. Guess what? Stations in Tulsa, Enid, and Oklahoma City put it on the air—and it went to number eleven on the Oklahoma country charts.

On New Year's Eve, Santa Fe played at the Bamboo Ballroom in Enid, Oklahoma, an airplane hangar that had been converted after World War II into a dance club. According to Matt O'Meilia, the band was paid a thousand dollars for the show—a fortune compared to what they usually pulled in for a gig.

The International Finals Rodeo, held at the Tulsa Fairgrounds, attracts rodeo enthusiasts from all over the world. Following Santa Fe's knockout performance at Tulsa City Limits back in September, they were booked to play again in January for four nights to coincide with the event.

The audience was primed for the great Santa Fe sound and the astonishing voice—not to mention stage antics—of its lead singer, Garth Brooks. The band played a couple of songs with Garth in the lead, then he turned over the lead singing duties to Tom Skinner. This didn't seem unusual to the audience members or the band. Garth often took turns with Tom.

Everyone cheered when Garth started singing George Strait's hit "Amarillo by Morning" but grew quieter when it became hard to hear his voice. They got quieter still when Garth began speaking, barely able to say that he was losing his voice and the band couldn't continue playing. He hoped the folks would come back and see them the next night.

Many of them did. And on the first song, Garth's voice was fine. But during the second song, he told the band to stop. To the astonishment of many in the audience, he said, "I can't do this to country music." He told them he was sorry, his voice was gone. He hoped they'd forgive him and his band.

It was sad for Santa Fe's many fans in the audience to watch Garth and the guys take down their equipment. Soon the audience began dancing to the club's stereo system. The musicians were really bummed—especially Matt O'Meilia. The Tulsa City Limits engagement would be his last with

Santa Fe and he'd wanted to go out with a great gig, not one that had to be canceled from the stage. Later that month, a drummer named Troy Jones, who had played with a bunch of other Oklahoma bands, took O'Meilia's place.

With Nashville on his mind, Garth wanted the band to get really tuned up for the big move. He booked them into every club, hall, ballroom, party, and school function he could find. They started saving money for the trip to Nashville and to have a little cushion while they got started there.

In April, Santa Fe played its last show at Willie's, basking in the good wishes of the crowd and the good-luck banners that filled the bar. More farewell shows followed at the Cimarron Ballroom and Bink's. The band returned to Tulsa City Limits, and this time Garth's voice filled the huge club.

The last show in Oklahoma, in May of 1987, was at Norm's Country Ballroom in Ponca City, where Norm told the crowd that Garth Brooks and Santa Fe were going to become the "biggest damn thing" country music had ever seen. He called them "the next monsters of country music."

CHAPTER TWO

THE DREAM

After that farewell, there was nothing to do but head east. Jed Lindsay and Garth drove to Nashville and stayed at the home of Bob Childers, a songwriter from Stillwater who had moved to Music City the year before. Childers had already made the acquaintance of Stephanie Brown, another songwriter who'd moved to Nashville from Florence, Alabama, and formed two music-publishing companies. Childers arranged for Garth and Stephanie to meet.

Like all music publishers, Stephanie Brown was always on the lookout for new songs to publish, new singers to create demos with, and new artists whose careers might become big enough to have a hit with one of her songs. Bob Childers had written a song he thought Garth could sing well. Stephanie agreed. That very night, they went to her apartment and worked for hours. Stephanie told Garth to just let himself sing the song as freely and emotionally as he wanted to. By dawn, Garth was tired but elated, and Stephanie had another cassette by a hopeful singer to add to her collection.

Let's hear it for the car's cassette player. In a town like Nashville, where you have to drive everywhere—and where the heavy traffic gives you even more time behind the wheel than you might want—music business executives listen to lots of music in the car. More than a great way to spend the time, it's a chance to assess how something will sound on the radio in the real world, outside the studio.

Stephanie Brown was blown away by what she heard in the car. She believed Garth had the best voice she'd ever heard and that he could become a huge star. As soon as she got to a phone, she called him and told him just that.

With that good news, Garth and Jed went looking for a house to rent. There would be five musicians, two wives, one child, and Garth and Sandy's dog, a Siberian husky named Sasha. They found a house in Hendersonville, about ten miles north of Nashville, with a brick front and a nice front porch. With five bedrooms and three baths, it had plenty of space. The rent was right, so they signed a six-month lease.

Sandy arrived as soon as the lease was signed and with Garth and Jed began getting the house ready for the rest of the band's arrival.

Troy and Jed and Mike lived downstairs, where there were three bedrooms. On the top floor, there were two other bedrooms. Sandy and Garth and Sasha took one. Tom and Jeri and their son, Jeremy, took the one that had its own bathroom.

Everyone also took jobs. Tom Skinner worked nights at a convenience store while Jeri worked days at Wal-Mart so they could alternate taking care of Jeremy. Troy worked mainte-nance at an apartment complex. Garth got a job managing a boot shop—his years at DuPree's had given him the experi-ence. Sandy got a job at the boot shop too.

There still wasn't a whole lot of money. Sandy and Jeri fig-ured out how to stretch their food dollars by buying what was on sale and making everyone in the house sign a sheet indi-cating when they'd be home for dinner. Each person had to pay from fifty cents to a dollar for a meal. The system worked out well for everyone.

With Sandy at his side, Garth had more strength to take Nashville on and believe that he'd get a chance. People in Nashville often say that it isn't necessarily the most talented people who make it, just the most persistent. It's also been said that if you have enough talent and wait, your turn will come. Garth realized that Nashville expected artists to make a commitment and that nothing came instantly. He also realized that having a commitment with Sandy didn't tie him down as much as he might have thought it would. Instead he had someone to struggle with and someone to bring him back down to earth if he got too impatient.

When they weren't working at their various jobs, the members of Santa Fe practiced their music, working on developing original songs. They figured, correctly, that Nashville wasn't looking for more cover bands. Their plan was to play at as many of the showcases they could, where managers, publicists, and record company executives were always on the lookout for new talent.

Stephanie Brown organized a showcase called Circle of Friends at the Sutler, a bar on Franklin Pike in Nashville. At Santa Fe's first showcase, the audience wasn't responding to their new songs, so they quickly changed their set and played the old stuff the audience knew. After a few more nights like this, the guys in the band were getting really discouraged. With four months left on their shared lease in the Hendersonville house, and perhaps realizing that the road to the top was bumpier than they'd expected, they decided to dissolve the band.

Now that he wasn't out playing music as much, Garth used the time to write more of his own songs. Stephanie Brown, growing more impressed with Garth all the time, decided to introduce him to Bob Doyle, who was an executive at ASCAP. Doyle had previously worked in the A & R department at Warner Brothers Records. While at ASCAP, the businessman in him saw the potential in song publishing, and he was getting ready to leave to start his own company. When he met Garth, the music man in him recognized immediately that this was a singer and songwriter with big potential.

When the lease in Hendersonville ended, Garth and Sandy moved into a three-room apartment in Stephanie Brown's house. Garth and Stephanie were writing songs together. He also began writing with songwriters Kent Blazy, Pat Alger, and others.

Growing up in Kentucky while his father worked for IBM, Kent Blazy was known even as a teenager as a musical whiz, the best musician in the school. The state that gave us great bluegrass was the backdrop for Blazy's musical development. Pat Alger, born in North Carolina, came to Nashville after a stop in Woodstock, New York, at the time home to such great musicians as Bob Dylan, The Band, and Van Morrison. Woodstock was often called "Nashville North" because of the importance placed there on songwriters and songwriting. Garth impressed these more experienced songwriters with the depth of emotion and drama he brought to his songs. From the start, he wanted his songs to do more than entertain: he wanted them to touch hearts and linger in the soul.

Garth did a lot of songwriting in 1987 and 1988, resulting in a strong collection of cowritten songs. This was a period of rich creativity in which Garth became engaged by the seductive emotional power of a good song. By doing a lot of writing himself and discovering what he liked in a song, Garth was also developing the skill of choosing songs written by others that he could interpret as a singer. The love of a lyric that "tears your guts out" and the incredible feeling of conveying that emotion to others while performing were what turned Garth on.

He met other new singers who were looking to break into country music, people like Joe Diffie, Billy Dean, and a singer from Georgia with a voice as amazing as his, Trisha Yearwood, to whom Kent Blazy introduced him.

Around this time, Bob Childers gave Garth some advice that confirmed what he already felt about performing. Childers told him that if he wanted the people in the audience to like him, he had to like them first. It was their money and time he was taking, after all. Childers told Garth to find something to like about each person in the audience and they wouldn't be able to stop loving him back. "Music is too powerful a force to be doing it without compassion and love," Childers told Garth.

Sandy worked at temporary clerical jobs while Garth continued working at the boot store. She also worked as a florist. They both had jobs cleaning a local church once a week. But Garth's impatience was getting the better of him. He was burning, yearning, and churning with desire to get started on the career and the stardom that he so fervently believed would be his.

One night they were driving home from work and Garth's frustration was overflowing. They had to pull over. "We were sitting in the parking lot of a damn fire station back in Hendersonville, Tennessee. I was beating my head as hard as I could, because I had snapped," he says. "I thought we weren't going to make it. I thought we were going to crash, trash out, go into debt, poverty, and stuff. It had nothing to do with music. It was two people, newly married, struggling against debt. I thought it was over."

Sandy knew that Garth felt he could make it in the music business, and she felt that way too. It was hard for them both, struggling to make ends meet, but she was prepared to hang in a little longer.

"Look, I was around when you came back the last time, and I'm not going through that again," she said. "I think you're good enough, you think you're good enough, so we're going to stay right here." Sandy had faith in Garth from the start.

"I'm not making this trip every year," she said. She told Garth that he was right to pursue his dream, that he loved the music, and that she believed in him. "Either we're diggin' in," she said, "or we're going home for good."

Thank goodness Garth had the sense to listen to his wife, a fine, strong woman who loved and understood him.

He was making some progress. In addition to playing at the many singer/songwriter events in clubs around Nashville like the Sutler and Douglas Corners, Garth sang on a lot of songwriters' demos, learning the ways of the studio and impressing everyone who heard him with his incredible voice. For a singer, working on demos not only helps pay the rent, it's a great way to showcase your voice so it can be heard by record labels. For songwriters, having a singer with a great voice demo your songs makes the songs sound that much better to artists who might decide to record them.

Joe Harris was born in Danville, Virginia, the son of a preacher. When his father was transferred to a new congregation in Bedford, Virginia, he met a young woman in church and decided that this beautiful young girl was the one he wanted to marry. Shirley Harris now says she gave him a little slap when he pulled her hair in church on Sundays, but, with a twinkle in her eye, she adds that she married him.

Two years after Joe and Shirley got married in 1954, Joe went into the service. (That's when Shirley found out that

Joe was really two years younger than she was.) By this time, the couple had a son, Joe Jr. Joe Harris would spend the next thirteen years in the United States Air Force serving his country with loyalty and honor. In Vietnam in the late 1960s when the truck he was driving hit a land mine, he was seriously injured. He was also exposed to Agent Orange, resulting in a series of illnesses that would be with him all his life. After his discharge from the service he was asked to go back to Vietnam, but his illness—and the fact that Shirley had lost a brother to the war—made him refuse.

While in Vietnam, Joe Harris booked big acts like Bob Hope and others who came overseas to entertain the troops. He enjoyed this so much, he wanted to do the same thing when he came home. But by this time he and Shirley had two more children, Lohoma, whom everyone called Sissy, and Glynis, whom he had nicknamed Peanut, so he had to defer that dream for a while. He worked back in Roanoke for Pet Milk, for the Mohawk Tire Company, and for the post office as a mailman. In addition to delivering the mail, he went to college on the G.I. Bill and began doing a little booking of acts in the local area. A band that another of Shirley's brothers was in, The Sportsmen, was one of his first acts.

Jim Prater, who was booking Charley Pride, George Jones, and Tammy Wynette, became aware of Joe and they worked together for a time. Another agent Joe Harris worked with to bring talent to Virginia was from Nashville. His name was Buddy Lee.

Joe Harris was a wonderful father. His son remembers one time his daddy had to punish him. Joe Jr. was about fifteen and had snuck out of the house one night when he was supposed to be sleeping. When his father found out, he gave his son a few smacks on the rear end with a belt. Then he told

Joe Jr. to do the same to him "so I would know how much it hurt him to hit me." Many kids have heard their parents say "this hurts me more than it hurts you." Joe Harris proved it to his son.

In October of 1979, the Harris family moved to Nashville at the request of Buddy Lee. Buddy Lee Attractions was already a pretty big agency in Music City, and Joe Harris began there by working in the mailroom. Soon, however, he moved up the ladder to become an agent. One of the first artists he met was George Strait. Joe was impressed from the start with the new singer from Texas and began booking him into the shows that kept getting bigger every year.

Joe left Buddy Lee Attractions for a while in the mid-1980s to work for some agents who had their own small companies. During this time, Joe worked to book comedian Jerry Clower and singer Boxcar Willie, two immense talents who have passed away in the last couple of years. Joe and Shirley were also working with Tommy Jennings, the younger brother of Waylon, who could really sing well. Shirley worked as a bookkeeper alongside her husband, and some of the practices they discovered in these companies bothered Joe's sense of ethics.

After trying to run his own agency, Joe Harris decided to return to Buddy Lee Attractions. He was booking the whole Buddy Lee roster, including Ricky Van Shelton, Willie Nelson, and Waylon Jennings, just around the time a new young singer from Oklahoma named Garth Brooks was trying to get his own career off the ground.

Bob Doyle had told people he was looking for writers and artists he could get excited about. When he met Garth in early 1988, he was ready to leave ASCAP. He formed his publishing company, which he named Major Bob Music in honor of his previous military service, and signed two writers. One was Larry Bastian, who had written songs for classic country singer Eddy Arnold and David Frizzell, the younger brother of one of country's greatest legends, Lefty Frizzell. The other songwriter was Garth Brooks. Garth received an advance against his future earnings, as all songwriters do. His was $300 a month.

Song publishing wasn't the only plan Bob Doyle had. He asked well-known Nashville publicist Pam Lewis to form a management company with him. Lewis, a native of upstate New York, had attended Wells College and majored in economics and marketing. As national media director at Warner Amex Satellite Entertainment, she was part of the original publicity/marketing team that launched MTV. She relocated to Nashville in 1984 to head the RCA Records Media/Artist Development Department, where she worked with top country stars like Dolly Parton, Kenny Rogers, The Judds, and Alabama. After her stint at RCA, Lewis founded PLA Media, her own public relations and marketing firm. PLA Media did projects for such clients as the Country Music Association, Steve Winwood, Steve Earle, and Lee Greenwood.

"All of this prepared me to do exactly the kind of work that managers do, nurturing a career," she says. "I'd had people say to me 'You'd be a good manager.'" When Bob Doyle approached her, she says, the timing was right.

Pam Lewis met Garth for the first time at Bob Doyle's office. Garth brought his dog—and his guitar—to the meeting. "Bob had kept telling me he had this 'boy' he wanted me to meet," Lewis says. "Bob talked about what a great voice this 'boy' had. Well, this 'boy' turned out to be a strapping guy, well-built with a firm handshake. He sat and played guitar and was amazing. What impressed me was his intensity—there was such intensity and an air of confidence about him."

In 1988, Nashville was in the kind of position it is in today: waiting for the next big thing to happen. The early eighties had been the "urban cowboy" era. The movie of the same name stars John Travolta as a young Texas farmer who moves to Houston to work in an oil refinery and then becomes a mechanical bull–riding regular at the real-life Gilley's honky-tonk in Pasadena, Texas. The movie's soundtrack was a huge hit, with songs by artists like Bob Seger and the Silver Bullet Band, Bonnie Raitt, Linda Ronstadt, and Boz Scaggs, all of whom mixed pop and country sounds. Suddenly, rhinestone cowboys and girls in fringed suede jackets were providing a market for the pop-influenced country music Nashville was turning out.

By the mid-eighties, with artists like George Strait, Randy Travis, and Reba McEntire, Nashville was the home of the so-called new traditionalists, whose music reflected the true roots of country and brought comparisons to George Jones, Patsy Cline, and Merle Haggard. With Strait, Travis, and McEntire now firmly in place, it was anyone's guess what the next trend in Music City would be.

Pam Lewis says that as she got to know Garth, she began to feel that his real strength was in making people believe in his dreams. "I also thought he had a beautiful and distinctive voice," she says, "and a lot of potential as a writer. I loved the songs he had written."

"Ignorance is bliss," Lewis said in an interview in the Music Row offices of her companies, PLA Media and Pamela L. Lewis Enterprises, in April of 1999. "I had some trepidation at first. Bob and Garth and I were all so different from each other. Finally I said this is too weird, it's so weird, it will probably work." Given the state of country music and the time, Lewis said, "Bob and I thought, 'Why not us? Why not Garth?' If we'd had any idea how hard it would be in the beginning, we might not have done it."

Doyle/Lewis Management signed Garth Brooks as its first client in January 1988.

Stephanie Brown introduced Garth to Amy Kurland, who ran the Bluebird Café. A nondescript club in a strip mall in the Green Hills section of Nashville a few miles from Music Row, the Bluebird is filled with photos of grateful artists who began their rise to the top there. Kurland held open auditions on Sundays, selecting from an often huge crowd of performers the talented few who would get their turn on the club's tiny stage.

Garth passed muster with Amy Kurland at his first audition. She gave him high scores for his song and an even higher one for his performance. He was given a slot on a writers' night, the first of many evenings he would join in the Bluebird tradition of presenting the best singer/songwriters to the Nashville music community. One night, the audience began applauding in the middle of a song Garth, Larry Bastian, and Pat Alger had written called "Unanswered Prayers." That kind of reaction was very unusual. It took a lot to impress the audience at the Bluebird.

Kurland thought Garth was great but told him, "I don't care if you're Kenny Rogers, it's going to take time. Slow down and be here for the long haul." Garth thought this was good advice, but it didn't make him any more patient. He regarded the opportunity to play at the Bluebird Café as "quite a compliment." He recognized what other songwriters had seen in Amy Kurland. She made them—and their songs—feel special.

Joe Harris was sitting in his office at Buddy Lee Attractions one day in 1988. Hundreds of hopeful artists were always sending their demo tapes or stopping in to audition at Buddy Lee Attractions. Like every great agent, producer, or manager who works more for love of music than love of the dollar, Joe Harris would listen to everyone—you never know where great talent will show up. Buddy Lee had heard the buzz going around town about Garth. Harris, too, had heard people talking about the young singer whose demos and performances at the small clubs around Nashville were drawing attention. So when Garth Brooks came in to see him, Harris was more than willing to give him a chance. Shirley Harris remembers what happened.

"Garth walked into Joe's office. He was real polite and respectful, and Joe said, 'So you can sing?' Garth says, 'Well, I try.' Joe said, 'Why don't you do something for me?' and Garth says, 'Well, I don't have my guitar,' and Joe said, 'If you can sing, you don't need a guitar.' So Garth started singing for Joe, and all the people in the office came in and wanted to know who was doing all that singing."

There was an instant rapport between Joe Harris and Garth Brooks. As they got to know each other better, Joe's enthusiasm grew—not just for Garth's talent but for Garth himself.

"He was just gung ho for Garth," Shirley says. "Joe said, 'He's gonna be as big as Elvis.' Joe had a little memo pad on his desk. So on that memo pad I wrote, 'Garth's number-one record' and put it up on Joe's wall." Shirley's handwritten note was right next to the gold and platinum record plaques of other artists Joe Harris had worked with, including George Strait.

Sol Saffian remembers hearing about the new act at Buddy Lee when he was working for the William Morris

Agency. Saffian was a native New Yorker whose long career in the music business had taken him first to Los Angeles and now to Nashville. Saffian had worked with all kinds of music and every kind of star—from Bobby Darin and Fabian, Louis Armstrong and Duke Ellington in the 1950s, to Neil Diamond and Felix Cavaliere and Motown acts like the Four Tops and Temptations in the 1960s, to Rod Stewart and Earth, Wind and Fire in the 1970s, all the way to country diva Reba McEntire in the 1980s.

"The other agents at Buddy Lee didn't think Garth could make it," Sol Saffian says. "Nobody thought he had a shot to the extent that it happened. Maybe he would be a mid-range artist, but nowhere did anyone think he would go through the roof." Because Joe Harris believed in Garth so strongly, Buddy Lee made Joe the responsible agent. Some of the other agents waited for Joe to be proven wrong about the kid he was so excited about.

It was time to begin the process of pitching Garth Brooks to Nashville's record companies.

These days in Nashville, demos are much more elaborate than they were ten or eleven years ago. There are often lots of instruments, backup vocalists, polished studio production, and fancy graphics on the CD and audiocassette covers that make it hard to tell they are even demos. Like a lot of other things in America, the demo process has gotten slicked up and image conscious.

But when Garth was creating his demo—the all-important demonstration of his talent that would sink or float his dream of a recording career—a simple guitar and vocal track were enough.

Producer Jerry Kennedy took Garth into one of the many smaller studios in Nashville that devote most of their time to demos. They chose songs that showcased Garth as both a singer and a songwriter.

To go with the demo tape, Pam Lewis and Bob Doyle had photos taken of Garth wearing jeans, boots, and a cowboy hat. Those clothes were not a costume—they were the same things Garth always wore.

"I remember doing photos outside. We found out quickly how difficult it is to shoot someone with a cowboy hat," Pam says. "We had a lot of photos that wouldn't work. Garth had this one hat he was so proud of, but the way he shaped the hat was to take a shower with it on, much to the dismay of Stetson makers across the country." Garth wanted to wear this hat for his photo, but he was finally convinced to get a new one.

Women buy a lot of records by male artists, so it was important to convey some sex appeal. "We asked Garth, 'Are you sure you want to put your wedding band on?'" Pam says, and adds she was pleased when Garth said, "Yes, I want to keep it on."

Writing the bio—the one- or two-page "pitch" that accompanied the photo and demo tape—was Pam Lewis's job. As an experienced publicist and marketer, she knew how to put the right "spin" on things, to shape an image, to craft an impression for the minds of, in this case, the A & R and marketing people in the record companies who, they all hoped, would want to sign Garth to a record deal as soon as they heard him sing.

In the case of Garth, she didn't have to spin that much. "By that time, he was a seasoned performer," Pam says. "He had played through college, he referred to himself as a human jukebox, he had worked the crowds. Garth knew pacing. He had a unique voice. He had beautiful, captivating blue eyes and a nice smile." The bio almost wrote itself. Pam

Lewis was able to talk about all of Garth's musical influences, from James Taylor to KISS, stressing the country singers he loved, like George Jones and George Strait. "He was the son of a singer, and also had been an athlete," Pam says. "There were lots of hooks and pegs."

Pam Lewis had done a lot of public relations projects for the Nashville record labels, and Bob Doyle had not only worked at one but knew everyone in town from his years at ASCAP. Garth's new managers had the connections and made the calls to all the right people. Sharp-looking packages containing the demo tape, photo, and bio were delivered to the very people who held artists' futures in the palms of their hands—or, more accurately, in their ears.

People were willing to listen to Garth's demo. In some cases, Pam and Bob were able to get him live auditions in the record companies' offices. One company that gave him a live audition was Capitol Records. After all of this work, Pam and Bob and Garth crossed their fingers.

Every label that listened to Garth's tape or saw his audition in their offices said no.

Joe Harris, Jr., worked nights at the Nissan plant outside of Nashville. His dad called him and told him there was someone he wanted him to meet, a singer he thought was going to be big. Joe Jr. drove over to Buddy Lee Attractions one night before going to work.

"There was this guy standing behind this old red pickup truck kicking on the tailgate because it wouldn't stay up," Joe Jr. recalled. He told the guy that wasn't how to make it stay up. His father had been standing at the window of his office watching the scene in the parking lot. The guy got the tailgate to stay shut, then drove away. "I looked up, and dad was standing there laughing," Joe Jr. said. "At the time, my dad just thought it was hilarious. He told me, 'That was the guy I wanted you to meet.'"

Every agent will tell you it is very difficult to book live appearances for an artist who doesn't have a hit. Without a record deal, it is downright impossible.

But the promoters out in America who buy talent for county and state fairs and the owners looking to fill the seats in their small clubs—including George Moffitt, the biggest buyer of talent for fairs in America—believed in Joe Harris as much as Joe believed in Garth. Harris told the promoters they needed to book Garth Brooks.

"Joe was getting favors from key buyers," Sol Saffian says. "They trusted Joe, and he sold them so many other acts that the buyers agreed to book Garth Brooks as a favor to Joe."

Robert Metzgar, a friend and associate of Joe Harris, was music director of a live Nashville television show called *American Country Showcase*. A lot of people already signed to record companies and many who got deals later, like Clint Black and Ricky Van Shelton, appeared on the show. During the time that Garth was getting all the rejections from the Nashville record labels, Joe called Robert Metzgar and asked him to have Garth on the show.

"There was something very special about Garth from the moment you met him," Metzgar said. "He had almost an angelic approach to people. He was very respectful and humble." He also put on a great show.

Music business executives roamed the clubs in Nashville, looking for talented singers and songwriters at the many showcases where hopeful newcomers gave it their all, dreaming no doubt that their big break was just one great show away.

One night in May 1988, the audience at the Bluebird Café was filled with even more than its usual share of music business executives. The Nashville Entertainment Association was sponsoring the evening's show. Its selection committee had listened to dozens of audition tapes submitted by publishers and songwriters, tapes that didn't bear the name of the artist. Garth was among the artists chosen to perform.

He was supposed to take his turn onstage later in the evening, but when Ralph Murphy, the artist slated to play second, didn't show up on time, Garth was asked to move up in the rotation. At first this seemed like a disadvantage to Garth. But it turned out to be anything but.

People at the Bluebird that night had an experience to remember. With only his own acoustic guitar accompanying him, Garth sang his first song of the evening. His performance and the way he connected with the audience had everyone sitting up a little straighter in their seats. Good thing. This way they didn't literally fall off their chairs when he finished singing his second song, "If Tomorrow Never Comes," which he had written with Kent Blazy.

Lynn Shults was in charge of finding acts for Capitol Records. He had, in fact, been present at Garth's audition for Capitol and was among those who'd made the decision to turn him down. In his audition at Capitol Records, Garth didn't impress Shults nearly as much as he did now, playing in front of an audience. When he heard Garth sing "If Tomorrow Never Comes" at the Bluebird, "Garth just blew me away."

"What went through my mind," Shults says, "was that I had just seen somebody who was as good as—if not better than—anyone I had ever seen."

Several record company presidents were in the room. But it was Lynn Shults who got to Garth first. He walked up to Bob Doyle and said, "How did we leave things with you?"

Bob Doyle told him, "You passed." The next day Shults told his boss, label president Jim Fogelsong, that he thought Capitol should reconsider the singer from Oklahoma. Fogelsong asked him if he really believed that much in Garth Brooks, and Shults replied that he'd never felt stronger about anything in his life.

Capitol Records gave Garth $10,000 to go into a studio and create four singles. After that, they'd see what happened. It was similar to the deal George Strait had been given in 1979 at MCA. Given how Strait's career was booming by 1988, Garth had every reason to feel satisfied with the opportunity he was now being given.

Garth had a booking agent and a record deal. The next step was to find a producer who could take Garth's talents and musical vision and influences and help create his own sound. Garth felt loyal to Jerry Kennedy, but Kennedy wasn't on good terms with Capitol's management and decided to bow out. Capitol Records and Garth's managers assembled a shortlist of producers for him to consider. Choosing a producer is one of the most important decisions an artist makes.

"I suggested Allen Reynolds," Pam Lewis says. "I had heard Garth talk about folk influences—he loved Dan Fogelberg and James Taylor. These were the kinds of music Allen Reynolds was doing. I also thought it important that someone would spend the time with Garth instead of having several projects all at once. Reynolds had his own studio and an integrity about him, and an appreciation for music besides straight country."

Born in Arkansas and raised in Memphis, Allen Reynolds had played and recorded with singer/songwriter Dickey Lee on Sun Records, Elvis Presley's label. He went on to write such pop hits as "I Saw Linda Yesterday" for Dickey Lee and "Five O'Clock World" for the Vogues in the 1960s. Along with Lee, Reynolds started a publishing and production company in Memphis. He also worked in a bank to support his family while writing songs and producing artists at night. In 1970 Reynolds moved to Nashville, where he produced Don Williams's first two albums and where he also purchased Jack's Tracks Recording Studio on 16th Avenue South, the studio built by legendary producer "Cowboy" Jack Clement.

Reynolds worked with Crystal Gayle, producing her special blend of country and pop music and writing songs that became hits for the longhaired singer. Other artists, including Waylon Jennings, also hit the charts with his compositions. He produced five albums and many hits for Kathy Mattea, including her Country Music Association Single of the Year in 1988, "Eighteen Wheels and a Dozen Roses."

In his office at Jack's Tracks on 16th Avenue South, Allen Reynolds graciously made time to share his recollections of what happened there more than ten years ago. "I was interested at the time in finding a male artist," he said. "I told my engineer, Mark Miller, 'Kathy's career is getting its legs. I wish I could find a male artist I would enjoy working with as much as I enjoy working with her.' Thirty days later or less, Bob Doyle called."

Reynolds had never heard of Garth Brooks and didn't know Bob Doyle that well at the time, but he agreed to listen to Garth's tape. After listening, he wanted to meet Garth.

"The way I work is to sit and talk with the artist. I try to get inside their head and see how they feel about music and see what they're wanting to do, to get some sense of whether or not there's a reason for us to do anything together," Reynolds said. "I was attracted by Garth's singing and the music, but I also liked the way he talked and how he thought. I'm just as interested in how an aspiring artist thinks, because that's going to have a heavy influence on how they survive and thrive. I liked the way he thought."

At their first meeting, Garth told Allen Reynolds, "I don't want anybody confused about where I stand. I'm a country singer, and that's what I want to be. I don't want to sit on a fence." He also said that two of his biggest heroes were James Taylor and Billy Joel. Reynolds told him, "That's not a problem. We don't live in a vacuum. Everyone is watching and listening to the same thing."

Garth liked Allen Reynolds immediately. He said he felt a sense of protection with Reynolds and a sense of peace.

At the end of the meeting, based on what they'd talked about, Allen Reynolds said he would be willing to get together and try to cut a few sides.

"We'll go into the studio and do a limited amount of work, put our best into it, and we might like each other very well but not work well together," Reynolds told Garth. "This connection you're about to make is important in your life. We'll do this, and at that point in time either one of us can say no thanks, that's not exactly what I'm looking for. If we like what we've come up with, we can go on."

*A*s they began working on the four sides, Reynolds learned more about Garth. "He told me for one thing he wanted to have at least one song with a rodeo motif on each album. I thought, 'This is cool. He's a western guy—they used to call it country and western.'" Something else about Garth stuck with Allen Reynolds. "He said, 'When it comes to the word *love*, it's like a four-letter word for me. I have a hard time using it in a song if it's employed like "I love you so much." I practically choke on the word.' Yet he was a real romantic guy and a really sensitive guy. I thought how refreshing and how interesting, because so much of the music that gets offered up is exactly that cloying, sucking-up kind of manipulative love song, and here was a guy who choked on the word."

By the time Garth met Reynolds, he had gathered many songs, some he'd written and some he'd discovered along the way by singing a lot of demos. Reynolds said he'd be glad to go through those sometime and give Garth his thoughts. "He brought a box-top lid mounded up with cassettes. He said, 'I hate to bring so many,' and I said I wouldn't mind. He had all these interesting songs that were very appealing to me on a lot of bases. I thought they were commercial and interesting and a little different." There were many "story songs" in Garth's box-top lid.

The more he got to know Garth, the more Allen Reynolds, like Pam Lewis and Bob Doyle and Joe Harris, became excited by Garth's intensity and enthusiasm.

A big part of a producer's job is to work with the artist to choose the musicians who will come into the studio and not only play the instruments but, it is hoped, become an integral part of the artist's sound. Reynolds and Garth talked a lot about the kind of musicians and sound they were looking for on the four sides they were going to cut.

Reynolds asked Garth if there were any musicians he had worked with in Nashville whom he was impressed with. Garth told him the only guy he really wanted was a bass player named Mike Chapman. "I said that's fine, I've worked with Mike and I really like his playing," Reynolds said, "and the drummer I would recommend to you, as it happens, grew up with Mike and they've known each other since first grade and played together all their lives. His name is Milton Sledge." Both musicians were from Muscle Shoals, Alabama. "If you've ever been around bands, having a drummer and a bass player who are that tight is a great asset," Reynolds said.

Reynolds also suggested other musicians. "I suggested Bobby Wood from Memphis, Tennessee, one of the most soulful, wonderful keyboard players I've ever known," Reynolds said. "I worked with him all my life down in Memphis. For acoustic guitar, I suggested Mark Casstevens, one of the finest acoustic guitar players in the world, bar none. For electric guitar I suggested Chris Leuzinger, who's originally from Florida but had been in Nashville for twenty-five or thirty years. I had worked with Chris a lot, and Garth was fine with him. That's the band we started with." A singer from the heartland got a great band from the South.

Both Memphis, the home of the blues, and Muscle Shoals have attracted musicians as diverse as Aretha Franklin and the Rolling Stones, as well as many country artists who enjoy recording with its vast pool of musical talent in a laid-back true southern atmosphere. During their heyday in the 1960s civil rights era, black and white musicians and writers who couldn't stay in the same hotels or eat in the same restaurants worked closely together in the studios of Memphis and Muscle Shoals to create a form of truly American music that is still exerting its influence today in modern country and pop.

Garth's agent, Joe Harris, was active with the Church of God in Cleveland, Tennessee. Right before Christmas 1988, Sheriff Richard Sutton of Sumner County called Robert Metzgar, the music director of *American Country Showcase,* and told him about a critical situation. The sheriff knew Metzgar would also alert Joe Harris.

A minister in Cleveland owed $4,800 in back rent to his landlord, who had obtained a dispossess notice and called Sheriff Sutton to evict the minister and his wife and children. "The sheriff did not want to go there two days before Christ-

mas and put these people and their furniture and three children out in the front yard," Metzgar says. Metzgar called Joe
Harris and Joe said he would, with the help of some people,
get not only the rent money but a little more so the family
could also have a Christmas. Robert Metzgar and Joe Harris
reached into their pockets to contribute $1,000 each.

"We went to all of our friends and said, 'Look, this is a
real bad situation,'" Metzgar says, "and we don't want these
kids on the street, so ante up. We called in our favors."

Metzgar went to see a friend of his, Bob Farr, at his car
dealership, Bob Farr Motor Company in Hendersonville.
Farr was happy when he received a phone call in April 1999
and was asked to remember what happened next. "Robert
said to me, 'I know from the past what's in your heart, and I
need help' and I said, 'Let me tell you what happened this
weekend.'" Farr's dealership had been broken into, his office trashed, and several thousand dollars stolen from his
safe. "Robert said, 'I hate to have to come to you after what's
happened,' and I said, 'What the hell's another thousand?'"
Farr gave his friend the money, and he says now, "It's paid off
a jillion to me."

Garth had received his $10,000 advance from Capitol—
some of which had gone for lawyer's fees and commissions to
his managers. But he reached into what was left and gave
$1,000 too. Through the very generous music community in
Nashville, the full $4,800 in back rent—plus another
$2,000—was raised in a very short period of time.

Joe Harris went out to the house to bring the family the
money and Garth went with him, according to Metzgar and
Farr. As they stepped onto the porch of the small frame
house, they saw and heard through the window that the
woman was on her knees, praying and asking God to please
work a miracle for her family. The family had been too proud

to tell anyone about the problem. If it hadn't been for the big heart of the small-town sheriff, no one would have known. As she knelt there praying, the woman didn't know that the miracle was just outside her door.

Joe Harris later told Robert Metzgar that this incident in Garth's life helped propel him to contribute to charity in a hugely generous way after he had been blessed with so much success. "It was a big turning point in his future," Metzgar said when he called to contribute the story to this book. "As we know, he has been one of the most charitable people in the music business."

The last demo Garth sang on after he got his record deal was a song written by Dewayne Blackwell and Earl Bud Lee. Dewayne Blackwell said Garth was so good at singing demos not only because of his great voice but because he really prepared himself by learning the song ahead of time and giving some thought to what the writers were trying to convey.

When Garth was done with this particular demo—which he did in one take—he told Blackwell he had just finished recording his album and said, "Where were you with this song two weeks ago?" Blackwell told him, "It wasn't quite finished yet."

Garth immediately started performing the song in his live concerts, and after about three months of seeing audiences go nuts for it, he put a hold on it for his next album.

By now, Joe Harris had plenty of dates for Garth and his band to play. Everyone in Garth's camp believed that fans who experienced a live Garth show, especially in the smaller clubs and fairs that were the only places an unproven act could play, would be primed and ready by the time Garth's album came out.

So Garth began to put together a touring band. In Nashville, most artists use studio musicians for their albums and a different band when they go on the road. Now that he had his big opportunity, the first musicians Garth tried to recruit for his new live band were from his old live band, Santa Fe. He was going to keep the promise he had made to his friends back in Oklahoma: if he got a shot at the big time, he had said, they'd get a shot too.

According to Matt O'Meilia's book, Garth asked Jed Lindsay to join the touring group. Lindsay wanted to tour with Garth but also wanted to play on the albums, something that Garth couldn't promise him, given the way things worked in Nashville. Garth also asked drummer Troy Jones to come back and play with him, but by now Troy had a steady job with Gibson Guitars and financial commitments that kept him from leaving it. Garth also called Dale Pierce, who couldn't join the band because he and his wife were expecting their first child.

The only musicians from Oklahoma who were able to take advantage of the opportunity to work with Garth were Ty England, who came on board to play rhythm guitar and sing backup vocals (and moved in with Garth and Sandy when he first came to town), and David Gant. David Gant was from Ada, Oklahoma, and had played in his junior year in high school with the Kiowa Country Band, in which Reba McEntire and her brother Pake were singers. After playing professionally in Oklahoma, he worked for ten years in Los Angeles with various bands. In 1989, he had just finished playing again with Pake McEntire's band when he heard Garth was looking for a keyboard player and fiddle player.

James Garver, from Concordia, Kansas, came on to play guitar. Pedal steel and electric guitar was played by another Kansan, Steve McClure, of Augusta. The drummer was Mike

Palmer, who hailed from Plant City, Florida. Tom Bowers was a bass player who also acted as road manager.

Pam says she was impressed by how Garth put his road band together. "For Garth it was less important how well they played, and more important whether they could get along and go on the bus together and not kill each other," she says. "It was what was in their hearts that counted. How would they look? How would they interact onstage? Were they easygoing, did they have a support system at home, or would there be a lot of upset on the road? It was a good and clever human way to look at it."

Garth and his band, which he named Stillwater to honor his college town, rehearsed in the basement of Bob Doyle's office in one of the many 1920s and '30s houses that make up most of the office space on Music Row. It was a dark and dingy basement. Pam and Bob would swing by at night to see how things were going. "One of the things I admired about Garth was he was a really good coach," Pam says, "good at motivating people to work together and rise to the occasion."

At the time Pam was using office space at the office of one of her clients, Airborne Records. She spent part of the day there and the rest of it at Bob's office, strategizing on Garth's behalf.

Before rehearsing with his band in the evenings, Garth spent his days writing with songwriters like Kent Blazy and Pat Alger. He was also going around Nashville and meeting people and sharing his dream.

"He already was smart enough to know he had to start waging his own political campaign with regards to winning people over and getting to know people," Pam said. "He had a lot of people rooting for him."

The four sides that Garth and Allen Reynolds and the studio band had set out to record were done. Capitol Records heard them and said, "Oh yes, let's make an album." So it was back to the studio, this time with even more excitement.

Reynolds suggested Bruce Bouton for steel guitar and Dobro. Then he asked Garth about the fiddle intro on the demo of "Much Too Young (To Feel This Damn Old)." "I just loved it, the fiddle line and everything exactly as he played it, and when we were going to cut that song I said to Garth, 'Who is this guy?' Garth said Rob Hajacos. I said, 'I love what he played. I don't know why we would call anybody else.'"

Over the course of creating Garth's first album, Allen Reynolds showed Garth the way he liked to work in the hope that Garth would agree with the method.

"I like to work as live as possible," Reynolds said. "When we were first working together, Garth referred to his vocal track as like 'tracking.' I said don't talk about that. The vocal that may happen when you're here in good voice while doing a song for the first time is often apt to be the magic vocal. I want you in here digging as hard as anyone else and flying with the whole group. That's where the magic comes from."

Allen Reynolds didn't like a singer to do a "scratch vocal," the term for when the singer puts down an often unpolished first vocal track to give the band some direction. "As an example, I pointed out that with Crystal Gayle on 'Don't It Make Your Brown Eyes Blue,' as with a lot of good records, the song came real quickly. It was the first time we rolled tape, maybe the third time we went through the song. Hargus 'Pig' Robbins, one of Nashville's legendary piano players, hit that little ba *da* ba da da and the band just congealed around it that quickly. Crystal's vocal totally moved me, but she thought it happened so quickly that maybe she could improve it. I said I don't mind trying, and she came back at least a couple of times and tried to improve until at last she was as satisfied as I was with the original vocal. It just had things that weren't there later. That's what I wanted Garth to understand."

Garth scratched the notion of a scratch vocal.

The first single, released to radio in March of 1989, was the song Garth had sung every chance he could back in the clubs and dance halls of Stillwater, Oklahoma. His original composition, written with Randy Taylor, about the tough life of a rodeo rider, "Much Too Young (To Feel This Damn Old)" showcased Garth's distinctive voice within the context of a favorite country theme.

Garth's voice was very much center stage. Allen Reynolds's masterful production kept all of the instruments proportioned in a way that surrounded Garth's rich voice, allowing the story and the message in the song to be conveyed. From the first song, Garth came on the scene with an incredibly developed style (all those nights playing in Stillwater had given him much more than $500 a week). The song's similarity to the George Strait hit "Amarillo by Morning" seemed like another plus in getting radio stations to play it.

Pam Lewis and Bob Doyle went to Country Radio Seminar in Nashville in February. Disc jockeys and radio programmers from all over the country come to this event to see what's new in country music and be barraged with promotional materials and performances of artists who know how important it is to have their music played, and played often, on radio.

J. D. Haas calls Country Radio Seminar a "schmoozefest." J.D. is one of the most energetic and enthusiastic people you'll ever meet. His Nashville-based company, J. D. Haas

Entertainment, provides first-class dream trips for country-music radio stations to use as prizes for contest winners. Stations all over the country put these contests on the air and offer them to local sponsors, like car dealerships or music stores, who get a lot of free advertising in exchange for contributing to the cost of the trips. Imagine being one of the lucky folks to win a trip to the Academy of Country Music Awards in L.A. in the spring or to Fan Fair in June or to Cheyenne Wyoming Frontier Days, where huge country acts always perform in July.

At the 1989 Country Radio Seminar, held at the beautiful Opryland Hotel, J. D. Haas had a ten-foot-by-ten-foot booth with a couch, a water cooler, and a comfortable rocking chair from which he sold his trip contests to radio stations.

"At the time Pam had just started up her thing with Garth. I hung out with Pam a lot and talked about Garth Brooks," J.D. says. "I love Pam like a sister, and she loved and believed in Garth." Very few people had booths at CRS, so J.D. shared his with Pam and Garth. This gave them a central location and a place to rest after running around and meeting people. J.D. was more than happy to accommodate his friend—and her new client.

"I met Garth and thought he was a real nice guy," J.D. said. "He was wearing chinos and a cowboy hat and a pressed shirt—he looked just perfect. What a guy, a great humble nice person."

Garth was the first one to arrive at Country Radio Seminar in the morning and the last one there at night. "He had an intensity about him like an aura," J.D. says, loving the opportunity to share his stories of an artist he loves. "Everyone has a different aura, and from the beginning, Garth had something. He had 'it'—you can't define it, can't taste it and know it, but Garth had it."

Pam and Garth were all over the Opryland Hotel—in the lobby, in the hospitality suites, doing interviews, talking to radio programmers and disc jockeys. "At the United Stations suite, Garth sang his heart out," J.D. says. "No one knew him, so it was very interesting to see him play that first year. Garth played 'American Pie.' Everyone could tell he was real and genuine."

Pam Lewis had buttons made up that said, in white letters on a red background, "We're much too young to feel this damn old." After a night of partying, many of the guests felt exactly that way when Pam pinned her buttons on them in the morning. Without an artist name or record company on the pin, the many record-company executives Pam placed the pins on didn't even know they were promoting a competitor's record.

Pam Lewis was grateful to J.D. for his help and enthusiasm, and also grateful for Joe Harris's help. "Joe was very sincere, and he was very religious and a family man, and that is an anomaly in this business," she says. "On the surface he was a country bumpkin, almost too naive for this business, yet he was very shrewd and principled. The promoters respected him and the fact that he had acts who stayed with him for years. I can remember I called him the Burl Ives of country music."

Garth's first album, titled *Garth Brooks,* was released on April 12, 1989. Capitol Records took a full-page ad in *Billboard* to herald the arrival of the guy everyone was starting to believe would be a huge success. Garth dedicated the album to the memory of two of his friends: Jim Kelley, his coach at OSU who had died in a plane crash, and Heidi Miller, a college friend of his who had died in a car accident.

"Much Too Young (To Feel This Damn Old)" was the seventh song on the album, and if you think Garth didn't plan it that way, well, you've never had a lucky number. Unfortunately, luck wasn't with him when it came to the song's climb up the charts: it made it into the Top 40 but then fell off. Although Capitol was pleased to have achieved a Top 40 radio hit with the first single from an unknown artist's first album, Garth and his managers were not happy at all.

Still, Garth was willing to do whatever it took to make good—not just for the memory of his friends, but to honor everyone who'd believed in him from the start. He would visit radio stations and retailers all day and play music all night. He played his heart out for even the smallest audiences. He shook hands, looked into people's eyes, called everyone "sir" and "ma'am." He was the guest of honor at the grand opening of a Wal-Mart in Raleigh, North Carolina, and played a full show the same evening at a local nightclub. He did the same for other retailers and record stores and gained a reputation early on as one of the most cooperative artists in helping stores sell his music.

As everyone who loves country music knows, the biggest party of the year isn't New Year's Eve. The real excitement happens in June, at Fan Fair.

Country music fans—the most loyal fans in all of entertainment—come from all over America, in buses, cars, motor homes, and pickup trucks, to gather at the Tennessee State Fairgrounds in Nashville for a weeklong festival of music and fun cosponsored by the Country Music Association and the Grand Ole Opry.

In brightly decorated booths erected by their fan clubs, country music stars—the most generous stars in all of entertainment—shake fans' hands, sign autographs, and pose for pictures with the folks who made them stars in the first place.

Tickets to Fan Fair entitle the holders to two free barbecue lunches prepared by the Odessa Chuck Wagon Gang of

Odessa, Texas, as well as admission to the Ryman Auditorium, the Country Music Hall of Fame, and Opryland, USA. The real value comes from the almost continuous live entertainment on the stage at the Nashville Motor Speedway, right on the edge of the fairgrounds. Here folks can see more live music in a week than they can all year long at home.

People who win one of J. D. Haas Entertainment's trips to Fan Fair—well, you can just imagine how excited they are. They are in for a week of lots of special activities above and beyond all the usual Fan Fair fun. They go backstage at the shows, have private concerts in J.D.'s office, and get to spend an hour or two of quality time with the stars. If they're really lucky, some of the stars will agree to have dinner with them.

In all his years of doing his contests, J.D. had found that most of the stars were really pleasant and generous with their time. But he had an awful time getting any of them to go to the airport with him to pick up his winners.

In June of 1989, contest winners from around the country who arrived at Nashville International Airport were met at all their gates by a tall, strapping guy who was "dressed to the nines," as J.D. put it, in spit-shined boots, pressed jeans, a starched shirt, and a sharp Stetson. He carried their bags to J.D.'s van or their rental cars. He sang for them right there at the airport.

That superfriendly, suitcase-carrying singing cowboy was Garth Brooks. Who?

Maybe the contest winners had heard his song "Much Too Young (To Feel This Damn Old)" on the radio. Maybe they hadn't. But it didn't matter to Garth. "Pam Lewis, genius that she is," says J.D., "had asked Garth to come to the airport. He wasn't one of these guys to say, 'Are they this kind or that kind of people?' He didn't care about politics, he cared about people—he just liked people, so when Pam asked Garth, he just came out to the airport. He was just wonderful."

All of J.D.'s winners liked Garth right away, even if they had never heard of him. "I've never met a person that hasn't just gotten who he was about," J.D. says. "He was just starting and only had one single, but he was willing to go out and get it while other people waited for opportunities to come to them."

J. D. Haas—who has met and spent time with dozens of important artists and stars—says he loves it when artists who are genuine and real make people feel important, when they take people they've never met and, confident that there's good in everybody, find something fascinating about them. "Garth had that ability," he says.

Chuck and Rose Wheeler, from Turlock, California, re-member their trip to Fan Fair like it was yesterday. Chuck owns two construction companies, and Rose, an aesthetician, owns a health and beauty shop, where she gives facials and massages. Native Californians, they are high school sweet-hearts who've been married for twenty years. Chuck says, "Had it not been for that trip, we would still not be country fans. Garth is how we got into listening to country music."

Chuck recalls the "cowboy with the hat who was so hun-gry, like all the other fellows on Music Row. He would play for anybody who would listen. Spending the week with him, he was just one of us. We found it so amazing that this tal-ented individual was so genuine in everything he did."

There was a welcome reception at J.D.'s office, and Garth brought Sandy. "There he was, holding hands with Sandy and carrying his guitar in his other hand," J.D. says. "The fans loved her."

These days, J.D.'s contest winners are treated to free shows at places like the Bluebird Café, but back then J.D.

couldn't afford to rent Nashville's singer/songwriter clubs, so the free concerts took place in his office.

Garth came and sat in J.D.'s rocking chair in front of twenty or thirty people and played for more than an hour. He sang the songs that would later become big hits. "People were sitting just mesmerized," J.D. says. "One of the winners, from Miami, Florida, asked Garth to sing 'Better Man,' not realizing it was Clint Black's big hit. Clint was Garth's biggest competition in the beginning. But Garth did 'Better Man' without any hesitation. He played it and he did a great job, and he didn't tell the woman who'd asked that it wasn't his song."

Garth had dinner with J.D.'s contest winners, and that night "has to be our best memory of him," Chuck says. Before dinner, Chuck and Rose went to Ernest Tubb Record Shop down on Broadway in Nashville and asked at the counter for some music by Garth. They couldn't find any, but they met someone in the store who said he was Garth's bass player and gave them a cassette tape.

"At dinner that night, I said, 'Hey, Garth, would you mind signing this for us?'" Chuck says. "He said, 'I've never given an autograph. This is my very first autograph I've ever given.'"

Chuck and Rose still have that cassette, which Rose has had custom framed, along with a lot of other Garth Brooks memorabilia they've collected over the years.

That year Garth made his first Fan Fair appearance as a new Capitol Records artist. When he was done, he signed autographs for the fans. "What was so amazing," Chuck says, "it was raining, incredible rains, and he was standing out behind the stage signing autographs up to his ankles in water. Everybody just loved him. He's an individual that, when you're connecting, it feels like just you and him. It's very intense."

"He had my contest winners in the VIP complimentary seats," J.D. says, "and then he took all of us backstage as his guests. He was the first artist ever to take us backstage."

All of J.D.'s contest winners became friends with Garth Brooks at Fan Fair in 1989. It was, says J.D., the treat of a lifetime for a lot of those people—especially after Garth became famous and they realized how great it had been to have had him to themselves for a week.

A gentleman from Valdosta, Georgia, asked if Garth had time to write a song with him, and Garth said yes. "Garth made time, he took the guy somewhere and spent two or three hours writing with him," J.D. says. "I always wondered what happened with that song."

"After Fan Fair, when we came back home, we started calling radio stations," Chuck says. "We told them, 'You've got to play this guy's music. We just saw him in front of twenty thousand people.' Then it seems 'Much Too Young' sprouted. We helped it along as much as we could."

Some months later, Chuck and Rose went to see Garth play at the Circle Star Theater in San Carlos, California. "He put on a great show, and after the show he was signing autographs," Chuck says. The line was so long that Chuck and Rose decided not to wait but walked by Garth and said hi. "He looked up at us and said, 'Chuck and Rose Wheeler, the radio station winners'! We couldn't believe it—him really remembering us was incredible."

Chuck told Rose after that show, "It's incredible. We've got his very first autograph and he's going to be a major superstar."

Garth Brooks and Stillwater spent the entire second half of 1989 on the road. They opened for a lot of other acts, including Steve Wariner, who was out performing the many number-one hits he'd gotten in the eighties, like "All Roads Lead to You," "Some Fools Never Learn," and "Life's Highway."

Out on the road, Garth was taking the experience he'd gained playing in all those clubs in Stillwater, Oklahoma, and working even harder to make himself and his show memorable. Joe Harris was getting the best reports an agent can ever get from the road—all the places Garth played wanted him back and were willing to pay more money to have him.

Garth did opening slots for people like Kenny Rogers and The Judds, fine-tuning the show in front of audiences who, in coming to see Rogers and The Judds, were open to new directions for country music. His managers started getting reports off the road, according to Pam Lewis, that Garth was "not just another cowboy."

Pam says Garth started doing things live that no country artist had done before. "He would leave the stage and come into the audience and sing," she says. "Most performers keep the barrier of the stage between themselves and the audience, but not Garth. He would sing to a girl in the crowd," Lewis remembers. "He jumped on tables, kicked beer bottles off the tables, sang and danced. He did a version of 'All the Girls I Loved Before,' doing Julio Iglesias's version with a Spanish accent, then a nasally Willie Nelson.

"Garth used his hat like a prop, threw it into the audience, tilted it to the side," Lewis says, "and had fun. It was no longer 'I'm a cowboy, you're the audience.' It was 'I'm not just going to stand and sing.' He interacted with the band, ran around the stage, grabbed the drumsticks and started playing drums. He would laugh and have a good time."

Audiences responded—and remembered.

One of the acts Garth opened for was the Ace in the Hole Band, the great group of players that back up George Strait in concert, at a show in Jackson, Mississippi.

Garth and his band were spending a ton of time in Texas, trying to woo the huge audience in Dallas to get a radio hit going in that huge market.

At a club called Cowboys on Gaston Avenue, Garth had the audience of two thousand people on their feet with an awesome show that was all the more dazzling because most of these people had never heard of him. Who was this guy standing on top of the speakers and singing from the middle of the packed dance floor?

One thing they did know: he looked as if he could be one of them. "Garth is so relatable," Pam Lewis says. "He looked like everybody's brother or son. He wasn't threatening to men. Mothers wouldn't mind if their daughters brought him home. Kids liked him, grandparents too."

Garth was all over Dallas. He played ten shows in three months at clubs with names like Crystal Chandelier, Nowhar But Texas, and Steppers. He also got to play at the king of all country bars, Billy Bob's Texas.

Over in the Fort Worth Stockyards, Billy Bob's Texas is the world's largest honky-tonk—and that's no bull. It has a 100,000-square-foot entertainment area and forty individual bar stations. The club opened at the height of the "urban cowboy" craze in April of 1981. There's never been a mechanical bull in Billy Bob's, but there have been more than twenty-three thousand live ones in the twelve-hundred-seat Billy Bob's Bull Riding Arena, which has live bull riding every Friday and Saturday night. Between the Billy Bob's Dry Goods Store and the Billy Bob's Texas Bar-B-Q, you never have to leave the place.

Garth put on a show at Billy Bob's that was every bit as big and bold as the club itself. The patrons went wild over the way Garth raised the ante on what constituted a country music show. Billy Bob's manager, Billy Minick, called him "one of the smartest, most aware artists I've ever dealt with."

Unlike a lot of other artists, Garth Brooks understood from the start that country music lovers could be loyal fans—if they loved you and you treated them right. He'd spend time meeting them and autographing for them after the shows and looking them straight in the eye, as though he was trying to remember them in case they ever met again.

When he played Nowhar But Texas before his first album was released, Garth had an audience of fewer than twenty people, but he played his heart out with the same intensity he would later display at bigger stadiums. Remember the famous line by Jon Landau in *Rolling Stone* about Bruce Springsteen? Landau wrote that he had seen the future of rock and roll in Bruce's show. Well, in those Texas clubs, long before anyone really knew the name Garth Brooks, people were saying they were seeing the future of country music.

The most fun was at Tulsa City Limits. Returning triumphant from Nashville, his first album finally a reality, Garth played to a crowd of his friends from Stillwater, including just about everyone who worked at DuPree's Sports.

"Hello, Tulsa Oklahoma!" Garth sang his songs from his new album with his new band. He ended the show as he'd always done at Willie's and the other places in Stillwater, singing "American Pie" with just his guitar. Then he signed autographs until two in the morning.

On the road, Garth liked to drive the bus late at night. It was calming to just sit behind the wheel, watching the highways disappear behind him. Being on the bus with the guys in the band, hanging out, listening to music, playing cards and just talking, was a way to feel normal despite the storms of change raging around him. Occasionally the bus broke down—and J. D. Haas would go out and pick up Garth and the band and help them get the bus fixed so they could go to the next gig.

The great reports that were coming back from radio stations to Capitol Records and what Joe Harris was hearing about Garth's knock-'em-dead performances were music to everyone's ears.

Pam and Bob went to Joe's office every Monday morning to talk about the weekend's shows. "I remember him drinking his coffee, and I'd say, would you like a little coffee with your creamer?" Pam says. "Joe was so wise, always giving us the best advice. He had a Holy Bible on his desk. What a grounded, spiritual, loving, decent man. We were very lucky to have him working with us. He told us it was important to have a big impact. We have to make sure people remembered what happened."

"I started a quote campaign," Pam says. "I came up with an idea: 'Garth Brooks, seeing is believing, hearing is believing, be a believer.' What set him apart was you had to see him to believe him." It wasn't Garth's looks, singing, or writing that put him over the top as far as fans were concerned, it was the live shows. So Pam Lewis started calling club owners and radio stations and asking for quotes about Garth. "Every week I sent out a press release using these quotes." The quotes attracted more people to pay attention, and once they did, they were hooked. "We had a groundswell of support and wanted to tell people about it. We were underdogs and wanted to work on the grassroots level. In the beginning we didn't have the label push and an unlimited budget to do some of the things we might have done in a different situation."

Given the great response Garth was getting from everyone who met him, Bob Doyle and Pam Lewis were eager to push the first single into the Top 10. "We hired radio promoters ourselves," Pam Lewis said, "and they worked their tails off, got the single back on the radio. There was still life in it."

By August, "Much Too Young" had peaked at number eight on the *Billboard* charts. Garth Brooks had a hit. According to Pam Lewis, the challenge now was to get the record company to realize there could be more and bigger hits to follow. "This label didn't know what they had," she says. "They hadn't had a hit in a while, they had to answer to a home office, and they couldn't just go demand two hundred fifty thousand dollars to promote Garth Brooks." Though they were coming off a strong song, Capitol couldn't get the albums in the stores fast enough to keep up with the demand Garth was generating with all his touring. So Lewis and Bob Doyle dug into their own pockets to supplement what Capitol was doing.

Even in the midst of all the work to launch his career, Garth insisted on going back to Oklahoma to play at the annual benefit for the Brush Creek Boys Ranch, an organization for troubled teens. He and Sandy didn't want to miss the event, where he had played for many years.

The New York Metropolitan Country Music Association (NYCMA) started out in 1983 as an organization of people who wanted a place in the Big Apple to listen to country music. They also wanted to be able to keep dancing to country music at a time when all the clubs that had opened in the city during the "urban cowboy" craze were closing down.

Brenda Giammanco, a past president of the association and its current treasurer, says that membership grew from a handful of people to about six hundred. "We hold dances every Saturday night in the Glendale area of Queens and hold several philanthropic events throughout the year. We tried to become a family organization and hold events children can be part of." An offshoot of the group, the Round-Up Dancers, is the only totally choreographed exclusively country line-dance group in the country.

The group holds free concerts in New York City's many parks—from Forest Park to Juniper Valley in the Middle Village section of Queens, to Cunningham Park, Astoria Park, Little Neck Park, and wherever else the New York City Parks Department is having summer concert series.

In late 1989, NYCMA worked with agent Dick Beacham, who, through Joe Harris, booked Garth to play at Forest Park in the late summer of 1990. At the time of the booking, Garth's only hit song was "Much Too Young (To Feel This Damn Old)."

After much debate about which song to release next, Capitol chose "If Tomorrow Never Comes," cowritten by Kent Blazy and Garth. The third track on Garth's first album showed what is so special and appealing about him—the ability to tap an unspoken emotion and express it in lyrics. The universality of the lyrics was attractive to all music lovers, whether they lived in New York City or Butte, Montana. Capitol also decided to make "If Tomorrow Never Comes" Garth's first video.

On the lawn outside a sweet Victorian house with lots of lovely gingerbread trim and a welcoming porch, a little girl and a woman—played by Sandy Brooks, looking utterly radiant—are frolicking in the sunshine. Flowers shimmer, the light is fuzzy. Their faces show joy just as intense as the somber gaze on the face of the man sitting inside, surrounded by all the pretty touches that make the house a home, singing about his fear he hasn't shown his love. What if he isn't able to before death takes him away unexpectedly? What if tomorrow never comes? The lovely scenes outside and the worried man inside come together just at the end when he embraces the little girl and the woman and the three walk together into the house. (Later Garth said that the house where it was filmed was one that he and Sandy had driven by frequently when they first moved to Nashville, dreaming that one day they could live in one just like it.)

Garth took to the camera like gravy to grits. He loved performing with Sandy and said it wasn't really a job, not like acting at all. It just felt comfortable and like a lot of fun, like filming real life as it was happening. But a few weeks later, when he saw the nearly final edit of the video at Scene Three Studios in Nashville, he just broke down and cried and walked out of the room. Soon people would discover just what had moved Garth to tears that were clearly not tears of joy.

"If Tomorrow Never Comes" hit the number-one spot in September. Here was only the second song to reach the public at a time when the album was not exactly flying off the shelves. Had more people bought the album over the first five or six months of its release, they would have found in it a wealth of great music to listen to.

A song like "Everytime That It Rains," written by Charley Stefl, Ty England, and Garth Brooks, showed one of Garth's greatest gifts—he could sell a song better than anyone, becoming the character whether it was something he had actually experienced or not. A story of young seduction set to a waltz, "Everytime That It Rains" is in truth autobiographical, a fact that made Sandy jealous even though Garth insisted that his experiences in life before he had met her were fair game for songwriting.

"Cowboy Bill," written by Larry Bastian and Ed Beghoff, is about the ability of young people to know who's real and who's false long before they've had their spirits clouded by skepticism. The song is like a movie in its rich visual sense, as is "Alabama Clay," by Larry Cordle and Ronny Scaife. "Nobody Gets Off in This Town," written by Larry Bastian and Dewayne Blackwell, and "Not Counting You," which Garth wrote himself, are as traditional as can be, the kinds of songs that could have been played back in any honky-tonk in Oklahoma. Sandy had contributed lyrics to "I've Got a Good Thing Going" and is credited as a writer along with Garth and Larry Bastian; the song is as listenable as a cool breeze on a spring day. Here was an album with a lot of rich, unique songs, and in the spring of 1989 everyone could only hope that more people would soon get to sample it.

So when "If Tomorrow Never Comes" hit that number-one spot, there was plenty of reason to celebrate—except that around this time Garth and Sandy were having marital problems, problems that Garth would ultimately make public, problems that were at the root of his tearful outburst when he saw the video of the song.

It was hard enough for the couple to be apart so much after having been constantly together for years, working and dreaming and striving toward this very moment of success. But worse still, Sandy was hearing that Garth was cheating on her while out on the road.

The temptations on the road are constant. There's no time to stop and think. Meals are fast food. Home is one hotel room after another. Every hour is booked with visits to retailers, press interviews, sound checks, phone calls back and forth to managers and record companies, and all the other details of trying to make a name for yourself in a short period of time.

Some enthusiastic fans would buy drinks for Garth and hand them to him onstage. Although he never liked alcohol, Garth often felt obliged to toast the fan and drink the drink—a big mistake in that it affected not only his voice but also his good judgment. Garth would get so hung up in all of his new-found excitement—staying up all night after the show, partying a lot—that he'd neglect to call home for several days at a time, adding to the problems between him and Sandy.

But the real problem was that what Sandy had heard was true: Garth had been cheating on his wife.

On November 4, Sandy called Garth. He was in Sikeston, Missouri, getting ready to play a concert the next night in Cape Girardeau, opening for Eddy Rabbitt and Kenny Rogers. She told her husband she knew he'd been cheating on her and was ready to leave him unless he came home to resolve their marriage. She'd packed her bags. She'd bought her ticket. Garth was devastated.

Sandy had spent two years of her life working as many as three jobs to help her husband achieve his dream. She wasn't going to stand for him acting as if that didn't matter.

When he went onstage the next night, Garth's voice was hoarse. He sang a few songs, including "Much Too Young (To Feel This Damn Old)." Then something amazing happened. Partway into "If Tomorrow Never Comes," nearly in tears, he stopped and told the audience his troubles. He'd been out on the road only a few months, but already he'd discovered how tough it could be. He talked about his love for his wife and alluded to some "bad things" going on.

Ty England, playing guitar, felt for his friend. He later said that the experience of seeing Garth go through so much pain in his marriage changed the lives of everyone in his band and organization. "We saw how much we could hurt somebody," England said.

After gaining his composure, Garth sang the song all the way through. When he was done with his set the audience, who didn't know him from Adam and had come to see the other two acts, gave him a standing ovation. Garth says he heard a woman's voice in the crowd during that show, a woman he couldn't see but to whom he would always be grateful. Her voice said, "Go home to her, Garth."

In late 1989, Garth Brooks and Stillwater joined the Kenny Rogers Christmas Tour. Garth and his band traveled the country through January of 1990 and were still able to go out to a mall or restaurant and blend into the crowds. Little did they know that this ordinary activity would soon become impossible. Being anonymous is what most of us take for granted. Garth Brooks wouldn't be unknown for much longer.

A fan club was organized for Garth by a friend, Tami Rose, around this time. Members could receive two backstage passes and a chance to meet Garth after his shows.

Something extraordinary was happening during the next few months—something that signaled Garth Brooks was a new kind of artist for Nashville.

Ira Fraitag is a music industry consultant, artist manager, and producer who has worked with many acts and major music companies. In 1989 and 1990, he was working on a project to promote David Bowie's Sound and Vision Tour and the rerelease of all of Bowie's albums around the world. EMI Capitol was Bowie's label. As part of the project, Fraitag spent a lot of time in Capitol's New York and Los Angeles offices as well as the company's offices in London, Paris, Berlin, Copenhagen, and Madrid. The same EMI staffers Ira Fraitag had worked with while on tour in Europe with Garth's hero Don McLean in the 1970s were now asking him about Garth Brooks.

"In record company offices in New York and L.A., Nashville was seen as a poor relation," Fraitag says. "But there was a buzz about Garth in New York, L.A., and even Europe due to all the talk about his live shows. Right from the start, he was different and he got noticed."

When David Bowie was playing a big arena in Dallas—and Garth was playing a much smaller hall in Fort Worth—Ira Fraitag heard people who'd seen Garth's show carrying on about him.

By the spring of 1990, Garth and Sandy had worked things out. Sandy understood that Garth had just been flexing his ego. She knew he was a very sexual person, but she also knew that his straying hadn't meant anything, that he really loved only her. That, coupled with the fact of how ashamed and embarrassed he was, made it easier for her to cope with his infidelity. Still Garth realized it had taken a "helluva human being" to forgive him. He promised he'd do everything to make their marriage work. He knew Sandy had given him the strength to succeed. And the bottom line was he knew how much he loved her.

But there was another storm to weather: the entire Capitol Records management had changed. Jimmy Bowen was hired to be president, replacing Jim Fogelsong. As was his style—he'd done it before at several other major Nashville labels—Bowen came in and dropped many artists. He also fired a lot of people, including Lynn Shults, the man who'd signed Garth. Bowen replaced Shults with James Stroud, a sessions drummer who had been his top A & R man at a previous label.

Born in the Texas Panhandle, Bowen had been a rock and roll musician in the 1950s (as part of the Rhythm Orchids he had a number-one hit with "Party Doll") and a producer and A & R executive in the 1960s (producing number-one hits for Frank Sinatra and Dean Martin years after their heydays). He came to Nashville in 1976 and, while running five different labels before coming to Capitol, he brought to Music City the more sophisticated record-production techniques and equipment used in rock and roll. He also urged artists to take more control over their music and careers, making them coproducers of their albums. He'd worked with many artists, from Mel Tillis and Conway Twitty to Reba McEntire and George Strait.

When Garth was getting rejections from record labels in Nashville, one of them had come from Jimmy Bowen and producer Tony Brown at MCA Nashville.

Jimmy Bowen always made it his business to go see his acts live. Already impressed with Garth's number-one single, "If Tomorrow Never Comes," Bowen was knocked out when he went to see Garth. When singing "If Tomorrow Never Comes," Garth had stepped off the low stage, taken a baby out of its mother's arms, and held it in his arms while singing the song. Jimmy Bowen told Pam Lewis and Bob Doyle how lucky they were to have Garth as a client and then proceeded to make everyone at the label go see him. Amazingly, very few people at Capitol had seen him perform. It's no wonder, as Pam Lewis said, that they didn't know what they had.

But Nashville in general didn't know what to make of Garth either. "He brought fun and frivolity and childish glee and sexuality to the music," Pam Lewis said. "Here's this guy, screaming, kicking, doing an Elton John song, then a Jim Reeves song." No one had ever seen this before in country music.

Jimmy Bowen decided to invest a lot of Capitol's time and marketing money in the kid from Oklahoma. He also told Garth he had listened to the first album. "Onstage you're this vibrant, electrifying presence," Bowen told him, "and that's not in the album." Garth said he did that on purpose, that he felt the album and the show had to be two different things. Bowen totally disagreed. If someone saw Garth live and got knocked out by his show, and then went and spent money on the album and didn't get that same emotional impact, why would they buy more records? The shows and the albums could be different, but the impact needed to be the same. Bowen also told Garth and Allen Reynolds that he wanted the next album from Garth sooner than they had planned to turn it in. Garth and Allen Reynolds said no, that they could not do an album to the standards they wanted that fast.

After Garth and Reynolds picked the songs for the next album, they made work tapes with just a guitar player accompanying Garth's voice. They didn't need to be perfect—no one but Garth, Reynolds, and the studio band would ever hear them.

Reynolds says that after hearing a singer do a song that way, "I'll get chill bumps if the song and the singer seem like that good a marriage."

Then they played the work tapes for the studio band. "The first time, the band just hears Garth with a guitar player, and that way they're not borrowing someone else's idea," Reynolds says. "Wonderful ideas come from the players—that's their specialty."

In order to try to get players to be free and uninhibited about offering up their ideas, Reynolds just tried to facilitate the communication and to stay out of the discussion as much as possible.

"In the case of Garth Brooks, he quite often has specific ideas about a song, but he understood, and it became his habit, too, to just lay back and listen to the ideas that came from the band," Reynolds says. "In Nashville it's second nature to musicians to collaborate—they just immediately are engaged. It's like a puzzle." Ideas can be added or subtracted as the songs take shape. "If the artist and I have found songs we are truly excited about, then when we go into the studio it's time to have fun. My only instruction to the engineer is to be ready so no one has to do it over because we weren't rolling tape."

By the time of the 1990 Country Radio Seminar, Garth was already too established to be part of its New Faces showcase. Still, Bob Doyle and Pam Lewis felt it was important that he get a chance to perform. So they convinced ASCAP executive Merlin Littlefield—the same guy who had given Garth a reality check on the music business when he first came to town in 1985—to allow Garth to make an appearance at ASCAP's big CRS luncheon.

Garth sang the song that was the last to have been recorded on his first album and then a song slated to be on his second album. That song was the one he had demo'd and hoped to record, one that would become a defining moment, another of his signature songs and one of the most played songs in the history of radio.

The crowd at the ASCAP luncheon was knocked out.

Garth was touring and getting the chance to open for big acts like The Judds. He was opening shows at state fairs for his Oklahoma comrade Reba McEntire. "He was so outlandish, so far beyond anything anybody did onstage," Reba said. "I thought it was weird, but I thought, 'It's classy, different, unique, and he's going to be a big star. This is what people want.'" He was one of the performers on the bill at Farm Aid IV—where he met one of his idols, Elton John, who left the show to sit at the bedside of Ryan White, the young boy whose death from AIDS brought attention to the tragic epidemic.

The Academy of Country Music on the West Coast gave Garth Brooks three nominations in 1990: New Male Vocalist, Single, and Song for "If Tomorrow Never Comes." Pam Lewis and her publicity machine went into action. "We worked on the people voting, wrote letters, made phone calls, and sent out postcards," she says. "We tried to do lots of media to create awareness."

On April 25, the Academy of Country Music broadcast its awards ceremony on national television. Garth was in the audience and managed to keep smiling as his name was called during the nominations but not called for awards. There was one highlight in the evening: one of Garth's heroes, George Strait, was named Entertainer of the Year.

"Garth was devastated," Pam Lewis says. "We were sad, too. James Stroud sat in front of us, and he was working for Capitol by then. He had produced Clint Black at RCA, and Clint was winning the awards." After the show, Garth and Sandy just left. Pam didn't go to any of the parties she'd been invited to, she says. "I went back to the hotel room and cried."

That night, losing in all three categories for which he was nominated, Garth might have wished he'd missed the pain. But he'd have had to miss "The Dance."

CHAPTER THREE

THE STAR

*A*my Kurland says it's wonderful when a singer or song-writer gets attention at the Bluebird Café, but her favorite thing is when a song gets noticed. One night, Tony Arata, a songwriter from Savannah, Georgia, who had once been an advertising copywriter, was on the bill. He sang a few songs and then introduced another one. It was called "The Dance." Garth was in the audience, still at a time when he was dreaming of getting a record deal.

"People were very polite when it was over," Garth said about the smattering of applause that followed Arata's performance, "and the voice inside me was standing up and screaming, 'Didn't any of you hear what I heard?'"

What Garth heard was a song of such depth and simplicity that it fulfilled what is often, sadly, the missed goal of every songwriter: to describe a feeling that is at once incredibly personal and completely universal. Garth asked Tony Arata for a demo and told him if he ever got a record deal he would record that song. But in all the excitement of the following months, he forgot about it until, toward the end of the sessions for *Garth Brooks,* producer Allen Reynolds reminded him about it.

"'The Dance' was and remains one of my favorite songs that I have ever been associated with," Reynolds says. "It was in that first group of songs Garth brought in. After I listened to it I said to him, 'There's a song in here, "The Dance"—it's a beautiful, economic poem that speaks on several different levels, depending on how you want to relate to it.' I asked him how he felt about it, and he said 'I love it,'" Reynolds says. "Well, if you love it, I think we ought to do it," he told Garth.

Reynolds still smiles at the memory of the recording sessions for "The Dance."

"When we went in to record it, at some point pretty early on Bobby Wood started playing that piano figure, and I remember Garth responding immediately to that and asking him to keep that up. He did, and it still is one of the prettiest things Bobby Wood ever played, one of most moving songs I ever heard."

To this day, Reynolds uses the story of how Garth discovered the song as an example when he talks to aspiring artists. "I tell them even though you don't have a record company, you don't have a deal, you've got ears," he said. "Be looking for songs, and arm yourself now with the moment you hope to get to later on."

Although it's not a country song, "The Dance" reflects Garth's love of such singers as Don McLean and James Taylor, who can be proud that Garth, like them, incorporated his musical influences and then took them a step farther. Garth doesn't copy the artists he loves but is able to take these influences and create something new from them. That's how music grows and evolves. Whether you're a singer or writer or painter, everything you've ever heard or seen becomes an influence.

The story in "The Dance" resonates for everyone who has ever wondered if the pain of a sad outcome was worth the happiness leading up to it. Garth brings so much passion to his singing of it amid a haunting instrumentation that gives its own power to the song.

When Garth's third single, "Not Counting You," was going up the charts, Jimmy Bowen and Allen Reynolds had a talk about what song to release next. Reynolds suggested "The Dance," but Bowen disagreed, saying that the radio promotion people in the company wouldn't go for a slow ballad that wasn't very country. But Allen Reynolds insisted "The Dance" would be a career record for Garth. He told Bowen that Garth was doing the song in concert and "you could hear a pin drop." "Garth wants this as a single," Reynolds told Bowen, "and if you put it out as a single, it will separate him from the other hats."

So just before Garth's unhappy evening at the ACM Awards in Los Angeles, Capitol Records released "The Dance" as the fourth single. *Billboard* called it "easily the most eloquently written and sensitively interpreted song of the past decade."

In April 1990, Garth asked his brother Kelly to come to Nashville to help handle some aspects of his touring and his business. Kelly wasn't sure he wanted to leave his banking job in Oklahoma, but when Garth said the simple words "I need you," Kelly was on his way. Garth also asked his sister Betsy to join the band as a bass player and singer, and a friend since second grade, Mickey Weber, to be his road manager. He figured these folks, who'd known him all his life, would keep him in line if he started getting too big for his britches.

By 1990, music videos were as common a part of an artist's marketing as touring. Whereas record companies had once devoted substantial promotion budgets to getting singles played on radio—and still did—they were now also driven to get heavy rotation of artists' videos on television. It was a no-brainer: touring cost tons of time and money, and despite the large stadiums where big shows could be held, still didn't get the artist in front of the millions of viewers that television promised. Rock stars like Madonna and Michael Jackson were as huge as they were due in no small part to the constant playing of their videos on MTV. Both CMT (Country Music Television) and TNN (The Nashville Network) were getting started at around this time, helping to fuel the rise of country's popularity.

Garth Brooks the music fan was still from the old school as far as videos were concerned. He didn't much care for them. As is true of many music-loving baby boomers, when he listened to songs and got lost in the story and lyrics, he preferred to imagine for himself what the characters looked like. Having his own vision of the song made it that much more personal an experience for him.

"If I was going to make music videos, I was going to give them a third dimension," he says. "And instead of funneling the sight of the vision, I was going to expand it to reach more people and, hopefully, reach more emotion."

Well, if listening to "The Dance" brought a lump to your throat, as it did for so many people who heard in its lyrics the message that the loving was worth the losing, watching the video pretty much brought a tear to your eyes. Here Garth took the concept of the song one step farther. The message of "The Dance" for him was that it was worth risking anything for a dream.

Instead of the artist performing the song or having actors replay the song's story, as is so common in music videos, in the video for "The Dance" there is actual news footage of dreamers such as Martin Luther King, Jr., and John F. Kennedy, two people whose vision and hopes for America galvanized the country into believing in its highest ideals and challenged its citizens to live up to them. Along with King and Kennedy, Garth included his own lifelong hero, John Wayne, who in movies and real life stood for the values of right and wrong. Garth had said that he'd like to carry the same messages in song that John Wayne did in his movies, because Wayne "stood for honesty" and his characters always knew right from wrong, whether they were the good guy or the bad guy.

As a symbol perhaps of all the musical heroes lost to death either through their own self-destruction or the madness of others—people like Jimi Hendrix, Janis Joplin, Jim Morrison, and John Lennon—Garth included images of the handsome Keith Whitley, dancing as he gazed in such sweet love at his wife, Lorrie Morgan. Whitley was a talented country and bluegrass artist who died of alcohol poisoning in 1989. Lane Frost wasn't well known to many of the video's viewers, but to Garth he was symbolic of the song's themes. Frost, who had achieved his dreams of winning a championship in the rodeo, earning hundreds of thousands of dollars in prize money, was only twenty-five when, just about a year before the video was made, he was killed by a bull at a rodeo in Cheyenne, Wyoming. Likewise, the incredible daring and tragic death of the crew of the space shuttle *Challenger* made their inclusion in the video a powerful addition to its heart-wrenching message.

Interspersed with these images was that of the newest American dreamer to capture the country's attention: Garth Brooks, the ordinary guy from Oklahoma with extraordinary dreams. And he ended the video with his own message.

"I'd never compare myself with the folks in this video," he says at one point in the video, his eyes fixed on what he hoped would be the faces of millions watching it, "but if for some reason I have to leave this world unexpectedly, I hope they play 'The Dance' for me, because I mean that's it, 'I could have missed the pain, but I'd have had to miss the dance,' and I wouldn't miss this for the world."

Country music has always been about the personal. Stories of love and heartbreak, stories about family, are as intrinsic to country music as the sound of a wailing fiddle. But Garth was taking these themes and, to use a popular phrase, kickin' 'em up a notch. With the exception of "Not Counting You," each of his first singles had in one way or another addressed truly existential themes. An aging rodeo rider worrying about the young bucks who are gaining on him at a time when he's growing too tired to care anymore. A man worried he might die before having the chance to tell his loved ones how much he cares. And an anthem to the power of a dream—the power to make you disregard even the risk of crashing and burning to achieve it. This was more than cryin' about your baby cheatin' on Saturday night. These songs went straight for the heart by way of the jugular.

One of the things that appeals to Garth about the songwriting skills evident in country songs—and appeals to country music fans as well—is the ability of the music to express deeply felt emotions. "There's a million things you can say that need to be said," he told *People* magazine, "messages that are of common sense, values, things people have to be reminded of."

Garth was offering songs that were real, that reported on real life as it was happening. Like the traveling, folksinging troubador that is so much a part of American myth and reality, he was observing life and then showing it to us anew.

Study Garth's face in this video and in the one for "If Tomorrow Never Comes." He is both completely relaxed as he sings his heart out and undeniably intense in his passionate communication of his song, his dream, and himself. People seeing him for the first time were intrigued by the apparent contradictions. Here was a guy who looked like someone who lived down the road, not a glamorous show business hunk at all, with a voice that could melt down steel, singing about the kinds of thoughts that keep you awake at night.

This was also a country singer who repeatedly said he appreciated women and hoped he would have daughters when he had children. He said he always felt women were extremely intelligent. Many country singers and songs glorify women—but not necessarily for their intelligence.

In mid-May, "The Dance" debuted on TNN. In early June, CMT put it in heavy rotation. The impact on fans was swift and dramatic. Many wrote heart-wrenching letters to Garth, to Capitol Records, and to CMT detailing the ways the song and video had personally touched their lives.

"The Dance" became Garth's second number-one hit. Now the whole music industry was buzzing about the kid from Oklahoma who was looking like the biggest overnight sensation to hit Music City in years.

On a June day in 1990, thousands of fans were crammed into the bleachers of the Nashville Motor Speedway at the edge of the fairgrounds. Throughout Fan Fair, each record label is given a block of time to put on its part of the almost continuous live music show that makes the price of admission a real bargain.

They were here to see Garth, and Garth gave them his all. These were the folks who had helped to make his dream come true.

Garth had always known that the record company, his managers, his booking agent, and all the others who were part of his success were just the beginning. The key ingredient was sitting out there right in front of him. If it hadn't been for them, and folks just like them back at home, Capitol Records president Jimmy Bowen wouldn't have been striding toward him on the stage holding the biggest prize of all: a gold record commemorating the sale of 500,000 copies of his very first album, *Garth Brooks.*

Joe and Shirley Harris, who went to Fan Fair that year, were amazed to find Garth standing there signing autographs all day. For hours and hours he stood, talking to the fans, making them understand how grateful he was to them for their support.

Pam Lewis had lined up a lot of interviews with the many reporters and news organizations that came to Fan Fair. "Garth had to be in three places at once," she says, "and the fans were lining up for so long in the heat that some of them passed out. It was hard for me to get Garth to take a break to talk to the press. He was adamant about seeing his fans."

One of the thrills for the winners of J. D. Haas's trips to Fan Fair is to go backstage at the shows at the Nashville Motor Speedway and meet with the artists when they come offstage. "I was looking at one line that was snaking around a building," J.D. says. "I asked, 'Whose line is that?' It was for Garth Brooks."

Garth's new fans got an even bigger thrill at Fan Fair in 1990. "We had a party for the fans at Douglas Corner," Lewis said. "The air-conditioning was out, and it was so hot. Sandy and some friends catered it with hot dogs and picnic food. We passed the gold album around so fans could have their picture taken with Garth and the album."

It was to be a Fan Fair that Garth and his fans would never forget.

It's always hot at Fan Fair, but that's nothing compared to how sweltering Nashville is in August. Still, artists and their organizations get the chills when the Country Music Association announces its nominations for that fourteen-inch bullet-shaped chunk of handblown glass, the CMA trophy that signifies the ultimate respect and love of your peers.

That year Garth Brooks received more nominations than anyone else—five in all: Male Vocalist, Single of the Year (as artist for "The Dance"), Song of the Year (as songwriter, with Kent Blazy, for "If Tomorrow Never Comes"), Video (for "The Dance"), and the Horizon Award (given to the artist whose career has shown the most growth in the past year).

He had garnered more nominations than Randy Travis, Hank Williams, Jr., Alabama, and even George Strait.

"This is like getting five invitations to a dance and not knowing if you'll get to dance or who with," he said when he got the news at a show in Springfield, Illinois. He added, "It's an award enough to be touring and fulfilling my dream, but this is great. Plus I get to rent a tux."

What a perfect time to release the second album, the all-important test of whether Garth Brooks was a flash in the pan or a beacon for the future. In late August, *No Fences* hit the stores. Its title would prove to be prophetic.

After the recording sessions had been completed, the last step in the process was for Allen Reynolds and engineer Mark Miller to mix the album. Sometimes there is overdubbing to be done at the end, but like most great producers, Reynolds didn't like to do that unless it was absolutely necessary. And if he did it with Garth's records, Garth was always there.

"Once you've got the record with the rhythm section and the singer, you know if you've got something that's got you excited," Reynolds says. "It doesn't become a record by adding other things to it. You can try things, try this idea if it doesn't work, no harm done. You've always got what you started with, which is the rhythm section. You continue to work with a cut until you've got it where you want it."

Most artists don't hang around for the mixing. It's a long, nitpicky process that sees the producer and engineer play the song over and over again.

"The way Garth and I worked," Reynolds explains, "was that Mark and I start with a mix in the morning and we know by a certain time in the afternoon we'll be reaching a point where we're closing in on it. That's when we need Garth to be there to give his imput about anything that we are doing. He's great. His ears are really good, so he always joins us after we've gotten it roughed out and to a point. Then we all collaborate on the final bit of drawing that mix together. And then you live with the mix for a while to make sure you're ready to sign off on it."

Having made such a strong statement with "The Dance," and given all that he had to celebrate, it was time for a party. After all, Garth Brooks hadn't popped on the scene just to be a philosopher.

The song that had so surprised the disc jockeys and radio programmers at the Country Radio Seminar back in March had been making the live audiences just as excited. It was the one Garth had sung the demo for when he could only dream of having the task of selecting a single from his second album. So picking the first single from *No Fences* was easy, and a new American anthem was born.

The song was called "Friends in Low Places," written by Dewayne Blackwell and Earl Bud Lee.

Over lunch on the afternoon of April 21, 1999, at Nashville's Sunset Grill, a music business hangout with fine food and wine, Dewayne Blackwell shared the story of events leading to Garth's recording of the song.

Blackwell, who was born in Corpus Christi, Texas, and brought up in California, is a veteran songwriter who moved to Nashville in the mid-1980s along with his brother, Ron Blackwell, who wrote "Little Red Riding Hood" for Sam the Sham and the Pharaohs.

Blackwell had written "Nobody Gets Off in This Town," which appeared on Garth's first album, with Larry Bastian.

Dewayne Blackwell was one of the first songwriters Garth had gotten to know when he came to Nashville. He loved Dewayne and admired his songwriting a lot. In fact, when Garth recorded his first album, he had surprised Dewayne Blackwell by cutting his tune "Mr. Blue," a song that had been a million-seller for the Fleetwoods years earlier.

"He did it without telling me. He just gave me a CD with the song on it. I went in the other room and listened to it, and tears started coming to my eyes," Dewayne said. "It really was a nice thing, and I loved what he did with the tune. Some people didn't—they don't like anything being messed with and changing the way you've heard a song. I think if you're not going to do something different with it, don't do it. But I like what he did."

Garth's version of the song added a really nostalgic moment to his first album.

Like many great songs, "Friends in Low Places" was born from a phrase tossed out almost offhandedly. Dewayne Blackwell and Bud Lee often spent time together in Nashville's restaurants and bars, and, as Bud said, "we were always looking for ideas for songs."

The time came one day to get the lunch check. "Bud was running up the bill, and a lot of time I'd get stuck with it before he had a hit," Blackwell said. He was quick to add, however, that since then Bud has picked up his share of lunch checks.

"I said, 'Bud, how are you going to pay for this?' And he said, 'Well, I've got friends in low places,'" Blackwell recalls.

"A feeling went from my backbone all the way up and stood my hair up on end after he said that. I took a drink and sat there thinking about that. I finally said to myself, 'I just can't leave and go write a song that was something he said.' So I said to him, 'Is this a song?' and he smiled at me and said, 'not yet.'"

Dewayne and Bud had written several song ideas on a napkin during that lunch, but the one about friends in low places was the only one they decided to expand upon later. "I really take my time with songs," Blackwell says. "I take it slow and think about things for a long time. But Bud's just like jumping on the couch and jumping on the ceiling and hitting the guitar and everything. Sometimes I wanted to Velcro him to the ceiling."

About a year later, Dewayne and Bud were having a champagne brunch at O'Charley's, and the pen and the napkin were on the table once again. Bud Lee says, "The first three lines of the song just fell out." After lunch they went back to Dewayne's house, and then, Bud says, "the chorus fell out as well."

Blackwell was pretty pleased with what they'd created. "The song wasn't my idea—it was his—but when he said it I knew it was a monster."

Although they'd been holding the song for Garth, Garth didn't go back into the studio for about eight months, because he was on the road so much. When he did get started recording his second album, he did three sessions without cutting "Friends in Low Places." By that time, one of the song's publishers thought Garth wasn't interested in the song anymore. When Garth found out he'd lost the hold, he called Dewayne.

"So I talked to him," Dewayne recalls. "I tried to explain I honestly had heard he'd been doing sessions and wasn't cutting the song, but I guess everyone jumped the gun. I think I really hurt his feelings. He said, 'Why did you do that? I told you I'd cut it. I thought we were friends.' I said, 'We are friends, Garth, but I wasn't going to hold you to it if you changed your mind.' But I said, 'If you want it, you're going to get it.'"

Garth cut the song soon after that. When it came time to finish recording the chorus, he wanted to capture the kind of party atmosphere the song was creating in the live shows.

"He brought about fifty people into the studio," Dewayne says. Sandy was there, as were Bob Doyle and Pam Lewis and Joe Harris and Garth's studio band, his road band, and some of their wives and girlfriends. "He had buckets of soft drinks and beer in the studio," Dewayne remembers. "Different groups of five or ten people were at the mikes, and he had us all singing. It was fun. It was a great idea."

If you listen closely to the song, you can hear the sound of a beer can opening.

Garth played the final cut for Dewayne before the song was released to radio. "You know that low note that he hits on there? He did that himself," Dewayne says. "When we were writing the melody I couldn't have gone down that low, so I didn't even try it. When it came out on the record and he hit that low note, I thought they must have VSO'd the track." VSO refers to a recording process that uses a variable speed oscillator, which works by taking a track at normal speed and playing it higher and faster, thereby raising the key. Then the artist hits that low note and the VSO mixes it down. "I said,

'Garth, did you VSO that thing?' He said, 'No, that's the way we do it in the show every time.' "

"Friends in Low Places" hit the *Billboard* charts on August 18 and just kept moving higher and higher.

The song, according to Pam Lewis, "exploded. It became a song everybody liked, not just country music fans." The college year had just begun, and many schools were having "Friends in Low Places" dance parties. Lewis says the song "became the anthem for parties."

Garth says he has a special affection for the song because it "tells about who I really am." Even though he was beginning to hang out with a lot of important and famous people, he still related more to "plain old folks," whom he calls the best people in the world.

Bud Lee thinks the song appeals to the rebel in everyone, "from nine-year-olds to ninety-year-olds."

Plenty of those plain old folks were thinking Garth was pretty wonderful too. In every town, county, and state, and in dorm rooms, barrooms, and rec rooms, "Friends in Low Places" was the song everyone was playing.

Before his first album had given Garth two number-one singles and two Top 10 hits, he had agreed to play at the Silver Spurs Gala fund-raiser in Arlington, Texas, for $10,000. By this time he was making ten times that much for each show. Many artists will want their fees adjusted when that happens, but Garth played for the amount he had agreed upon months earlier. Then, after the show, he donated his check to a charity that benefits cancer research.

A similar thing happened in New York. The New York Metro Country Music Association, which had booked Garth Brooks when he was a relatively unknown but wonderful country artist back in 1989, now had country's biggest star coming to New York to do a free concert in Forest Park in Queens. What excitement!

Forest Park was set up to hold 2,000 people for a concert. The biggest crowd the park had ever seen was 5,000 people for Barry Manilow. But on a hot August day in the summer of 1990, a crowd estimated by police to be 12,500—if not more—was cheering to the sounds of Garth Brooks.

"They had to close the park and the street," Brenda Giammanco recalls. "There were people lined up all over Woodhaven Boulevard. It's six lanes, almost a highway, and they had to close it. People were standing on the street and sitting in the trees."

Country music in New York City! Brenda and the NYCMA knew there were fans, but this was amazing. Before and after the show, Brenda and some of the others in the NYCMA hung out on Garth's bus with him and Sandy, who, Brenda says, "was really sweet." And Garth? "He was just a wonderful, sweet kid," Brenda says, "with a lot of humility."

"Friends in Low Places" was flying up the charts and, Brenda says, "Garth was so amazed. He didn't know if people here knew who he was, and here was this crowd of New Yorkers singing along with 'Friends.' He said, 'I can't believe you guys know all the words.'"

After the show, Garth and Sandy and Pam and Bob joined one of Pam's New York friends for a ride on the Circle Line, the boat cruise that goes around Manhattan on the Hudson and East Rivers. Wearing those funny foam Statue of Liberty head things, they laughed so much that Pam still laughs when she recalls it. "Things were really starting to happen for us," she says. The dream was starting to come true.

For No Fences, Garth wanted to choose songs that would continue to showcase his talents. Like all singers who have hits, he had to make sure the songs he chose were ones he'd be happy to sing in concert for years to come if he was lucky enough to have more hits. What did he look for in a song?

"It has to mean something to me," Garth says. "I would rather have one song that was from the heart than eighty songs that were clever and went to number one on the charts."

Stephanie Davis was the daughter of a Montana sheep farmer and had graduated from the University of Montana with a degree in journalism. After that, she worked as a cook in an oil camp on Alaska's North Slope—a job she got after the previous cook had been mauled and killed by a polar bear while taking out the garbage. From Alaska, she moved to San Francisco, playing all kinds of music as an accomplished fiddle, piano, trumpet, and guitar player. She had moved to Nashville in 1987 because she figured it was the place to get serious about her songwriting—and where, she hoped, she could land her own record deal.

Garth had heard Stephanie Davis sing a song at a singer/songwriter showcase, and when she was done he walked up to her and said he was looking for material for his second album. He told her he wanted to use the song, and she agreed. The song was "Wolves," and Garth made it the last track on No Fences—the place that had been so lucky for "The Dance" on his first album. The song is a heartbreaking story, telling first of the cattle that get lost to wolves in nature's own dance of wisdom and pain, and then talking of a family losing their farm as the bank takes over the land they have worked for generations. The song's narrator acknowledges that God has reasons for everything that happens but ends with a plea. The last line—"Oh, Lord, keep me from being, the one the wolves pull down"— is sung by Garth with complete conviction that communicates the full meaning of the song. Stephanie Davis writes with an economy of words that conveys maximum emotion. A video could not have illustrated the sentiment better than the spare lyrics. Garth showed that like his idol, George Strait, he knew how to pick the very best material.

"Wild Horses," written by Bill Shore and David Wills, is another song about choices—the rodeo rider's decision to promise Diane he'd have his last go-round and his inability to keep that promise. It's the wild horses that drag him away from her—and he is powerless to change who he is.

"Same Old Story," by Tony Arata, who wrote "The Dance," is a classic tale of one person loving too much.

By choosing and recording songs that went deeper into new emotional territory than even the most heart-wrenching songs in country's past, Garth Brooks was starting to make a big difference.

Jimmy Bowen had hired Joe Mansfield to be vice president for sales and marketing at Capitol Nashville. Capitol was going to spend money on advertising and on making sure there were plenty of CDs and cassettes in all of the stores—and in places where consumers could see them prominently displayed. This in turn prompted Garth to go out and make believers out of the folks who would be selling his music to the fans.

"We worked really closely with Capitol's regional sales guys and Joe Mansfield," Pam Lewis said, "and I think part of the reason Garth was so good about doing retail was that we had languished so in the first year and a half of the record deal. When we finally had people who believed enough and a label head who spent dollars, Garth was going to make sure he'd do his part."

Garth and his band went to Bentonville, Arkansas, to do a show for all the Wal-Mart employees at the company's corporate headquarters. Even after he was established and didn't have to go out to stores anymore, Garth continued to do so. "He would do in-store signings, bringing his guitar and playing a little bit," Pam says. "He personalized everything he signed instead of just signing 'Garth Brooks.'"

Before the official release date of *No Fences,* a radio station in Oklahoma called Pam Lewis and asked for an advance copy of the album. "I said I had no authorization to give it out. You'll get it when everyone else does," Pam recalls. Bill Catino, the head of promotion at Capitol, had to make sure all radio stations got the new album at the same time. "So the station called Colleen Brooks and tricked her. They told Colleen, 'We've talked to Pam, and she said to bring it over.' Colleen, who had recorded at Capitol Records in the fifties, didn't think twice, and she was more than happy to oblige," Pam says. "She told them you can't play the album, but on the way home, she heard a song from the album in the car. She was all upset and crying, and Capitol was furious. This was a month or six weeks earlier than it was supposed to be out."

Jimmy Bowen was in Hawaii. Pam called him, and at first he said Capitol would issue a cease-and-desist order to keep the station from playing any other songs from *No Fences.* But Pam says she thought, "This is fabulous from a PR and marketing standpoint. It always used to happen in rock and roll. Now, this country album was so hot people were playing it early on the radio." Pam asked Bowen if they had a similar story here. "He liked it, and he said—these are his exact words—'We'll get that son of a bitch right out.'" Capitol started shipping, and Pam called *USA Today.*

Where were you in October 1990? The world was busy. The United States announced it was strengthening its forces in the Persian Gulf as the crisis following Iraq's invasion of Kuwait was mounting. The words "East" and "West" had been dropped from "Germany" after the Berlin Wall came down in 1989, an event some people attribute in part to the influence of music on the hearts and minds of German citizens. Newspaper editorials were complaining about the "nasty" tone political ads were taking.

And Garth Brooks was on top of the world. On October 4, eighteen months after its release, his first album, *Garth Brooks,* was certified platinum. It was the first country album ever to go platinum in so short a time.

On October 6, Garth joined the Grand Ole Opry. It was very unusual for an artist to be asked to join that revered establishment so early in his career. Pam said she had started bugging Hal Durham, the manager of the Opry, right from the start to invite Garth to join. Joe Harris also called Durham, who was a friend of his, to let him know about Garth.

Garth Brooks was an artist whose first album had already started pushing the boundaries of country music—and whose future work would take country even more in the directions of rock and pop. By now, however, the Opry was more open to change than it used to be.

Bob Wills and His Texas Playboys arrived in Nashville for their first appearance at the Grand Ole Opry in 1944. Opry musicians who usually performed in overalls and straw hats loved the Playboys' stylish western suits, cowboy boots, and Stetson hats but didn't welcome their horns and drums, instruments that had been all but banned from the Opry stage. Wills refused to play without them. The Opry relented and let him play his full show that night, but they never invited him back. Still, the Opry musicians did begin wearing sharper clothes like Wills's, leading to the western fashions in country music that artists like George Strait and Garth Brooks so handsomely exemplify today. (Nashville didn't want to hold a grudge about the incident at the Ryman Auditorium, and neither did Wills. In 1968, he was inducted into the Country Music Hall of Fame.)

Garth was moved beyond measure when he became a member of the most esteemed organization in country music.

He said he considered his induction in the Grand Ole Opry his "greatest achievement." He felt so much reverence for being permitted to play where the greatest country artists had played for the past sixty-five years. He stood proudly on the circle on the stage of the Opry House that was taken out of the floor of the Ryman Auditorium when it was moved out to Opryland in 1974. Playing where Hank Williams and Roy Acuff and Minnie Pearl had first played, standing on that circle of wood was "the most wonderful feeling in the world," Garth said. He would not perform the wild show he took on the road when he was playing the Grand Ole Opry. He wanted to uphold what the Opry had worked so hard to establish: morals and manners.

The very same day that Garth received that high honor, "Friends in Low Places" hit number one. It stayed there for four weeks and went on to become the most played song in the history of country radio.

And just in case anyone in Garth's world thought they would have time to catch their breath, on October 8, they were all dressed up and seated in the audience at the Country Music Awards.

Getting seated was an adventure in itself. Garth had told Pam Lewis he would take care of getting the tickets to the show. Pam told him he really didn't need to, that she would take care of it, but he insisted.

"Bob and myself, Garth and Sandy were backstage at the Opry, about to come out," Pam says, "and I said to Garth, 'It's a big night, do you have your tickets for your parents?' Well, he'd never ordered tickets for Sandy's parents or his parents. Now we needed four tickets, and it's the night of the CMAs." Pam worked some magic and got four tickets. It was forty-five minutes before the telecast. Then it was time for Pam and Bob to find their own seats, but because of another mix-up there were no seats for them. "Now it was fifteen minutes to telecast. The Bellamy Brothers didn't come, so we got their seats," Pam continues, "and they had all these camera angles for the Bellamy Brothers set up, so we were on television more than Garth was."

Joe and Shirley Harris were also in the audience at the CMA Awards that night. Garth and Joe had joked before the show that they had to wear "monkey suits," but they both looked great in their tuxedos. Garth was wearing a white tuxedo, and Joe was dressed in black.

Garth sang "Friends in Low Places" for the millions who were watching on TV.

He won the CMA for Video for "The Dance." What was easily the most powerful political message ever contained in a country music video—featuring the richest, most eastern, and only Catholic president of the United States and the black reverend whose fame was based on his resistance to the prejudice against blacks in the South—had won the highest accolade from the country music establishment in Nashville, Tennessee, often called the buckle of the Bible Belt and, not incidentally, the city that is home to the Southern Baptist Convention headquarters.

When the winner was called for the Horizon Award, once again it was Garth. This time he didn't go to the stage alone to accept the award. He took Sandy's hand and brought her with him.

"I'm not much good at it," he said, "but when I don't sing, I try to be a husband. This is my wife, Sandy."

Garth thanked George Jones, George Strait, John Wayne, and his father.

Backstage, Garth met the press and told the world what he had learned so far: that some of the biggest awards are found far away from the official podiums. It had taken him a while to realize that, he said, but once he did, he began to obtain the awards.

What a month, right?

Oh, there's one other thing. By October 9, five weeks after its release—*five weeks!*—*No Fences* had sold a cool million copies.

One reason the album is so good is that there was such a high confidence level in the studio. The success of the first singles from *Garth Brooks* and Jimmy Bowen's total enthusiasm for Garth had released everyone from the struggle. Bowen had told producer Allen Reynolds to bring to the album the kind of excitement and personal power that Garth displayed so amazingly onstage.

Garth felt the album was completely different from his first one, and that's something every artist loves—to be able to stretch in new directions, to not be stuck in one mode.

On October 13, Garth played to about 35,000 fans at the State Fair of Texas in Dallas. It was his biggest show to date, and the place to display all of the techniques he had borrowed from rock and roll. Like David Bowie and Madonna, he was wearing a wireless microphone—only, his was attached to his cowboy hat. Free of the traditional microphone and cord, he could run up the lampposts—just like Pete Townshend of The Who. He could fall into the audience like Peter Gabriel or swing across on a rope like David Lee Roth.

When country audiences saw this stuff, they were blown away. They'd never seen anything like it. They left the show changed—changed into fans of Garth who couldn't wait to come back for more!

"*I* think this guy is great," said Jay Leno in his capacity as guest host of *The Tonight Show Starring Johnny Carson* on October 16. Jay was holding up a copy of *No Fences* as he told the audience that Garth had just won two Country Music Association Awards.

Wearing faded jeans and a blue and white striped shirt, Garth Brooks turned America's favorite late-night show into a regular honky-tonk, singing "Friends in Low Places" with an exaggerated drawl and a whole lot of swagger. He didn't even blink when one of his guitar strings broke partway through the song.

When Garth was done with the song, he took off his hat, shook Jay's hand, and sat on the couch while Jay teased him about all the pretty women who come to his shows. Do they make you nervous? Jay asked country's newest superstar. Yes, Garth said, because usually his wife was with him at the shows. A guy who'd never been on a big national television show—and *The Tonight Show* was about as big as you could get—Garth handled himself like a pro. He also looked as surprised as anyone by his own success. As the show broke for a commercial, Jay said to Garth, "Hey, will you autograph this for me?" and Garth signed the CD of *No Fences*.

On November 3, the second single from *No Fences* debuted on the charts. Written by Pat Alger, Larry Bastian, and Garth, "Unanswered Prayers" tells the simple story of a guy who, with his wife at his side, runs into his old girlfriend at a hometown football game. Remembering how much he'd prayed to win her heart for life, he realizes how glad he is that things didn't turn out that way and how happy he is with his wife. It prompts him to thank God for some of his "greatest gifts," the prayers He doesn't grant. It's a turnaround of an old theme, one that says be happy for what you've got instead of always regretting the past or worrying about the future.

Years before Americans would heed Oprah Winfrey's call to keep a "gratitude book," each day writing down the things and people we are thankful for, Garth Brooks had captured that message in a song that was capturing America's heart. On Thanksgiving, he had even more to be thankful for as he rode in Macy's Thanksgiving Day Parade right down the very heart of America's entertainment capital—Broadway, New York, New York.

Next month, Joe and Shirley were at a Christmas party at Garth and Sandy's small house in Madison. For Christmas, Garth had made a special tape of songs for Joe and Shirley Harris. Shirley says, "He told Joe, 'If I didn't have a daddy, you would be my daddy.' That's how he felt about Joe—he was that close to him. Joe was very close to Garth and had a lot of faith in him. Garth was good to us. He treated us like family."

The Harrises thought Garth was somebody the Lord had put into their lives. Joe Jr. says, "My dad thought Garth was just super. He said he was something he'd been working for all his life . . . to have that kind of talent. My dad had always told me you don't ever let the entertainer forget who got them there, and Garth was naturally that kind of person that didn't forget."

Pam Lewis was also at the Christmas party. "I asked Garth, 'Looking back on this year, so much has happened, what was your favorite part?' and he said, 'My induction into the Opry—I will always be an Opry member.' It was very moving and nostalgic."

During the winter, Garth and Sandy bought a four-thousand-square-foot colonial-style house on a hill sitting on eight acres in Goodletsville that had previously been owned by the former mayor of Nashville, Richard Fulton. The local newspaper estimated that the Brookses paid close to half a million dollars for it. It was an hour out of Nashville, but a world away. In that home, Garth could remember he was just a guy and a husband whose wife would make him take out the garbage and help keep the place clean. A good place to keep things in perspective and remind him that stardom was one thing, real life quite another.

It's every son's—and daughter's—dream to be able to buy his or her parents something special in return for everything they've done as parents. Garth bought his mother and father a 160-acre spread in Edmond, not far from Yukon, with a long, low ranch house. It had beautiful flower beds, trees, a fish pond, and a pool. Colleen loved the place. She rode around the property in a purple golf cart with a red basket full of gardening tools.

"I'm grateful for the success, but I really don't have a clue why it happened to me," Garth says. "What I deserve and what I've gotten are totally off balance." Garth thinks his success must have had something to do with "divine intervention."

Just before Christmas, a woman driving home along Interstate 40 in Oklahoma had a flat tire. She waited in the rain for two hours and no one stopped to help her, despite the big "Help" sign she'd put in her window. Finally a bus pulled over and a couple of guys got out and changed her tire. She was invited onto the bus to warm up before continuing home and discovered that the bus belonged to none other than Garth Brooks.

By the end of the year, the sales of *No Fences* had doubled. Two million copies of one album in three months.

Happy, happy New Year! Nobody in America had more to celebrate than Garth Brooks—and, because of him, Nashville and the country music business had plenty to celebrate, too.

In January 1991, "Unanswered Prayers" hit number one. Garth admitted that the song was autobiographical and that he'd changed only one fact: he ran into his old flame at a crafts fair, not a football game. It was Garth's fourth number-one single.

"Two of a Kind, Workin' on a Full House" was released as the third single from *No Fences* in early February. Written by Bobby Boyd, Warren Dale Haynes, and Dennis Robbins, it is an easygoing tale of a man happy with his woman and celebrating the simple little moments of life. Who couldn't relate to a song that puts daily life on a pedestal?

The Gulf War was raging in early 1991. In February, Garth helped out with "Voices That Care," a record and video sold in record stores that raised money for the Red Cross and USO. Garth joined stars like Michael Bolton, Celine Dion, Sheena Easton, Little Richard, Luther Vandross, the Fresh Prince, Debbie Gibson, Paul Anka, Meryl Streep, Whoopi Goldberg, and Richard Marx on the project.

Playing the Houston Livestock Show and Rodeo for the first time, in February 1991, was a huge thrill for Garth. This Texas-size party is one big blowout that lasts for eighteen days, beginning with the Downtown Rodeo Parade, in which thousands of trail riders join forces with dozens of elaborate floats and marching bands from all over the state. The crowds go from there to fiddlers' contests, a hay-hauling competition, quilting contests, crafts exhibits, and, of course, the all-important livestock competitions. This just helps them work up their appetites for the World Championship Bar-B-Que Contest, which attracts cooks from all over the state.

Each night these happy revelers pack the Houston Astrodome for concerts by country music's top acts. Being invited to play these spectacular shows is a sign you have arrived. In February 1991, when Garth made his first appearance, the Gulf War was at its height. Garth came out onstage waving an American flag, and the crowd just loved him. Just a year before, he had played a small club on his first visit to Houston.

Once he became a headliner, in 1991, Garth demanded that promoters keep his ticket prices down to a maximum of $15 at a time when most were around $25.

"I believe in the Wal-Mart school of business," he told *Forbes* magazine about a year later when that distinguished publication did a story on country music's rise—and put Garth on the cover. "The less people pay for a product that they are happy with, the happier they are with it."

Next, Garth went on the True Value Grand Ole Opry American Tour, performing at each show with some of the classic names from the Opry: Minnie Pearl, Holly Dunn, Bill Monroe (the "Father of Bluegrass"), Ricky Skaggs, Patty Loveless, Riders in the Sky, Mike Snider, and the Whites. The rare, ten-state tour brought the Opry's barn facade to stages and presented acts in the typical Opry format. One act played "host" to three others. Minnie Pearl, perhaps the Opry's best-known ambassador to the rest of America, called the Opry "a wonderful family of entertainers" and said the tour showed off this family's diversity. In 1990, the Opry had done a smaller tour that included one big event: they played at the Economic Summit of Industrialized Nations in Houston, Texas, at the request of President George Bush, a long-time fan of country music.

Garth was back in Oklahoma again on March 16 as one of the hosts and the musical guest at the Thirtieth Annual Western Heritage Awards, held at the magnificent National Cowboy Hall of Fame.

Around this time, Garth and Sandy decided to do some renovations on their house, expanding it and customizing it to suit their wants and needs. The work was so extensive that for a while they were living in a trailer on the property. Garth, who often sang about the struggles and daily moments going on in his fan's lives, was now demonstrating that much the same things went on in his. So the fans related to him more than ever at this time, and they saw that even if it was on a slightly grander scale, he was just one of them.

When the Academy of Country Music announced its nominations in March of 1991, Garth received seven: Entertainer of the Year, Male Vocalist of the Year, Single of the Year (for "Friends in Low Places"), two nominations for Song of the Year (for "Friends in Low Places" and "The Dance"), Album of the Year (for *No Fences*), and Video of the Year (for "The Dance").

One thousand dedicated fans were assembled in the Yukon High School auditorium on March 16. Back on February 13, the Yukon City Council had approved a plan to paint "Home of Garth Brooks" on the city's water tower on Vandament Drive near the interstate. Councilman Frank Wagner said, "We're honoring a fine gentleman." Finally, Garth would get to see his name as he'd fantasized he would when he pulled into Nashville the first time back in 1985—only this time he'd see it in his hometown. The city spent $1,500 on the project but expected to see a lot in return in terms of the national publicity Yukon would receive.

"The town adores Garth, and he adores it," Colleen Brooks said, adding that Garth was "thrilled to death" with the honor.

Garth came home to Yukon for the dedication of the water tower. Mayor Jerry Shelton proclaimed March 16 Garth Brooks Day in honor of his contributions to country music and to Yukon.

Mayor Shelton told the crowd, "We have a tradition here in Yukon where we put winning sports teams on a water tower. Well, we varied from that a little bit, because you brought recognition to our town and you stand for what Yukon means."

Garth was also remembered by one of the Brooks family's neighbors. "The first sounds I heard from Garth's garage were rock and roll," Jack McCurdy said. "Even then he played a mean guitar, and he had a damn loud drummer. We can all be very thankful that he turned country."

Returning to Yukon was like coming home to family, Garth said. He was amazed at the number of people who had come back to Yukon to walk or ride past his childhood home and to take pictures or to be bold enough to knock on the front door. He said that was the one thing about his success that had affected the people of Yukon. Otherwise, they still saw him as their son and their brother, not as the hottest thing in country music.

After the ceremony, Garth and Sandy met with family, fans, and media backstage to sign autographs and answer questions. It was a great day for Garth and Oklahoma—but also a tragic one.

© O'Brien/Globe

© Djansezian/AP

© AP/Milwaukee Journal by Mark Gail

© Alan Mayor/Gamma Liaison

This is how

he does it!

© Luongo/Shooting Star

© Crosby/Shooting Star

© Norton/Shooting Star

Awards

The awful news broke on Sunday morning: a plane had crashed outside San Diego, killing seven members of Reba McEntire's band and her tour manager. For the rest of the year, Garth and the other members of Stillwater wore black armbands to commemorate the awful loss.

In Nashville on April 2, along with fifty other country acts, including one of his heroes, George Jones, Garth recorded a song, "Let's Open Up Our Hearts," for a campaign to encourage kids to stay in school. Local schoolchildren sang backup vocals. From there Garth went to Norfolk, Virginia, to play a free "yellow ribbon" concert for the families of the troops still serving in the Persian Gulf.

On April 24, Chuck and Rose Wheeler went to the Academy of Country Music Awards with J. D. Haas's trip winners. They were backstage during rehearsals.

"Garth ran up to the top of the stairs and said hello," Chuck said. "He sat with us for a few minutes."

Garth won a record six trophies: Entertainer of the Year, Male Vocalist, Single for "Friends in Low Places," Best Video and Best Song for "The Dance," and Album for *No Fences.* He almost spent more time onstage than in his seat!

Backstage, Garth told reporters he was about to release a new video and said he was "gonna get a lot of conflict over this video because it's about real life."

Garth and Sandy and Pam and a friend of Pam's, Terry Brown, returned to the Sheraton Hotel in Los Angeles after the show.

"We pulled up, and there was bedlam," Pam says. "You would have thought the Beatles had pulled in. People were pulling on Garth and Sandy, and he was really scared for his wife. People just wouldn't stop." Pam says this sort of thing was starting to happen more and more with Garth's fans. "Women would faint and cry hysterically around him. I felt like saying, 'You ought to see him with his stinky socks on.'"

Garth says he woke up crying at four A.M., realizing the magnitude of what had happened that evening. The year before, he had lost in all three categories for which he had been nominated. This year he had won six of the seven awards. Even with that huge endorsement by the country music community, the adventures of being Garth Brooks were only beginning.

In May of 1991, *Billboard* magazine's charts began reflecting the real sales of different kinds of music. Those bar codes that were showing up on all kinds of consumer products were now on CDs and cassettes, so it was no longer a matter of talking to some key retailers to assemble the charts. A new company out of Hartsdale, New York, called Sound-Scan, revealed the truth: country music was selling lots more than anyone had thought, and Garth Brooks was selling the most.

Garth's managers and record company hosted a party at the Country Music Association's new building—still under construction—on Music Circle. They made a huge laminated blowup of the *Billboard*–SoundScan chart and celebrated country's new prominence in the world of music. The whole industry was invited, and the heads of most major labels showed up. Garth's victory was their victory as well. Country music was no longer a poor distant relative in entertainment; it was now taking center stage.

The same week, *No Fences* hit number four on the pop charts, the first country album to make it that high since Willie Nelson's *Always on My Mind* in 1982. Garth didn't even have a single on the pop charts when that happened.

Meetings with the label, monitoring the charts, talking to the press, answering fan mail—things started to get really busy in Pam and Bob's offices. Sometimes when Joe Harris called, Pam had three or four phone lines lit up. "He would talk really slowly and ramble around," Pam says, "and I loved him, but I would say, 'Joe, what do you need to tell me? Please hurry up' and he said, 'Do you know why I do this on the phone? It's to slow you down.'" These sweet reminders from Joe Harris helped everyone keep their feet on level ground during the storm of excitement that accompanied Garth's unprecedented success.

The first thing listeners heard when they popped *No Fences* into their CD or cassette players was the roar of thunder. "The Thunder Rolls," written by Pat Alger and Garth, turned out to be as daring a country song as had ever been put out by an artist at the start of his career. Telling the story of a cheating husband driving home in a storm to a wife who knows in her heart where he's been, it is delivered with all the drama and urgency Garth could bring to his voice.

Sticking to his opinion of music videos—that they should add another dimension rather than simply illustrate a song—he created a dramatic short film for "The Thunder Rolls." It took three days to shoot the video in Los Angeles and about $100,000. Directed by Bud Schaetzle, it also starred Garth—and not just as the singer.

Garth says he wanted to play the part of the cheating, abusive huband in the video because he wanted to fully convey the evil of his character. "My goal," he says, "was to make this man hated so much that every person in America wished it was them pulling the trigger."

Trigger? Well, yes. There was a verse to the song that wasn't part of Garth's recording, a verse in which the betrayed wife makes sure her husband won't ever cheat on her—or anyone else—again.

Garth Brooks was playing by his own rules, bringing a new dimension to country music and daring his listeners to join him in being real.

Sandy didn't like the fact that Garth was going to play the role of the cheating husband in the video. She was especially upset when he did the love scenes himself. But her true anger was reserved for the decision to have the child in the video witness the violence between her parents. On that basis, Sandy refused to watch the video.

CMT was waiting for Garth's latest video. Given the huge success they'd had with "If Tomorrow Never Comes" and "The Dance," they were planning to make "The Thunder Rolls" the "Pick Hit of the Week." In fact, for a few days CMT and TNN were broadcasting it six times a day to 53 million households in the United States.

But then something shocking happened: TNN and CMT announced they would stop airing the video for "The Thunder Rolls." It was, according to the networks, too graphic and violent. There had been some negative viewer response, according to CMT's director of operations, Bob Baker. "We are a music channel," said Baker. "We are an entertainment medium. We are not news. We are not social issues. We are not about domestic violence, adultery, and murder." A TNN spokesperson said the video was great "but it doesn't offer any help or hope to anyone in an abused situation."

The network wanted Garth to add an explanation to the video, but he refused. Pam Lewis thought it was inappropriate for Brooks to add the message to the video. "If there's a problem with the video and if TNN feels there's something they want to say about it, that's fine. If they want to run an 800 number or have someone from a woman's group possibly do some sort of video afterwards, feel free," she said at the time. "But we don't feel it's Garth's place to do it."

Jerry Bailey, a spokesman for TNN, said, "If Garth creates a controversial video, he needs to be willing to take responsibility for its social implications."

"TNN has standards; I have standards," Garth said. "For some crazy reason, on this occasion the two did not cross." Garth said he was disappointed that the networks wanted to see the good side of real life but were turning their backs on the bad side.

What Garth objected to most, he said about the media furor that followed, was that "every major channel that showed the video put fifteen seconds of the worst part together and showed it, and that was it." Garth said the video had been put together in such a way as to "make these decisions with the characters as they went on." He also said the video shows "nothing they don't see on the ten o'clock news."

Back in Yukon, Colleen Brooks told the *Daily Oklahoman,* "Wife abuse has been pushed aside by a predominantly male society for too long. Maybe this will give some women the courage to get out. Or if this helps one man stop what he is doing, it's worth it."

In Nashville, the Tower Records store played the video continuously for hours each evening for a week after TNN and CMT banned it. Radio stations ordered copies of "The Thunder Rolls" video from Capitol and held screenings for their listeners. It turned up on *This Is VH-1 Country.* Barry Kluger, vice president for public relations for VH-1, said, "We found it was an acceptable video within our standards."

Garth issued a statement saying he refused to do ordinary videos that would "waste the viewers' time and the label's money....This video is a side of real life people don't really want to see."

On May 26, Garth joined fellow Oklahomans Vince Gill, Joe Diffie, and Restless Heart in a benefit concert at the Myriad Convention Center to help financially distressed farmers. The sold-out concert raised almost $300,000.

Garth spent the summer of 1991 touring to the big venues, sometimes as an opening act but mostly now as a headliner, continuing to keep ticket prices low. Now the guy who had played the little clubs dreaming of the big arenas was actually playing in bigger concert showplaces all the time. He began to crank up the show even more, adding more flourishes, more energy, more excitement. He told his band that the folks in the audience could listen to his music on CD or the radio all the time—but they were coming to the live shows for something bigger and stronger. Garth loved the visual aspect of the shows. He also began to see the guy onstage at a Garth Brooks concert as someone different, separate from the guy he saw offstage. He remembered what he felt like going to live shows by the musical heroes he had looked up to. He wanted his fans to feel the same way about him.

Out on the road all summer, Garth was drawing fans like no one else—not even the big rock acts were coming close to his amazing sellout shows. As he continued to wow audiences, the albums continued to sell. As the albums showed new listeners what all the excitement was all about, the shows continued to draw huge crowds.

Trisha Yearwood, whom Garth had met when they were both singing demos to earn a few bucks and who had sung some backup on his albums, was his opening act. Trisha had come to Nashville from Georgia to attend college and had worked as an intern at MCA Records. Her voice was dazzling the crowds who came to see Garth. Her debut album, *Trisha Yearwood,* became the first debut album by a female country artist to go gold, selling 500,000 units. Her first single also had gone to number one. "She's in Love with the Boy," written by Jon Ims, rang true for every young woman in love with someone her parents didn't approve of.

Garth's shows drew from every corner of the musical map—from the same wealth of material that had so dazzled the folks back in Stillwater. He played everything from Willie Nelson to Julio Iglesias, from Chuck Berry to George Jones. An unabashed fan of Billy Joel, Garth put his own stamp on the Joel classic "You May Be Right" and on a Joel song that had been an album cut but never a single. That song was "Shameless."

The more Garth performed "Shameless" onstage, the more he loved it. He kept raising the level of intensity with each performance, loving the feeling he got as he screamed the line "I've never been in love like this," stretching out his hands and getting lost in the excitement. The line between moments like these and the rest of life was growing larger for him.

The little boy at home on "funny night" was coming out again. He had a simple philosophy about music that he spread farther with each show: "It's all about the listener having fun."

In July, the Recording Industry Association of America (RIAA) certified that in less than a year *No Fences* had sold four million copies. No other album in the history of country music had sold that many copies that fast.

The economy was in a recession, but Garth's low concert ticket prices and his amazing sound on records was fueling its own boom—and leading a rise in interest in country music. In spite of the fact that the pop music industry was spending millions on acts like Michael Jackson, U2, Hammer, and Guns 'n' Roses, country music was the new star of the show.

SoundScan had a lot to do with it. Finally, real record sales were being measured and reported. Rap music also was proving itself to be no small phenomenon. Real people buying real music about their real lives were finally being heard.

Every big success is a tough act to follow. Garth had been touring so much that he hadn't written any new songs in a while. Though the first album had gone platinum, it was *No Fences* that everyone would be comparing his third album to. But he didn't want to repeat himself. Allen Reynolds helped him to focus by advising him to "keep taking the chances" and to move in still new directions.

Garth hadn't been doing much writing, but he did have a lot of compositions that hadn't been included on his first two albums.

In July, Capitol Records released a compilation of Garth's three videos in a package titled *Garth Brooks*. They added some footage from Garth's live shows so that those who hadn't attended could see what all the fuss was about. They also took the opportunity the video package offered them to give viewers a few moments of Garth talking to them about himself and how he felt about his videos.

"The Dance" leads off the collection, even though it was Garth's second video. Like all who'd seen it on TNN and CMT, newcomers to the Garth juggernaut were mightily impressed with an ordinary guy from Oklahoma's choice of images. With "If Tomorrow Never Comes," they saw the softer side of Garth. And then they got to see—and finally judge for themselves—"The Thunder Rolls." About a month after its release, the video was number one on *Billboard*'s Top Music Videos chart.

In August, the folks back in Oklahoma saw Garth Brooks in a very different kind of video once again. To kick off that year's

United Way fund-raising campaign, a video was put together. In it Garth told the story of three families aided by United Way agencies. He said that ninety cents of every dollar donated to the United Way in Oklahoma went to help Oklahomans.

The first single from Garth Brooks's eagerly awaited third album was a song called "Rodeo," written by Larry Bastian. If there's a theme that is ingrained in Garth from his child-hood, it's the rodeo, which was a sport in his high school just like basketball and football. Long before he was old enough to gain the insights to sing about love and choices, the rodeo was a part of his life. This song makes you feel and hear and smell the rodeo. He didn't make a video of it, but it doesn't need one. The mark of a great singer is that you see the story—that is, it is so richly told that it is played visually in the listener's own mind. Hearing that new single on the radio made fans just as excited.

Ropin' the Wind—a fairly apt description of what Garth was doing—was released on September 10, 1991. Even though it was the first of his CDs to cost $10.98, after a price increase of one dollar (money the record company spent on marketing) that Garth fought against, it went flying out of the stores. "I screamed, I begged, I pleaded with the record company," Garth says. An executive at the record company said he'd give Garth a dollar for every complaint that came in. Then the exec reached in his pocket and gave a dollar to Garth, saying, "You're the first one."

Retailers were so eager to have the album on sale that they had already ordered more than a million copies. It was one thing for an album to go platinum—but now Garth was *shipping* platinum. *No Fences* had spent eighteen weeks at number one; what new milestone could Garth conquer with his third album?

"*I* have huge respect for Garth as a songwriter," Allen Reynolds said. "I like the way he thinks about writing songs. He sees pictures and he approaches the business of writing songs strictly from a good place. He's not like a songwriter who sits around writing greeting cards, little ditties. His songs come from his emotions and mind." Clearly Reynolds felt that the songs Garth cowrote on *Ropin' the Wind* were solid choices for the follow-up to the hugely successful *No Fences*.

He wouldn't have simply indulged his artist's ego, because Reynolds never wanted to work with singer/songwriters who weren't open to songs that might come along from other writers. "I don't think many songwriters can pull it off and be the only ones writing the songs they sing," he said. "Garth had hoped he could be able to write as many as half the songs on his albums, because that would personalize the albums in a way that appealed to him. At first he'd felt he didn't want his name on more than half the songs, because he didn't want to send a message to the songwriting community that he wasn't open to their songs."

Reynolds felt this stood Garth in good stead. "If he had any other attitude," Reynolds said, "he wouldn't have had 'The Dance,' or 'Friends in Low Places,' two of the songs he did not write that have been huge for him. That's been a fundamental asset in his career. He's a fan of songwriters."

Garth was extremely proud of *Ropin' the Wind*. He said, "If I've got to come to the plate to follow *No Fences*, then *Ropin' the Wind* is the bat I'd grab." He said he wasn't interested in one album being a "sequel" to another. Instead, he wanted to explore new musical territory each time.

In this album, Garth really hit his stride. He was more confident and comfortable in the studio and with his song choices. He stretched his talents in new directions; for example, on Billy Joel's "Shameless," he took a Long Island songwriter's song and made it sound as country as if it had been written in Oklahoma. For the first time you can hear Garth just letting go in the studio, bringing some of the excitement of the live show inside.

Allen Reynolds questioned Garth's choice of "Shameless," even though he knew Garth did an incredible job with the song live and that it totally resonated with his country audiences. He reminded Garth that at their first meeting, Garth had told him he choked on songs about love. But Reynolds had a deal with his artists, and unlike some producers, he did not insist on picking the songs for inclusion on albums. Instead it worked like this: artist and producer could each suggest a song. If the other didn't love it, it could be suggested again at another time, but the bottom line was that neither party would be pressured into working on a song he didn't love.

Reynolds felt that Garth was violating his own rule about not singing blatant "I love you" songs. Reynolds would not have thought to present a song like "Shameless" to Garth, and in fact had told other songwriters and song pitchers that this wasn't the kind of song Garth liked. But when Reynolds listened to it, he could see what Garth loved about it. By this time, Garth had been playing it live and getting raves for it, so Reynolds decided to go with Garth's instincts. Then he went ahead and produced one hell of a cut.

The song list on the back of the CD has one white letter in each song. Though not in perfect order, they spell out "God Bless You."

"What She's Doin' Now," written by Pat Alger and Garth, is a classic ballad that people will still be playing twenty-five years from now along with standards like Glen Campbell's "Wichita Lineman." "We Bury the Hatchet," written by Wade Kimes, sounds like a song about making up after a fight—

until you come to the line about leaving the handle sticking out. "Cold Shoulder," written by Kent Blazy, Kim Williams, and Garth, is a truck driver's lament, the story of a guy out on the road on a snowy night, wanting to be home holding a woman instead of hugging the cold shoulder of the road. "In Lonesome Dove," written by Cynthia Limbaugh and Garth, is another short story, completely cinematic in its telling of love, loss, renewal, and revenge.

"Papa Loved Mama," written by Kim Williams and Garth, is a classic story of jealous revenge that makes plenty of sense when you listen to its lyrics. It was going to be the album's first single, but after all the uproar over "The Thunder Rolls," Garth and his managers and record company decided to simply release the song with the rest of the album and see if radio decided to play it. A lot would depend on whether the fans requested it. "If it's the people's choice," Garth said, "I think it will fly." It did.

Reviewers of Garth's shows and albums, as well as other media pundits, critics, writers, and commentators, were raising questions. How could Garth call himself a country music singer when he sang pop-ish songs, played rock-ish concerts, and sold in such "mainstream-ish" numbers? Garth heard this criticism, and one day, as he was leaving Jack's Tracks Studio, asked Allen Reynolds about it: "Garth said, 'I hope what I'm doing is helpful to country music and not harmful.'" Reynolds told him, "All I know is this—country music has to change or it becomes a museum piece. If it doesn't change, it's dead in the water."

When it comes to the "definition of country music," Allen Reynolds is passionate. "Nobody—no authority in Nashville, no authority at the Country Music Association or anywhere else—can give you a definition of what is country," he said. "Everybody has an opinion. But no one can tell you what is country. To some people what is country is cheatin', barroom, drinkin' songs. Well, to me that is one motif in the long and wonderful history of country music—and nothing more. Comedy is one motif. There are many motifs. Waylon Jennings probably gave the best definition. He said, 'Country is the singer. I'm country, and I can sing whatever song I want to.' He said that in response to people giving him grief for singing 'MacArthur Park.'"

Allen Reynolds believes a country singer is as good a thing to be as any other kind of singer, and that country singers have the right to sing any kind of songs they want to sing.

"Garth Brooks has done some songs that may be a little outside of country clichés, or the country idioms that a lot of writers are quick to grasp on to, like drinkin' and cheatin,'" Reynolds says. "I'm saying that these people who think that's what country is are the ignorant ones—they are not very well informed at all, or they would know that country is many more things than what some people say."

If Garth was trying to respond to the people who thought he'd been pushing things too far in his videos and stage show—country purists who were worried about where Garth was taking their beloved old music—he couldn't have found a better song than "Against the Grain." It was written by Bruce Bouton, the pedal steel guitar player, Larry Cordle, who sings backup on the album, and Carl Jackson, who also sings harmony. Garth also added to this album classic bluegrasser Sam Bush on mandolin and Jerry Douglas on Dobro.

In response to talk of Garth being a maverick, of not being diplomatic where the traditions of country music were concerned, and of making his own rules, the song challenged listeners to do the same. Making a difference meant leaving your mark, Garth sang, and that sure is just what he was doing.

If "The Dance" had been Garth's first true "career song," then "The River," cowritten by Garth with Victoria Shaw, was going to be another one. Garth takes his love for the rock influence and makes it work in a beautiful intro that takes you higher and higher into his dream. You just want to sail along with him, wherever his vessel is going. What he does is convince even the most tired, defeated, and bitter among us to give it one more chance. Dreams and inspiration—it got Garth there, and he wants us to get there, too.

Garth's devotion to his fans—"the people"—is what has driven everything he has done. He did his wild concerts to please us. He made the records he thought we would want to hear. He kept his ticket prices down so more folks could afford to come out and see him play. And he has often talked about how the fans' response to his shows is what made him want to make those shows even wilder. He has said he wants his material to be appealing to fans but, more important, he wants to treat them right. "If you treat the people the way they want to be treated," he says, then the good material will make the difference between whether you are a hit or a might-have-been.

On September 20 and 21 Garth played two sold-out concerts at Reunion Arena in Dallas, Texas, and filmed them for the NBC special *This Is Garth Brooks.*

After *No Fences* made history by becoming the fastest-selling country album in history, what would *Ropin' the Wind* do? Well, on September 28, Garth Brooks made country music history once again when *Ropin' the Wind* entered both the *Billboard* Country Albums and the *Billboard* 200 Top Albums chart—the chart that puts all categories of music together in one big shooting match—at number one. Other new releases by such standard hitmakers as Kenny Loggins, Diana Ross, and Dire Straits were left in the dust. The only other country album ever to reach number one on the pop chart had been Kenny Rogers's *Greatest Hits,* but that had taken many weeks to happen.

"It's a historic accomplishment," said Geoff Mayfield, associate director of retail research at *Billboard* magazine. "As best as we can determine, it's the first time it's ever happened."

CHAPTER FOUR

THE HERO

*G*arth was in Dallas when he heard the news that *Ropin' the Wind* was the top album in America. He was asked if country was going pop. "I don't think we're going anywhere," he said. "I think the crowds are coming over to country . . . the people who listen to rock and roll are coming over to country."

Before the 1991 CMA Awards, people were coming up to Garth and telling him he was going to win everything. Garth didn't like that at all. He said he'd rather have people tell him he was a bum than to be bombarded with all that praise. It just didn't make him feel comfortable.

Colleen Brooks was asked about all the comparisons of her son to Elvis Presley and about Garth's nomination as Entertainer of the Year. She said all that was fine and she hoped he'd win but she really wished he'd just be more careful and not hurt himself when he ran around the stage. It was well-known in Yukon, she said, that Colleen Brooks was a protective mother. That's probably why, when a national tabloid did a story on Garth that would have upset his mother, the local grocery store personnel hid all the copies when they saw her coming.

On the night of the CMA Awards, the many folks gathered in Yukon at the "watch parties" saw the camera panning the audience. Colleen Brooks was all dressed up, her nails decorated with silver paint and teeny gemstones that matched her dress, courtesy of Jacque's Family Hair Styling back in Yukon, where she had also had her hair done. Jacque's is in the Town Plaza shopping center at Fourth and Elm in Yukon, and its interior walls are covered with photos and posters of Garth. It is owned and run by Jacque Weber, the mother of Garth's road manager, Mickey.

Also sitting out there in the Grand Ole Opry was President George Bush. Bush, a country music fan from way back, was seated in the second row with his wife, Barbara, and country stars Crystal Gayle, Roy Acuff, and Gatlin brothers Larry, Steve, and Rudy. The Bushes received a standing ovation as they entered and took their seats in the second row.

Even with all of the security at the Grand Ole Opry that night due to the President's visit, Garth and Pam made sure that J. D. Haas's contest winners got in to see the rehearsals. "Garth always made time for us," J.D. said, "he never turned us down. There were dogs, armed people, and still we were able to meet Garth backstage right near where the President was receiving people."

J.D.'s trip winners changed a flat tire on Trisha Yearwood's car that night outside the Grand Ole Opry. They loved helping her out.

Garth brought down the house with his performance of "Shameless." It was a great idea to show audiences all over America what Garth could do with that song. Sales of *No Fences* and *Ropin' the Wind* accelerated even more after the show. By the way, TV ratings for the CMA Awards broadcast showed an increase of 20 percent over the previous year.

What sweet satisfaction indeed when "The Thunder Rolls" won Video of the Year. Then Garth won Single of the

Year for "Friends in Low Places," and Album of the Year for *No Fences.*

The last award of the evening is the one everyone waits for. When the CMA members are sent their ballots, they are instructed that in voting for Entertainer of the Year they consider an artist's overall accomplishments in recording, touring, and in general excellence in the field of country music.

Johnny Cash was the presenter of the award that year. He called out the name Garth Brooks, then provided comfort to a weeping Garth onstage.

Garth became the first artist in the history of the CMAs to win the Horizon Award one year and Entertainer the next. Garth praised two of his heroes, George Jones and George Strait. "I love my Georges," he said, then added, "No offense, Mr. President. I didn't think about that."

Backstage, Garth told reporters, "Man, this is cool. It's funny how a chubby kid can just be having fun and they call it entertaining."

Shirley and Joe Harris were just as proud and happy as they could be. "It was a very awesome feeling," Shirley said.

The Judds won their seventh consecutive Best Vocal Duo Award, fiery rebel Tanya Tucker was named Female Vocalist of the Year (and watched her standing ovation from a hospital, where she was due to give birth to her second child). Garth's fellow Oklahomans Vince Gill and Tim DuBois won Song of the Year for "When I Call Your Name," and Vince won for Male Vocalist.

At the end of the show the President and First Lady took the stage, and once again they received a standing ovation. President Bush said, "Country music gives us a window on the real world." He said he and the First Lady would always be grateful for what the country music family did for the troops and their families during the Gulf War. "It's easy to see why America loves country music," the President said. "Country music loves America."

Garth came home to Yukon High to do a concert to finance new pig barns for the Future Farmers of America club. He made a large contribution to the Oklahoma State University athletic department and continued to support facilities for needy children in Tulsa and Amarillo, because his mother had always had a dream of building a "boys' home."

Even with the the CMA awards in hand, Garth realized that fame, as they say, can be fleeting. He'd seen many artists hit it big, get some awards, and then be forgotten a year or two later. Garth Brooks did not want to be forgotten.

In October, the second single from *Ropin' the Wind*, Billy Joel's "Shameless," was released to radio. Some Top 40 radio stations played Garth's version of "Shameless" without any prompting from Garth or Capitol Records' radio promotion staff. And Billy Joel paid Garth a great compliment when he told *Billboard*'s Debbie Holley that Garth's version of the song "expanded my perception of what country artists can do."

By now the little yellow house on South Duck Street had a sign on it that said "Garth Brooks and His Wife Sandy Lived Here." Landlord Ken McWherter had fixed it up after he heard someone was spending $100,000 to refurbish Lawrence Welk's old house.

Colleen Brooks was being interviewed by seemingly every newspaper and magazine around. She told the *Daily Oklahoman* about her son: "He's religious, polite, educated. The kid doesn't smoke, doesn't drink, doesn't cuss. The only vice he has is grease. He loves to eat. Garth's a little bit of everybody. He's a complete package."

Around this time the RIAA announced that *No Fences* had reached five million in sales. And in November, *Ropin' the Wind* became the first album of any music category to go gold, platinum, double platinum, triple platinum, and quadruple platinum within one month!

"I like to bypass the listeners' ears and hit 'em in the heart," Garth said. Well, he was doing just that, and they were responding in kind.

In November 1991, Garth's duet with Trisha Yearwood, "Like We Never Had a Broken Heart," written by Garth and Pat Alger, was high in the charts. And speaking of duets, in November at the O'Connell Center in Gainesville, Florida, Billy Joel joined Garth onstage. With Joel on piano, Garth sang "Shameless" with even more passion than usual, if that was possible.

To add to all their blessings, Sandy was expecting the Brookses' first child. At the *Billboard* Music Awards show in December, after winning five more awards to add to the bundle he already had from the other major award-granting organizations, Garth told reporters he was going home to Nashville to be with his wife.

"This is my first baby. I'm scared," he told reporters. "I don't know if I'm ready to be a father, but here it comes."

In December, Garth Brooks was named one of *People* magazine's "25 Most Intriguing People of 1991." The magazine noted that Garth had "accomplished what no Nashville performer had ever done before" when *Ropin' the Wind* debuted at number one on both the country and pop charts. Garth was quoted as saying that his success was evidence that the American dream is very much alive. He was just an ordinary guy who had been extraordinarily lucky that his talent and hard work were paying off.

He also took out a full-page ad in *Billboard* thanking Capitol Records for his new contract—one that increased his royalty rate on his records to one more in keeping with his huge sales performance. The kind of contract given to new artists no longer applied.

Winter in Nashville. If you thought that just because it's the South it stays balmy all year, you'd be wrong. Temperatures frequently drop down into the thirties, although the coolness of the air is still tempered by the high humidity, which is a constant in middle Tennessee. There isn't much snow, but even a quarter of an inch—or the threat of it—can cause schools to close, roads to become treacherous, and supermarket checkout lines to snake all the way back to the meat department as everyone stocks up on supplies. A lot of albums are recorded in the winter, when artists don't go on the road as much. Nashville has fewer tourists and only an occasional big event, and it's a great time to lay back.

So for the winter of 1991–92 Garth stayed in Nashville. He had already proven what he could do on the road—sell out 98 percent of the seats wherever he showed up to play. His album sales were spectacular: 14 million in one year, figures unheard of in country music and amazing for music of any kind. Sandy was pregnant, so they stayed in and watched a lot of TV and got to know each other again after the whirlwind of the past year or so.

"We found that inside our house, it was just me and her," Garth said. "I introduced myself to her, and she introduced me to one of the neatest people I've ever met."

On Friday, January 17, Garth and Sandy—and 28 million other people across the country—turned on the TV set at 8 P.M. Central Time to watch a television special called *This Is Garth Brooks*. It was the show that Garth had recorded in Reunion Arena, and it showed the country what this country boy could do.

"The singer effectively did away with decades of country stereotypes and helped usher the music into a new era," Karen Schoemer wrote in the *New York Times*.

This Is Garth Brooks gave NBC-TV its best Friday-night ratings in two years. What really told the tale was that on the same night CBS had a special on Michael Jackson—and Garth's ratings exceeded it. His special was among the ten highest-rated shows of the week.

All those television viewers got to see what concertgoers had been raving about for years.

They also got to see Garth in the shirts that had been getting so much attention. Garth was wearing all kinds of odd-colored shirts. Some were half red and half black. Some had giant black and mustard-colored checks. Big wide stripes, lots of tiny checks…Where was Garth getting these shirts?

Well, he was designing them himself and having them made right back in Apache, Oklahoma, by Maury Tate, a calf roper. Tate had noticed that whenever he found a sharp shirt to wear to a rodeo, he'd show up and see half a dozen other ropers wearing the same thing. He wanted to have some originals.

His friend's mother, Ruth McDaniel, was a seamstress, so Tate bought some fabric and designed a few shirts, which Mrs. McDaniel sewed for him. He wore these new shirts to the rodeos, and now people on the professional rodeo circuit were asking him where they could buy them.

In 1986, Tate took orders and Ruth McDaniel made about two hundred shirts. In 1987, Tate started selling the shirts in his mother's beauty parlor and his father's real estate office in Apache. In 1989, *Western Horseman* magazine ran a story on Tate and his shirts and the business really took off. Tate was only twenty-three.

In the early nineties, a friend of Maury Tate's introduced him to Mickey Weber, Garth's road manager. Maury told Weber he wanted to give some shirts to Garth. Garth and his band liked the shirts because they were different—and because the band members could each design their own. Maury's company, which was now called Mo Betta Shirts and had about a hundred people sewing, still crafting one shirt at a time, would make whatever shirts Garth and his band designed. Maury Tate, a veteran Professional Rodeo Cowboys Association roper and 1991 Dodge National Circuit Finals Rodeo champion, was now a very successful businessman (his mother helped run the Mo Betta factory in Apache) as well. World champion calf roper Roy Cooper and Garth's own country singing hero, George Strait, were also wearing the shirts.

"*Our* house is a house for loving, for fighting and making up, for learning, for screaming at each other, for laughing—it's not a house for music." Garth said that music had given them their house but that the house was just for Sandy and him.

In that house on the following Sunday night, Sandy and Garth were watching the United Cerebral Palsy telethon in Nashville. They decided they'd like to donate ten cents for each dollar raised locally.

"We just jumped in the truck and got down here 'cause we saw it on TV," Garth said. When they got there, Sandy wrote a check for $25,000 ten minutes before the benefit ended. That brought the total raised locally for United Cerebral Palsy to more than $275,000.

Ropin' the Wind stayed at the top of the pop charts through the end of the year, keeping such acts as Guns 'n' Roses, U2, and Michael Jackson from spending more than a week there.

At the American Music Awards in Los Angeles at the end of January, Garth was scheduled to be a musical guest. But on the flight from Nashville, Sandy became ill, then began hemorrhaging at the airport. She and Garth had to put up with news photographers who took pictures (even as Pam Lewis was trying to swat them away with her large leather handbag) that were later published in the tabloids.

Both Sandy and Garth were terrified as she was taken to Daniel Freeman Memorial Hospital in Inglewood upon arriving at Los Angeles International Airport. Was her pregnancy in danger?

Garth canceled his performance and didn't attend the ceremony. He did win three American Music Awards: Country Single for "The Thunder Rolls," Favorite Country Album for *No Fences,* and Favorite Male Country Artist. Bob Doyle and Pam Lewis accepted the awards for Garth.

After Sandy was released from the hospital, she and Garth returned to Nashville on a tour bus he was able to charter. It took three days to get back to Nashville. Doctors told her to stay off her feet for eight weeks.

In February, Garth was still too concerned for Sandy's health and her pregnancy to return to L.A. for the Grammy Awards. So he didn't get to personally accept his Grammy for Best Country Vocal Performance, Male, for *Ropin' the Wind.*

In March there were more awards—and more kudos for country—as Garth and Reba McEntire triumphed over pop stars like Michael Bolton and Mariah Carey to win Best Performer Awards in addition to country honors at the Eighteenth Annual People's Choice Awards.

Backstage at the awards, Garth told reporters, "Sandy is not so much of a part in my business life—I can't put that on her. But she listens, and I just talk, and she gives me what she thinks." He added that "she's someone I can vent to, yell at, and scream with." A good wife, a good friend, a good partner.

In April, Garth was out in Los Angeles again, for the Academy of Country Music Awards, this time with Sandy. They drove out because she couldn't fly, even though everything was all right by this time with her pregnancy.

Garth won awards for Male Vocalist and Entertainer of the Year.

After the show, he and the other performers were told that riots had broken out in L.A. following the acquittal of the four police officers who had been captured on video-tape beating Rodney King. Garth and Sandy decided not to spend the night in L.A. and instead got on the bus and drove back to Nashville. While they were on the bus, they watched the reports on TV of the unprecedented destruction going on in the City of Angels. Garth had a lot of feelings about what he saw—ranging from the sense that taking the law into one's own hands was dangerous no matter how justified by events, to the feeling that the people of Los Angeles had little choice in light of the outrage the acquittal represented.

During that period, Garth and Stephanie Davis had been working on writing a song called "Our Time Will Come." In the aftermath of the riots, they were compelled to finish it. It would have a new title when it was done and be another landmark song in the Garth Brooks collection.

Garth took some time off in early 1992, despite the fact that he was at the height of his popularity and there were millions of dollars in concert money just waiting all over America to jump into his pockets. Having grown up in a family that never had a lot of money, Garth felt the money he'd made in the last two years was "more than enough." For a while he "no longer had any hunger for the road." So he stayed home. He would soon be, like so many other working parents, struggling with the conflict between work and family. He felt that no one would want to leave their kids home to go to work unless they had to, and he was at the point where he never had to leave home again to support his family.

But there were still enormous demands on his time. NBC wanted to do another big TV special. Companies were clamoring to give Garth big endorsement deals. He was also in the middle of renegotiating his contract with Capitol—again. He felt that his numbers were so huge that even the new contract he'd received in 1991 wasn't adequate. He was aware of the kinds of royalties other artists at his level were getting, and he and his managers felt he deserved that too.

When Garth had first signed his deal with Capitol, he was a new artist grateful that anyone wanted to put out his music. When he got the second contract, he was happier. Now he saw how much money he was making for the label and felt he should share in it a little more equitably. Garth says he felt it was unfair that, after signing a record deal predicated on sales of two million records and going on to sell so many more, he was still receiving a royalty rate based on the lower sales projections. He had seen his record company move into fancy penthouse offices in Nashville and spin off three new labels. He'd heard he was responsible for 68 percent of the label's entire income. So he decided to fight for more—not just for himself, but for all the people who worked so hard for him.

By the end of 1992, Garth had worked out a joint venture with the record company that gave him control over his music. He would pay for production and packaging himself, own his masters, and give them over to the company for marketing and distribution. He was also free not to record, and he retained the option of not releasing a record if he was unhappy with the label's handling of his marketing.

He told everyone he needed a break, and he rearranged his touring schedule so that when he went out again, he and the band could spend part of most weeks at home. He also knew—much as he hated the prospect—that he would no longer be able to spend countless hours after the shows signing autographs for fans. For a star so devoted to his audience, that was the biggest loss. The more the fans wanted to be with him, the less time he could afford to spend with them.

What Garth wanted most was for people to continue coming to see him for bigger and more spectacular shows, but to still regard him as a guy who had stayed real and hadn't let success go to his head. "This business has a way of changing you," he said, "until you are a different person."

While he was off the road, Garth turned his attention to his next album. He knew he was already a tough act to follow.

Garth wasn't the only country artist who was gaining in popularity and bringing country music a new profile in America. Vince Gill, another Oklahoman, had taken his incredible singing voice, guitar skills, and songwriting genius to a platinum level with his first two albums, *When I Call Your Name* and *Pocket Full of Gold.*

And the woman who had begun as one of Garth's backup singers, Trisha Yearwood, became the first woman in country music to have her debut album, *Trisha Yearwood,* certified gold within a few months of its release.

The *New York Times* took notice of this new trend and sent a reporter to Nashville to see what was going on with "Mr. Brooks," as the *Times* called him—the "slightly pudgy fellow with a twangy voice and a 10-gallon hat." Jimmy Bowen, the president of Capitol Nashville (which he had renamed Liberty Records to reflect his new stewardship), was happy to talk about why country was eclipsing rock and pop music in the national spotlight.

"For years it was old—old acts, old consumer," Bowen said. "But now the youth of America is saying, 'Wow, I think I like that music.' There are millions of Americans who can't relate to rap and most of the dance lyrics. They haven't all come to country, but they've come to a few of our acts."

Country music had always spoken a universal language, although its songs' stories were those of the small towns, not the big cities. But the songs had never taken on subjects like adultery and abuse, sexuality and philosophy in quite the way Garth had. And the music hadn't been fused with so many rock and pop elements. Garth was able to unite the country with the city in a new way that brought city listeners to his songs. The fact that so much of what was coming out of the radios in the cities were the technology-driven sounds of rap and dance music meant that listeners looking for easy rhythms and acoustic guitars—and lyrics that spoke to the simpler issues of love, work, and family—could find them only on country stations.

"Garth Brooks debuting on the pop charts at No. 1 helps all of us," Trisha told the *Times.* "It's neat that we're having an appeal to pop audiences without having to compromise our music."

The music wasn't being compromised. These new artists didn't have to pretend they were in touch with America's suburbs—most of them were from the suburbs. Most of America—even in cowboy country like Oklahoma—was becoming the suburbs.

The suburbs had helped to foster the "urban cowboy" trend of the early 1980s, when the movie of that name had the malls crawling with people in star-spangled cowboy clothes, feather-trimmed hats, and lots of big hair, and bars replaced their disco balls with mechanical bulls. Nashville artists got plenty of attention in that era, but no one had broken through in quite the same way that the artists of the nineties now had.

Now bars with names like Denim & Diamonds were opening in Manhattan and in Santa Monica, California. Instead of going to discos and getting blasted and going home with strangers—not such a great idea in the age of AIDS—people were getting sober and doing country line dancing. Now there were thirty-three country albums that went gold in one year—and thirty-five that went platinum—as opposed to 1985, when only sixteen country albums sold the 500,000 units that would give an artist that prized gold record to hang on the wall. Now there were more than 2,500 country radio stations, as opposed to 1,800 in 1982.

Television was helping, too. The creation of TNN in 1983 had helped fuel the growth in country music, and the network had grown continuously—from only 7 million subscribers at the start to almost 53 million in 1991. Country music awards shows like the ACMs in April and the CMAs in October were enjoying higher ratings each year.

Country stars had made it on TV before—prime-time series hosted by Tennessee Ernie Ford, Eddy Arnold, Jimmy Dean, Johnny Cash, Glen Campbell, Barbara Mandrell, and Dolly Parton had found sizable audiences. They had done so with plenty of rhinestones and country flair, and had seemed amusing and nonthreatening to what was still called mainstream entertainment. Country's longest-running program was still *Hee Haw,* which only reinforced the hayseed image of such sitcoms as *The Beverly Hillbillies, Green Acres,* and *The Andy Griffith Show.*

But in the nineties, country wasn't so hayseed anymore. Thanks to artists like Garth, Vince, and others, America would have a new chance to discover the rich heritage and high quality of our own unique, homegrown music—the American folk art that was now moving toward dominance of popular culture.

The message was driven home even harder when Garth appeared on the cover of *Forbes* magazine on March 2. A country star on the cover of the nation's leading business magazine? The headline was even more startling: "Led Zeppelin Meets Roy Rogers." It was a quote from Jimmy Bowen. *Forbes* looked at the money side of the country music business and found it quite healthy indeed, remarking on the low production and marketing costs as compared to those of rock, and noted that the category appealed to fans in a wider age range—from twenty-one to sixty.

Later that month, *Time* magazine put Garth on its cover, only the second country artist (the other was Merle Haggard) to ever achieve that distinction—a huge honor for Garth. He joined some other famous Oklahomans who have graced the cover of *Time,* including former U.S. House Speaker Carl Albert, sports great Johnny Bench, and Will Rogers, who was shown in July 1926.

Time magazine called Garth an "unlikely new country superstar, with his acetylene eyes and chipmunk cheeks, stalking the concert stage, acting up, acting crazy, climbing the rigging and blitzing the crowd with bravura . . . the audience lets itself go nuts with him. Nicely nuts. Mannerly nuts. Country nuts."

Garth told *Time* he was as amazed at his success as everyone else. "I have always come in through the back door rather than the front," he said. "It always seems like I am standing outside of me, watching the whole thing go down, whatever I am doing."

Many of the other national publications that were featuring Garth Brooks in their pages were at once celebrating him and country music and giving their success a somewhat sardonic, tongue-in-cheek put-down. But there was no getting around how Garth felt about what he was doing.

"The only time I know I'm really alive and doing something on God's great earth," he said, "is when I'm in between those speakers and the lights are up and the music is loud. I never want to get down; I never want to get off the stage."

Why would he want to get off the stage? With all the lights and smoke, with his heart pumping and his body rocking and his soul being loved by thousands of people—it was unbelievably thrilling.

Ask any woman who has been involved with a musician and she'll tell you that often his mistress is the music. (Perhaps the husbands of today's female music superstars feel the same way.) You can make love to the music, get close to the music, have fun with it, change it as much as you want to, and it always loves you back. The music is always there for you. For Garth, add the frenzy of the stage and you can see why he might talk about quitting from time to time but probably couldn't ever really say goodbye to it.

"If I have my way, I'll do this until I die," he says.

Garth appeared on the TV sitcom *Empty Nest,* playing himself. During the filming of the episode, he took a few days off to go to Elkhorn, Nebraska, to sing at the wedding of his pianist and fiddle player David Gant. Gant told the *Daily Oklahoman* that Garth "showed a lot of class" and "played it low key, not wanting to take away from mine and Susan's wedding."

It was Garth Brooks Appreciation Day in Yukon, Oklahoma, and the town's most famous native son had come home for a visit. Three thousand fans were waiting on a rainy Sunday on the last day of May, much to Garth's surprise. Sixty of them had camped out all night in front of the Fine Arts Auditorium at Yukon Mid-High to get the best seats.

"If I was waiting out there in the rain, it would be for someone a hell of a lot more special than me," Garth said.

Just as the city of Memphis had done for Elvis, Yukon was naming a street for Garth. The dedication of Garth Brooks Boulevard was the idea of the city's 2000 Committee, and the Yukon City Council had approved it overwhelmingly. Now Eleventh Street, also known as Cemetery Road and State Highway 92, would be known as Garth Brooks Boulevard from State Highway 66 south to the city limits, which lie just south of Interstate 40.

Garth's hometown fans gave him a roaring welcome. The governor of Oklahoma, David Walters, was there. The superintendent of schools, Darrell Hill, presented a plaque on behalf of the Yukon Public Schools Foundation for Excellence. Yukon mayor Dave O'Bannon presented Garth with three souvenir signs, one each for "Garth Brooks Blvd.," "Sandy Brooks Ave.," and "Taylor Mayne Brooks Pkwy."

The school choir sang "The River." When Garth appeared, he told the crowd he loved coming home to Yukon because people treated him the same as if he weren't a big star.

Sandy was doing fine. By this time Garth and Sandy had chosen the name for the daughter they were expecting: Taylor Mayne Pearl. The name Taylor was in honor of one of their musical heroes, James Taylor. Mayne was because the baby was conceived in Maine. Pearl would be the child's third name because, as Garth said, "Sandy loves Minnie Pearl." He told his hometown paper that the baby better come soon or she might wind up with even more names.

From Yukon, Garth went to Denver, Colorado, to open his 1992 tour on June 2. This tour was going to have even more exciting stage antics for his fans.

"When Garth started to make money, it was like 'How can I top myself?'" Pam Lewis says. "He wanted everything to be bigger and better. He attracted a lot of young people because of that, and it became hip to dress like him."

In June of 1992 at Fan Fair, Sandy joined Garth onstage during his show at the Nashville Motor Speedway. Fans gave them lots of baby gifts. Then Garth spent nine straight hours signing autographs, spending up to five minutes with each fan. After closing time, he insisted on keeping open the building where his booth was located. He went out of his way to give some time to J. D. Haas's contest winners, and when he realized later how long these people had had to wait on line to see him, he sent ten pizzas over to J.D.'s offices with a nice note.

He also brought more national press to Fan Fair than had ever been there before. In an interview with CNN he talked about the coming birth of his child and alluded to the possibility of quitting the music business, as he had also done at the ACMs back in April. He said if it weren't for the people who came out to see him, and his great love for them, he would have quit the business soon after he had become successful.

In July of 1992, tickets went on sale for a Garth Brooks concert to be held at the Reunion Arena in Dallas on October17. Nineteen thousand seats sold out in less than thirty minutes.

The 1992 tour really gave fans something new in country music concerts. Garth would enter through an elevator coming up in the center of the stage. Lights would flash and twirl. Rumbles and explosions would rattle the rafters. Then a very regular-looking guy would appear and joke about the size of his own behind as he shook hands with fans, gathered their gifts, and began to sing his heart out for them.

Although country music songs are filled with laments about the sadder side of love, and even though Nashville is no stranger to gossip about "who's cheatin' who and who's bein' true," as one song's lyrics put it, Garth Brooks's public admission early in his career that he'd been unfaithful to his wife was still remarkable. It's one thing to sing about it, quite another to talk about it.

In an interview with *Ladies' Home Journal* published in June of 1992, Garth talked about it even more. He told writer Marjie McCraw that "being true to someone carries a heavy weight on it. At the time, I didn't think so. I thought, I love my wife to death, she's the only woman I could live with, so me messing around doesn't mean I love her any less." Looking back on it now, Garth said, he realized that was "bunk."

And looking forward to the birth of his first child, he added that of all the things he remembered as a kid, "it was the attention I remember—to know that someone was interested in what I was doing."

He told the *Saturday Evening Post,* which also featured him on the cover, that he'd always had a wife who understood the big weight he put on music, "but a child will not, and I understand that."

Taylor Mayne Pearl Brooks was born on July 8, 1992. "The second that little girl popped out in this world," Garth said, "the one thing that I hit on right away was . . . nothing is as important as human life." He later said his respect for his wife "went up about a bazillion notches" after she gave birth. "I could never even think about going through that. If it'd been me who had the baby, I'd still be lying there today."

Garth also said that being in the delivery room with Sandy and witnessing Taylor's birth had him "hooked" and "pumped"—the same words he uses to describe his feeling onstage.

The renovations on the house were not yet done—the nursery was being decorated in a Mickey Mouse theme—so when Garth and Sandy brought Taylor home from the hospital, they lived for the first few weeks in the house trailer they had brought to the property when the renovations began. A national tabloid made a big deal about the famous country superstar bringing his wife and new baby home to a trailer.

Becoming a father changed Garth in all the same ways that becoming a parent changes anyone. Suddenly, he and Sandy weren't the only people in the family. He remembered how well his parents had raised him, how he and his siblings were the most important people in their lives. "That is what I must give my girl," he said. "The fact that we have millions of dollars means nothing to her."

Martina MacBride was Garth's opening act during most of the summer 1992 tour. It was really a thrill for the up-and-coming singer. McBride was from a small town in Kansas, a former farmgirl with the opportunity of a lifetime.

John McBride, Martina's husband, had started as a soundman on Garth's tour and later became his production manager. After one of her waitressing jobs ended in 1991, Martina joined the Garth tour then in progress and sold merchandise. Garth knew she was trying to get a record deal, although she never imposed on him with her musical ambitions. When she got a recording contract with RCA, Garth offered her the opening-act slot on the '92 tour. Suddenly she went from singing in small clubs to singing before huge crowds.

What would have also amazed audiences, had they known, was the fact that when the Garth Brooks tour pulled into their towns that summer, one of the guys unloading and setting up equipment was—Garth Brooks! "He wasn't raised to sit and watch other people do things that he could do himself," said his tour manager and friend Mickey Weber. "Garth doesn't want to separate himself from the guys."

It was around this time that Garth began his somewhat curious practice of referring to himself in the third person. He wrote in the souvenir booklet for the tour that Garth was not difficult to understand if you looked at him as two different people—as Garth, the guy who loves to hang around the house, and GB, the artist who loves everything about the fantasy world of being a big star.

At one of his many press conferences on the tour, Garth told reporters he was interested in making his stardom last. He hoped to be out for thirty years, playing arenas as the Rolling Stones still did, he said. He didn't want to be "a trivia question in twenty years" that no one would know the answer to. The press hung on every word Garth said, and he was constantly in the news.

Garth's tour was so hot that scalpers were getting ahold of tickets and selling them at prices up to $750. This outraged Garth. His publicists issued a statement from him saying, "I've seen the prices that scalpers are asking for tickets to my shows. I've seen the show—it's not worth it. Please do not pay a scalper's price."

On August 23, Garth held a news conference at Billy Bob's Texas to announce that one dollar for each copy of *Beyond the Season,* his first Christmas album, would go to an organization called Feed the Children. He was also making a sizable contribution himself. This kicked off a seven-city mini-tour to promote the album and its cause. Liberty Records shipped 1.6 million copies of the album following his press conferences.

The same problem that had been in the news back when Garth was born in February of 1962, that of farmers growing more food than the United States could consume, was the guiding principle behind Feed the Children.

Feed the Children is a wonderful organization, head-quartered in Oklahoma City, Oklahoma. It was founded by Larry Jones, who visited Haiti in 1979 and saw the terrible suffering of hungry children there. Realizing that the many kinds of surplus food available right here in the United States could make a difference for these hungry kids, Jones and his wife and partner, Frances, decided to devote themselves to delivering this surplus food to those who needed it the most.

The organization provides thousands of children with food, supplies, clothing, medical assistance, and educational opportunities through schools, orphanages, and homes for the physically disabled as well as church-related feeding programs. Feed the Children has also been active in providing emergency disaster relief throughout the Third World, as well as in industrialized nations in Europe, Asia, Africa, and Central and South America.

But lest anyone think hungry and suffering childen are only in other countries, Feed the Children has for years documented the alarming rise in the number of poor and hungry children right here in the United States. The poverty rate of families with young children has more than doubled since 1973.

"People think that hunger is something found just in Ethiopia," Garth has said. "The more I've traveled, the more I've found that poverty and hunger can be found all across this country."

Feed the Children has earned the praises of Presidents Ronald Reagan, George Bush, and Bill Clinton. What impresses everyone is the organization's ability to collect and ship donated food and supplies within seventy-two hours of receiving them from the thousands of organizations—and millions of people—who donate them.

Garth's booking agent and dear friend Joe Harris saw a television program on Feed the Children back in 1988. He called Larry Jones and said he wanted to do something with Feed the Children in Nashville. For years, Harris had worked with local churches, food pantries, and social service agencies to distribute food to hungry children in Nashville. Joe Harris and Garth, along with Pam Lewis, shared a love for the organization from Oklahoma City that was doing so much to help hungry children.

Joe Jr. remembers the many times he and his dad would get into their pickup truck and drive to different churches, making sure each church had enough of each kind of food. "When he first come back from Vietnam," Joe Jr. says, "I was a little thing. I remember him telling me I needed to be grateful for eating the way I did because he saw so many children over there who didn't have anything to eat. I could tell by the way he talked it was something he felt inside."

With Garth bringing the attention of music fans to the problem of hunger in America, throughout his 1992 concert tour fans brought food to be collected right at the shows. They felt good knowing that what they brought in went to ease hunger right in their own communities.

"What I like about Feed the Children is that the money and food collected stay here," Garth said at the time. "And by having people drop off food, it's an effective way to have people think about what's going on and to get involved."

There was often more food dropped off at concerts than Feed the Children's trucks could contain. Because Garth was traveling with six huge trucks of stage and sound equipment, the decision was made to use those trucks during the many hours they were sitting empty at a concert arena to deliver food to the local agencies that distributed it to the public.

At the press conference in Billy Bob's, Garth also revealed he was working out plans to film his next TV special—at Texas Stadium late in the summer of 1993. It was amazing he had kept quiet about it for that long; back in November of 1991, he and Joe Harris had called Glenn Smith, a promoter in San Antonio, to talk about the idea of a Garth concert at Texas Stadium. By April of 1992 Glenn Smith had approached Texas Stadium general manager Bruce Hardy to talk about playing one night. No one thought Garth would need more than one night or sell more than the 65,000 seats in the stadium. But when the production company that would film the TV special said it would be better for them to have two nights for shooting, the idea of a second night was considered.

"Dallas was the first city to really embrace what Garth was doing," Joe Harris told the *Dallas Morning News,* explaining why Garth wanted to film his TV special there. "His whole deal in concert is to feed off the energy of the crowd, and Dallas audiences are always the most excited."

Garth's remarks to the press about retiring were getting almost as much attention as all the work he was doing. He had said if he did quit, it would be permanent—if he couldn't be both a father and a musician, he would be a father. He said his goals were now for his daughter to say he'd always been there for her and for his wife to say he'd been a good husband.

He was struggling, just like all his fellow baby boomers in the 1990s, with the issues of family versus career. It was interesting that whether you were a couple struggling to get by on two modest salaries or a superstar with millions, the same issues presented themselves: time, time, and time. If he wanted to keep doing what he loved, even money couldn't get Garth more time with his family than anyone else had.

Garth didn't seem to ever censor himself, even when some of his advisers told him he was saying things in public that he should have said to a more private counselor. Other artists might have heeded that advice, but Garth often didn't realize what a big artist he was. He felt so close to his fans, as though each was a personal friend—which in a way was true—that he could say whatever was on his mind.

"Sometimes he would say things and later would regret he said them," Pam Lewis says. "He never went to media training. He wouldn't have gone if we'd wanted to send him. He's a colorful, opinionated man."

Garth also knew that it was better to have these personal things coming from him right out front than to have the press get ahold of them first. By being so frank and open about the most personal aspects of his life, Garth was stealing the thunder from the negative journalists and tabloids always looking for dirt and finding new ways to dish it.

He talked often about his regrets over hurting Sandy in the early days of his success, and also of losing some friendships. But he also spoke of making the best of his second chances. That didn't make him all that much different from the rest of us who slip, fall, reflect, and hope to make a fresh start.

Garth was in a position few are lucky enough to find themselves in. His dream had come true. When he was starting out, he had had nothing to lose. Now that he had everything—in a reverse of the Bob Dylan lyric—he had everything to lose.

When he found himself wanting to tell Taylor, who was about nine months old, some of what he'd learned in life so far, he thought he would tell her to push herself toward a dream, to keep her head up, and to lean into the wind. Instead he just whispered to her, "Be happy." He realized how simple it was, and that even with all of his success, he wasn't feeling so happy about his own life.

No doubt there are people who will say, "What the hell did Garth Brooks have to be unhappy about?" "How can a man have so much success and be out there doing what he loves to do and still say he's unhappy?" Well, there's clearly more to life than money and success, and it took a man of some depth to realize this principle while he was at the very height of that success.

In this way, Garth wasn't that different from the rest of us: wanting to struggle a little, enjoying the angst just a bit, being happy with being unhappy, and wanting to see a stronger future even while trying to be at peace in the present.

He loved the intensity of his life and missed the intensity of the stage when he wasn't on it. He adored the precious moments with his wife and daughter and wanted to have as many as he could. So he wasn't consistent; he was as confused as the rest of us.

But these were momentary thoughts, because at the time Garth said some other things as well:

He said if he wrote any songs during the first months after his daughter was born, they would all be sweet and sappy.

And he said that looking five years ahead, he hoped he would be a good husband, a good father, and a good son to his folks.

If you saw a Garth Brooks concert in the first few weeks after Taylor was born, you might have missed the wild stage antics he'd become known for. He was being more careful, because he had a little girl who was counting on him to come home. After a while, though, he and Sandy had a talk. They decided that the guy onstage just had to be himself, and that letting loose onstage and giving his fans a wild show were what made Garth Garth.

He also understood he was a role model for his fans, just as James Taylor and Dan Fogelberg had been role models for him. He had based a lot of his decisions in life, at a time when he was coming of age, on what he heard in the music. He felt it was the duty of artists to be socially aware and to use their celebrity to make things better.

Less than a month after Garth's tour to raise money for Feed the Children, Indiana congressman Dan Burton stood on the floor of the House of Representatives in Washington, D.C., and blasted him. The reason: At one of his concerts, Garth had not been able to meet with a twelve-year-old girl from Burton's state who had brain cancer. The girl had since died.

Burton's official statement said, "We ought to care about kids in this country. And people who are leading musicians in the country-and-western field and others should be willing to take the time to say 'Hi' to a dying girl. And Mr. Garth Brooks, I hope you get the message." Burton also told a reporter that although Garth may have been a great star and had the praise of millions, "he's not much of a human being, because the little girl is dead now. I think that is a shame. It's a real shame."

For an artist like Garth, who went out of his way to meet his fans, this was awful. It turns out that Garth had been given four names in connection with the young girl, and since he couldn't spend time with all four of them, he arranged for them to have free tickets. Clearly he didn't know that among them was a terminally ill girl.

Outraged by Burton's attack, numerous people rose to Garth's defense, pointing out that he was working hard to raise money for Feed the Children, that he went out of his way to meet with fans to the point of exhaustion, and that he gave enormous sums to charity. In fact, several charities issued a joint press release praising Garth's efforts on their behalf.

Larry Jones of Feed the Children said, "There would have to be a hundred Garth Brooks and four hundred hours in every day" to meet every request the singer gets. David Skepner, manager of the group Riders in the Sky, said of Garth: "He's probably done more to help children and people with difficulty than the entire United States Congress combined."

Congressman Burton's attack on Garth occurred around the time of the release of the first single from his upcoming fourth album, a song he'd been performing all summer at his concerts. The fans were showing even more enthusiasm for the tune than they usually gave Garth's songs, and he was pleased that they loved it so much.

"We Shall Be Free" was the final title of the song Garth and Stephanie Davis had been writing back in the spring during the riots in Los Angeles. When Garth came back from L.A., the two songwriters had sat on a hill behind Garth's house and written the song without musical instruments, because, according to Allen Reynolds, Garth wanted to make sure the message was the most important thing about the song.

"I was hearing some of the lines as it was going on, and I just thought it was a wonderful piece of work, and I still think it's a wonderful statement," Reynolds says. "It's not preachy at all. It starts out 'This is not coming from a prophet, I'm just an ordinary man, when I close my eyes I see what could be' . . . I love the lyric to that song. 'When nobody walks a step behind, then we shall be free.'"

"We Shall Be Free" is an anthem that gives voice to the hopes that children will be fed, the air will be clean, people will not be judged by their skin color, and that everyone is free to worship as they please—pretty much everything America is supposed to be all about. The song rocks and is strengthened by the chorus behind Garth: Donna McElroy, Vickie Hampton, Yvonne Hodges, Debbie Nims, Gary Chapman, Howard Smith, and Johnny Cobb. Donna McElroy and Vickie Hampton are in-demand session singers who sing on many albums, including Wynonna's.

"The song is right down the spinal cord of where Milton Sledge, Mike Chapman, Bobby Wood, and that element of the band grew up," Reynolds says, "and the background singers—a mixed choir, mixed black and white—seemed appropriate because of the message that was being delivered in the song. It has a little bit of a gospel feel."

The song contains a line about another hope: being free to love anyone we choose. It was that line that got all the attention. And a lot of the attention was not positive. Though Garth said the line was about the choices people make, whether in interfaith or interracial couples or homosexual couples, the public focus was on homosexuality.

The song was released to radio but didn't make it to the Top 10 on the *Billboard* radio airplay charts. Garth said he wasn't upset when some stations that played it either didn't get requests for it or stopped playing it in response to listeners' objections. What bothered him was that some stations made the decision without giving listeners a chance to weigh in.

Allen Reynolds is still bothered by radio's response. "It was surprisingly controversial with radio—not with the fans, let me point out, but with radio, the chickens of the world, the cowards of the universe. They backed off, and the song didn't get past the twenties. But from the day it came out his country audience has loved that song and sung along and waved their hands in the air, and it's still a high point in his concerts. It was written from such a sweet, honest, caring point in his life. It was terrible for radio to inflict that kind of pain on him for something that was so genuine and loving on his part."

Newsweek said of the song, "Brooks has taken a leap out of the shelter of country tradition—where men can go astray but are forgiven if they repent—and into the dirty reality of modern life." The *New York Times* said Garth "used his megastar pulpit to attack some of country's longest standing attitudes . . . in so doing, he poses a direct challenge to country's traditionally conservative positions on sexual preference, political affiliation and religious persuasion."

Garth told the *New York Times* he thought the Republicans' big problem is that they believe family values are June and Ward and 2.3 children. "To me it means laughing, being able to dream," he said. "It means that if a set of parents are black and white, or two people of the same sex, or if one man or one woman acts as a parent; that's what family values are." Garth said it is possible to hear the song and not get that message, but that's what he meant. "My thinking is that if I get shot down for saying this, I need to be away from the people that object. You have to do what you believe."

Garth also released a video with "We Shall Be Free." Using real news footage again, as in "The Dance," the video features celebrities like Marlee Matlin, Harry Belafonte, Lily Tomlin, Jay Leno, Reba McEntire, Elizabeth Taylor, Colin Powell, and Martina Navratilova, among others, who look directly at viewers and offer advice and messages of hope. Garth appears in the video with a beard and longish hair. The shot of a wall with a big peace sign gives a feeling of the sixties all over again. Garth wanted to make a point with the video, and he did: he felt that people were moving more toward brotherly love than away from it. "Life is a team sport," he said, "and we all have a role to play."

Garth's fourth album, *The Chase,* was released on September 22, 1992. It took the number-one spot on the *Billboard* Top 200 Albums chart within a week.

"Brooks demonstrates that the true country performer can do as he wishes," the *New York Times* wrote. "By concentrating on the more introspective side of the rock that he adapts to country, Brooks arrives at his most persuasive collection. *The Chase* combines the '70s singer/songwriter approach with country's understanding of entertainment." That review had to be a dream come true for Garth Brooks.

Out on the other coast,the *Los Angeles Times* also praised *The Chase:* "Good news. Brooks demonstrates in his most consistent and most fully satisfying album that unprecedented success hasn't dulled his ambition or instincts," Robert Hilburn wrote.

Once again, Garth chose songs and stories that may not have had the intellectual depth of Paul Simon, the abstractness of Bob Dylan, or the sweetness of James Taylor but were stories of experiences that could have happened to any one of his fans. He is singing the stories of his fans' lives, and his voice carries them with such great emotion that you can't help but be spellbound while listening.

Take "Somewhere Other Than the Night," written by Kent Blazy and Garth. Country songs have talked about love, but when the man comes in and finds his wife with nothing but her apron on, that's taking the love theme a few steps farther. This beautiful song probably awakened the long-dormant love between plenty of couples. "Learning to Live Again," by Don Schlitz and Stephanie Davis, is like a short story, with characters and telling details, little dramas that become large in Garth's interpretation. A man's first date in a long time (we aren't told what has gone before, but it is either divorce or death of a lover) shows him as nervous as can be.

"Mr. Right" is a song Garth wrote back in 1988 in the vein of Bob Wills, and it is a fitting tribute to Wills, a hero of Garth's own hero, George Strait. "Walking After Midnight," the Alan Bloch and Don Hecht hit for Patsy Cline, gets a new interpretation from Garth, as does "Dixie Chicken" by Lowell George and Martin Kibbee, which was a hit for Little Feat. "That Summer," by Pat Alger, Sandy, and Garth, is another totally specific story that is also completely universal—a younger boy's initiation into the ways of the flesh by an older woman who has her own needs. Trisha Yearwood's harmony adds to the depth and richness of the song. Once again, Garth is taking the themes of love into deeper levels.

At the CMA Awards on September 30, Garth sang "Somewhere Other Than the Night," the latest single from *The Chase*. For everyone who'd seen or heard about his wild live shows—and for the viewers who remembered his rendition of "Shameless" at the CMAs the year before—this was a chance to show his more tender side. He sang the song with so much conviction and passion that he left no doubt why pop fans were turning to him in droves. Vince Gill and Reba McEntire, fellow Oklahomans both, were cohosts of the show. His friend Trisha Yearwood sang "Walkaway Joe," a duet with the Eagles' Don Henley that was written by Vince Melamed and Greg Barnhill.

Even more thrilling for Garth was to watch as George Jones was inducted into the Country Music Hall of Fame. It brought tears to Garth's eyes, as the millions of television viewers saw when the camera swept the audience. *Ropin' the Wind* won Album of the Year and Garth received his second consecutive Entertainer of the Year Award.

On October 17, 1992, when Garth played the Reunion Arena, he asked the crowd what they would think about his playing Texas Stadium in 1993. The roar of approval was deafening.

It was just as satisfying when *Beyond the Season*, which had entered the *Billboard* Top 200 Albums chart at number four, rose to number two and stayed there. It was a huge hit that raised a lot of money to feed hungry children. It has continued to do that every holiday season since.

In December, it was announced that *Ropin' the Wind* was the number-one album of the year. Period. Not just of country but of all albums. Ahead of Hammer and Kris Kross, Michael Jackson and Michael Bolton, U2 and Metallica. The number-six album of the year was *No Fences.*

That album was playing at a party in the tiny town of Wyoming, New York, when Taya Branton was in the tenth grade at Pavilion Central High School. "I first became a Garth fan in the tenth grade, because I was at a party and someone put on 'Friends in Low Places,'" she says. "I really liked the song; it was such a happy song. Some people at the party knew it and were singing and dancing. Everybody was having a good time. So a couple of months later, for my birthday I asked for *No Fences.* That soon became all I listened to."

The town's name has no relation to the state, but there isn't a more country place on earth. Huge farms surround a charming town center where the streetlights are still powered by gas—a gift from the local gas company, which said it would provide continuous gas for the lights when it won the town's business many years ago. Every fall the AppleUmpkin Festival attracts folks from miles around who also stop in and visit the year-round Christmas Shop.

The school bus driver played country music and it could be heard in many stores in Wyoming, but it wasn't considered cool among the town's students. Taya hadn't really listened to country music before, but after she heard Garth Brooks, "I changed my radio stations over to country, which was a pretty radical move at the time, as the rest of my classmates didn't get into country until about a year later, if they ever did at all."

By the end of 1992, it was reported that Garth Brooks was the most popular solo artist in America and that the most popular form of music was country. Country music had doubled its share of U.S. record sales in the three years since 1989. Amazingly, country radio had overtaken the Top 40 format among listeners nationwide. In 1989 and 1990, only seventy-six country albums had gone platinum. In the next two years, 1991 and '92, 157 country albums went platinum. Media pundits on both coasts who never really paid attention to the vast country of America in between were rushing around trying to explain how that had happened.

It was an ordinary night in the eastern New Mexico town of Clovis in January 1993. Clovis is famous as the town where Buddy Holly recorded many of his songs. A club called Clovis City Limits was practically empty, but a few people had shown up to hear a performance by a new country band called Yukon Jack. The ads had said Yukon Jack was an up-and-coming contemporary band on the verge of signing a major record deal. One of the patrons in the club that night did find it odd that this new band had a lot of very fine, very expensive sound equipment.

Clovis has about 34,000 residents and is home to Cannon Air Force Base. Folks tuning in to their radios that night at around nine-thirty heard some of the band members on the air, asking listeners to come on out for the show.

When the band was announced and the crowd had quieted down in anticipation of the evening's entertainment, Garth Brooks walked out onto the stage. People were in shock—and then they went wild. Everyone who had a cell phone called anyone they could think of. Radio station KSEL, from nearby Portales, began to broadcast the show live, and within minutes about nine hundred more people showed up.

The show had been arranged by Joe Harris, who hadn't told even the club's owner whom he was really bringing in. Joe did it for Garth, who'd been wanting to play a small club for a while. Everyone who knows Joe can just imagine him laughing at the surprise of the club owner, who had booked this "new" act on the strength of Joe's say-so.

There was one group in the audience who were also enjoying the trick. Shirley Harris was sitting with Sandy, Taylor, and Colleen and Raymond Brooks, who were celebrating their thirty-fifth wedding anniversary. Joe and Shirley had come from Tennessee with Garth and Sandy and would continue on with them to their next shows after the stop in Clovis.

By the way, tickets to the show were $3 each. So it had come full circle: now that Garth was playing in the hugest arenas in the country, he yearned to play a small club again.

From a little club in a small New Mexico town to Los Angeles, California.

First Garth won another American Music Award as Favorite Male Country Artist. Then he did something he'd been planning ever since he'd been in the city during the riots.

"We didn't come here to make speeches," Garth told the audience at the Forum in Los Angeles. "We came here to raise some hell and have some fun, as always."

They had also come to raise some funds. Garth was putting on two benefit concerts to raise money for rebuilding Los Angeles after the devastating riots that began the night he was in town to play at the Academy of Country

Music Awards. But he didn't make a big deal about his generosity, and there was no ceremony with a public official accepting a giant-size check. Instead, Garth gave L.A. his usual spectacular show. He didn't even showcase "We Shall Be Free," choosing instead to play it early in the show and then move on to his other big numbers.

Speaking of big numbers, the shows raised $1 million for the citizens of Los Angeles who needed it the most.

On Saturday, Garth performed a nationally televised concert at the NFL Experience theme park. And on Sunday, he sang the national anthem at the Super Bowl in front of an estimated worldwide audience of one billion people. Actress Marlee Matlin translated into sign language.

But Garth almost refused to go on. He had spent countless hours editing clips from "We Shall Be Free" into a tape, which NBC then said had arrived too late to air. Garth said if they didn't run the clips, he wouldn't sing the national anthem. They ran the clips.

At the Houston Livestock Show and Rodeo in February 1993, Texas Stadium general manager Bruce Hardy stopped in at the sound check to let Garth know how excited he was about Garth's plan to play the stadium. Garth just gave him a big hug.

In the spring of 1993, Garth had another hit single with "Learning to Live Again," written by Don Schlitz and Stephanie Davis. By the summer he'd have another hit, called, appropriately enough, "That Summer."

Garth spent the first part of 1993 trying to lose some of his girth. Like millions of Americans who found the most shocking part of their thirties to be the fact that their waistlines were expanding, and like the millions who knew full well that all the fast food and sugary treats they were indulging in were the reasons why, Garth put himself on a diet.

By May he had lost about forty pounds, and said he felt a lot better. Like his fellow dieting Americans, his biggest fear was that he'd put the weight back on. He said he was afraid the pounds he lost were "waiting at a truck stop out there."

Fans across America had something else to love about Garth. It wasn't just in his heart that he was like them. It wasn't just his soul that struggled with the same issues they did. It was right down to his pants size and his worries about it that Garth Brooks was one of us.

CHAPTER FIVE

THE ICON

*L*ooking back on his first meeting in Nashville with Merlin
Littlefield of ASCAP—the time Garth stayed in Nashville a
full twenty-three hours before heading back home with his
tail between his legs—Garth had a new perspective. He realized what a favor Littlefield had done in showing him the
sometimes harsh realities of the music business. Had Garth's
fantasy come true—had he been given a record deal instantly and made it big right away—he might have lost Sandy.
He also might have turned his back on his family, his town,
and his roots. Now he understood just how much he was a
part of his people and his home state, how important they
were to him, and how none of the success he was enjoying
could have happened without them.

Rolling Stone magazine sent a writer to Nashville to interview Garth at one of his favorite restaurants, The Pancake
Pantry in the Hillsboro Village section of town on Twenty-first
Avenue South. Even the biggest rock and roll magazine of our
time had to acknowledge the phenomenon that was Garth
Brooks. Garth talked about his band, Stillwater. He said his
musicians were definitely country players—two guys from
Kansas, three from Oklahoma, playing steel guitar and fiddle,
wearing hats, Wranglers, and Ropers. He said sometimes
they'd rather play George Jones and George Strait than even
Garth's own songs. "We're just a real, dirty band," he said.

"We're raw and we're tough." None of them were top-scale, top-line musicians, he said. But, he added, you can go get those top-line musicians "and see if they can entertain like us."

Every March along with the Academy Awards comes a "Barbara Walters Special," in which the queen of American TV journalists interviews the biggest newsmakers and noisemakers in the world of entertainment.

Barbara Walters had been calling Pam Lewis for a Garth interview for a while and had even sent Garth a personal letter telling him she wanted to include him in the pantheon of stars, world leaders, and American personalities it was her specialty to profile. In 1993, Garth sat down with Barbara for a special that also included Sharon Stone and Denzel Washington.

Garth told Barbara that he felt there were plenty of singers who looked better, played better, and sang better than he did. For that reason, he felt he had to pull every trick out of the hat to satisfy his audience. He told her that being onstage was like sex (he excused himself for saying this to her, but there was no other way to describe it, he said). "It's just a thousand miles an hour, the wildest thing, and then in the flip of a heart, it goes to this nice tender soft thing and you find everyone leaning in and then all of a sudden it's *bam!*" Garth said he felt he could really fly when he was onstage. It was wonderful, he said, and "very addictive, too."

Of course, Barbara asks those questions everyone wants to know about, and Garth was no exception. She asked him what he had learned about the road—and from the devastating experience of having his wife discover he'd been cheating on her. Garth told Barbara the lesson was "stay clean, stay straight," and to remember one thing: that during the ninety minutes onstage there are no rules, but that after that, there are.

When Barbara asked Garth about the song "We Shall Be Free" and whether he had intended the line "When we're free to love anyone we choose" to be about gay people, he answered by telling her that his sister Betsy was a lesbian. He added that he loved her to death and that, sorry, but he couldn't condemn somebody simply for being in love with someone else. Pam said she offered to ask Barbara to edit the comment out (whether Barbara would have or not is another matter), but that Garth said not to.

Garth made headlines for "outing" his sister, and plenty of people criticized him for doing so. "In his mind," Pam said, "it was nothing to be ashamed of, there was nothing wrong with it. He had put out 'We Shall Be Free,' a song about tolerance. But he didn't stop and think about how it would affect his family."

Before the show aired, Garth called his sister to tell her what he'd said. Betsy said she was afraid at first that hateful people would "blow up the bus or something." Later she said that a lot of good had come of it.

For a country superstar to use his fame to advocate tolerance in the area of relationships—and Garth said he was talking about interfaith and interracial relationships as well—was so new as to be revolutionary. He was helping to break the stereotype of the prejudiced Middle American white guy as well as turning a brighter light on those who'd been discriminated against. He was showing you could be from the heartland, be from the "majority," and still not impose your moral stand on other people.

Garth made another remark on the Barbara Walters show that brought him some flak. Barbara asked why he thought so many other artists played it safe in their music while Garth was always taking chances and stretching its limits. He told her he felt those artists wanted to keep doing what they loved and perhaps felt that playing it safe was the way to do that.

Then he said he had more money than his grandchildren's grandchildren can spend. This remark also seemed to offend a lot of people, particularly since it was taken out of context and reported widely without the words that followed. All Garth was saying was the truth: Unlike some stars who want more millions all the time to keep proving they are important, this ordinary guy from a family of modest means realized early on that the money he was making was enormous—and enough. He was already free. Why shouldn't he follow his musical instincts now that he didn't have to worry about paying the bills?

Garth added to his assessment of his financial status that he also had a wonderful home and family—his daughter and his wife. What could anyone take away from him?

In April 1993, Garth visited Texas Stadium with representatives of the film production company that would record a concert there for Garth's TV special *This Is Garth Brooks, Too.* They reviewed blueprints. They examined seating charts. Garth climbed up to the highest point in the stadium so he could see what kind of view a helicopter would have. He walked on the catwalk to see how the show would look from there. What other artist would take the time to sit in every section of the stadium to see what the view would be for fans in each seat? He decided not to sell the first two rows so he could give those seats away to some of the folks who had tickets up in the rafters. What a cool idea—imagine showing up at a concert expecting to sit in what some people called the "nosebleed seats" and then landing up in a front row.

After checking out the stadium, Garth asked Bruce Hardy, Texas Stadium general manager, to reserve the weekend of September 24. The next day, the Dallas Cowboys football team asked the National Football League to schedule back-to-back away games on two Sundays, September 19 and 26. By May 1, Garth had received word of the NFL schedule: Texas Stadium was his.

On June 6, Garth held a news conference in Texas Stadium to announce the concert. Sitting in front of the stadium's 65,000 empty seats, he told reporters he was nervous about selling that many tickets. "What if the first show sells out like that?" asked a reporter, snapping her fingers. Garth said if that happened, he would "do something to take care of the rest of the people." He was too nervous to mention the words "second show."

On June 12, 1993, tickets went on sale. Dallas fans bought 65,000 tickets to Garth Brooks's Texas Stadium concert in ninety-two minutes. Thousands of fans were left waiting on line.

Garth called Bruce Hardy at home to say thanks. Hardy's wife answered the phone and "even though he'd met her before for only a minute or so, Garth remembered her name and they talked for about five minutes before he asked for me," Hardy said.

On June 14, Garth announced that a second show had been scheduled, for September 25. Tickets for this concert went on sale five days later, and did take a little longer to sell out—ninety-three minutes.

On June 22, Garth appeared on the TNN television program *Crook & Chase* and announced a third show, which would be played on Thursday, September 23, making it actually the first show. Tickets to that show went on sale five days later, selling out in an hour and fifty-eight minutes.

Promoter Glenn Smith said, "This has been like a fantasy so far." The three shows would be the biggest concert event in Texas history. Not even rock stars who could pack stadiums full of fans had ever done this in Texas. And no one in country had ever come near it. But Garth wasn't finished yet.

In July, Garth went on *Crook & Chase* again, this time to say he would give away 65,000 tickets for a fourth show in Texas Stadium, scheduled for Sunday, September 26. Free. For this show, he would be lip-synching to tapes of the previous three nights for close-ups and retakes for the cameras. Garth also hoped the free show would devalue scalpers' tickets.

Garth opened his 1993 world tour in Cheyenne, Wyoming, at Cheyenne Frontier Days, one of the most exciting annual events in all of America. Thousands of people converged on Cheyenne, as they have every July since the event was first held in 1897 as a way to bring civic pride and provide an economic boost to Cheyenne. Day after day of spectacular events included air shows by United States Air Force Thunderbirds and grand parades featuring one of the world's largest collections of horse-drawn vehicles. Free pancake breakfasts started each day for the tens of thousands of people who came for a taste of the authentic Wild West.

While those events were taking place, a stage sat at one end of the biggest rodeo arena in the country. In the evening, the stage was pulled into full view of the fans who had come to see Garth Brooks live—the biggest western party since Buffalo Bill's Wild West Show performed in 1898 to a cheering crowd.

After doing his usual blockbuster show, Garth climbed up onto the scaffolding and, with the wind blowing all around him, belted out the Grand Funk Railroad anthem "An American Band." At this, the opening of his world tour, he reminded everyone there that his roots were right here in the American West. It was a night as big as the West itself—a night neither Garth nor the thousands of people in that rodeo arena would ever forget.

Like many other gifted singer/songwriters, Stephanie Davis had been unable to land her own record deal for reasons having more to do with commercial expectations than artistic merit. Garth had offered to help Stephanie—his cowriter on "We Shall Be Free" and the writer of "Wolves" and other songs on Garth's albums—to get a deal, but she wanted to wait and get one on her own merits. Finally she did, when Asylum Records decided to record and release a Stephanie Davis album. The CD, titled simply *Stephanie Davis,* received great reviews.

For his 1993 tour, Garth asked Stephanie to be his opening act. Although she had played numerous showcases—where you were lucky if a hundred people showed up—now she was going to play in front of the kinds of crowds only Garth Brooks could attract.

Davis knew that as Garth's opening act, she wasn't the reason the crowds were there, but still she wasn't satisfied with the way the crowd received her on her first night of the tour. The next night, however, the fans were on their feet cheering after her last song and calling for encores. What made the difference?

Well, Stephanie Davis had gone back to her hotel room after the first night's set and written a brand-new song—an up-tempo number that she taught the band to play the next morning. The next night she closed her set with it to huge applause. Pretty impressive, right?

Back in Yukon on September 11, the second annual Garth Brooks Boulevard Craft, Antique and Music Festival took place. By this time Rick's Donuts was filled with autographed pictures of Garth. Yukon Trophy, located at Garth Brooks Boulevard and Main Street, was selling Garth souvenirs, including hats, T-shirts, key chains, and street signs, along with replicas of the water tower complete with the words "Yukon:

Home of Garth Brooks." The store was the brainchild of Bea Johnson, a longtime resident of Yukon whose son, Todd, used to play with Garth and Kelly Brooks. Bea told everyone who asked that Garth had been a real nice kid.

In Pieces, Garth's fifth album, was released in September of 1993, right in the middle of his tour. One of the songs he had been performing on tour, "American Honky-Tonk Bar Association," was getting the same great reaction "Friends in Low Places" had when he had introduced it live before releasing it to radio as the first single from *No Fences.* The song is a celebration of the ordinary person who feels overworked, overtaxed, and underappreciated. It is Garth's tribute to the folks who wear hard hats, drive a truck with a gun rack, and wave the flag, and it contains a line about tax dollars going to people standing on a welfare line. Some people took offense at that. Others loved the line that exhorts people to "rejoice, you have a voice" if you care about "the destination of this great nation." Garth was telling his fans they had the power to change and shape America and suggested that they use it.

But no one could argue with "Standing Outside the Fire," written by Jenny Yates and Garth. Like "The River" and "The Dance," it challenges everyone to jump into life and take risks, rather than live in the relative safety of untested dreams. The song sums up Garth's philosophy of life: If he isn't doing something huge and risky, he doesn't feel he is living at all. The video, with its story of a boy who has Down's syndrome deciding to compete in a race with so-called normal kids, makes the point that anything is possible.

In "The Night I Called the Old Man Out," written by Garth with Pat Alger and Kim Williams, a rebellious son takes on his strong dad and learns that even when his father asserts his power, it hurts him to do so. It's kind of like the lesson Joe

Harris, Jr., learned from his own dad when he was a teenager. And teenage boys aren't the only ones who rebel, as is made clear in the rollicking "Ain't Going Down ('Til the Sun Comes Up)," by Garth with Kent Blazy and Kim Williams. This time a girl does exactly what she wants to do all night— which are all the things her mama has forbidden. It would become another number-one single for Garth. In "The Night Will Only Know," Garth, Stephanie Davis, and Jenny Yates tell an even more disturbing story. A man and a woman, "both belonging to another," are unable to help a woman in trouble because to do so would reveal their tryst.

"The Cowboy Song" was something Garth had been playing since before he made his first album. Bob Doyle had actually found it in a trash can when he was working at ASCAP. He knew Garth liked cowboy music, so he decided to play it for him. Written by Roy Robinson, the song had been cut once with Garth's regular full band, but now they decided to cut it a second time—with Roy Huskey on bass, Sam Bush doing mandolin, Rob Hajacos on fiddle, Bruce Bouton on Dobro, and Chris Leuzinger and Mark Casstevens on acoustic guitar. The song was recorded live over a single day. Garth put it into the "ten spot of the album, which is my favorite spot."

The combination and variety of messages in the songs on *In Pieces* seemed to reflect the constantly changing emotions inside the artist himself. "I'm a guy who's still confused about life," Garth said. "I've got this wild side, where I really want to rip things up, and I've got this side that's aimed at manners and being polite and following the rules. I'm a mixed-up guy, but I can only be me, and the inner turmoil inside me spills out on these records."

The album's title reflects the fact that the whole album "came to us in pieces," Garth said. "Some songs were still being written the day we were cutting, and some songs came out of left field."

One song on the album gave Garth a chance to record with a group he loved. "Callin' Baton Rouge," written by Dennis Linde, had been recorded years before by New Grass Revival. Garth and Allen Reynolds had been thinking of cutting it for the first track of the album but didn't. Then, six months later, they had a change of heart and decided to cut it. "I think New Grass was a band that was thirty or forty years ahead of their time," Garth said. Pat Flynn, Sam Bush, John Cowan, and Bela Fleck hadn't been together in years, but they all told producer Allen Reynolds they would love to join Garth on the song. Everyone had a great time in the studio, and a song that almost didn't make it onto the album became one of its biggest singles.

It was a special experience to work with the guys from New Grass Revival. On this, his fifth album, Garth was still working with the same studio musicians who'd been with him from the beginning. The only significant additions in the studio from time to time were string players, The Nashville String Machine, who were the premier studio string musicians in Nashville and had appeared on numerous gold and platinum albums. Charles Cochran took care of Nashville String Machine's arrangements, which were always carefully written out in advance, because, as Reynolds said, "violin players don't wing it."

Allen Reynolds said, "Garth knows my tendency is to occasionally make changes in the band rather than stay with exactly the same players. I find now and then it's helpful to bring someone fresh in." By this time, Reynolds was perfectly happy with the existing band and would consider changes only on principle. "Garth never wanted to change," he said. "He was always so thrilled with the way these guys responded to him. His words to me were 'These guys have never let me down.' They certainly have covered for him a wide variety of musical forms and feels, and they've been wonderful. I never argued at all."

"On this album we went in totally free, jumped off the cliff, smiled, and just said let's see what falls together," Garth says, "and *In Pieces* fell to what it is."

One thing that fell into the album was "The Red Strokes," a picture of love and a description of what seems to stand out most when passions run high. Lisa Sanderson, who is listed as a cowriter of the song with James Garver, Jenny Yates, and Garth, had told Garth about a painting she saw at the Louvre in Paris, one of the world's greatest art museums, a painting in which red brush strokes were dominant. The blue strokes represented the blues, the green ones envy, she said. Sanderson wrote a poem about these observations and sent it to Garth, who thought it would make a wonderful song. It did.

It also made for one of the most dramatic videos ever seen. In a stark white room with sunlight streaming through the windows, a white baby grand piano rises up with Garth sitting at it wearing a white tuxedo and a white Stetson. A pool of red paint is on the floor. As he plays the song, the red paint becomes part of the story. At one point blue paint oozes from the piano keys and green paint from the piano's pedals beneath Garth's bare feet. As the passionate lyrics of the song ring out in Garth's rich voice—the line "thundering moments of tenderness rage" is pure Garth Brooks—the red paint streams around and eventually splashes onto him like a rainstorm.

While making the video, Garth had to be lowered into a pool of the paint and then rise out of it. On the first day of shooting, the paint was so cold that he began hyperventilating. The piano also got stuck because the paint was so thick, and Garth says it was truly "the hand of God" that kept it and him from sinking altogether. Filming the video required eighteen full tuxedos, twelve white Stetsons, six baby grand pianos (each of which had to be used twice and therefore completely cleaned and repainted between shots), and five thousand gallons of mud mixed with thirty-five gallons of red paint. It was filmed over six days in Nashville, Los Angeles, and New York. Later, the pianos were auctioned off to benefit various causes.

Garth said he had always prided himself on the ten cuts on his albums being different from one another. On *In Pieces* the styles of music were even more different. He said he felt the songs from this album would be the ones he'd most enjoy performing.

Taya Branton got *In Pieces* as soon as it hit the stores in Wyoming, New York. She was still trying to convince her friends of the greatness of Garth Brooks. "No matter what he's singing, he's totally into the song," she said. "If what he's singing is upbeat—or, on the slower songs, sad—he puts his entire self into it. He has an amazing voice. He's a simple and honest guy that everyone can relate to." Taya's friends didn't want to listen to country in the car, so she listened at home. It was there that Taya Branton began turning her mother, Terry, into a country music fan. She wasn't having any luck with her brother, Mark, or her father, Denis, but she kept trying.

In August of 1993 Garth was asked about the money he had raised for Feed the Children with his Christmas album, *Beyond the Season*. By this time the album had raised about $2 million after only one season on sale. The money had been sitting in an interest-bearing account. Garth wanted to use it to buy gas for the trucks that transported the food distributed by the organization. Garth said, "It's a great organization, and I feel that it has a great goal to it. I feel good to be a part of it."

Garth felt good to be alive, too. He was on his way to Texas Stadium.

On September 4, preparations began for the biggest concert in the history of Texas and the biggest show in the history of country music. Garth Brooks's production equipment—tons and tons of it—began arriving in Irving, Texas, home of Texas Stadium. As soon as the Dallas Cowboys finished their game on September 12, stage equipment would start coming in.

The crew was in the stadium and ready to get started on September 13. Ironworkers welded two trusses across the opening in the stadium roof. The huge steel braces would help to hold the 200,000 pounds of sound and light equipment that would be suspended from above. The football field was covered with tarp and plywood. Risers were put in that would angle the floor seats for better sight lines. The year before, Guns 'n' Roses and Metallica had come into Texas Stadium on a Saturday, but even with their huge shows, the Cowboys were able to play football the following Monday. Bruce Hardy told the *Dallas Morning News* that there was no way the team could play so soon after the kind of production that would go into this concert. The stadium would be out of commission for two weeks.

One of the guys working to set up for the show was Garth Brooks himself. Over the next several days, much to the great concern of everyone around him, he was climbing up, jumping down, roaming around, and generally lending his hand to all but the most dangerous construction tasks. When he wasn't worrying the daylights out of his managers, staff, and crew, he was walking around the stadium checking camera angles.

Whether Garth's show in Texas Stadium would be the biggest film shoot in history was debatable, but it was definitely the biggest film production shoot of 1993. Kodak said the project would use the most film—400,000 feet—ever shot in such a short period of time.

Just after midnight on September 18, Garth was rehearsing his Texas Stadium show in Las Colinas when he got a call from his brother.

"Garth, you'd better get over here right away," Kelly said.

The stage roof supporting the lighting and sound equipment had collapsed. The huge space-frame that everything hung from had just snapped right in the middle, and when a lighting truss fell from the roof, eighteen crew members had been injured.

Garth listened, then asked Kelly if anyone had died or had lost any limbs. He was told it didn't appear that way. Then he and Sandy rushed over to the stadium.

Ambulances were already on the scene. They took the crew members—some from Garth's organization and some local—to the hospital, where they were all treated for mostly minor head, back, neck, and leg injuries. In Garth's organization, safety is always a prime concern, and he was shaken by the accident. As if that wasn't enough, on the Wednesday before the show, at about one P.M., another crew member fell seven feet to the floor after he stepped backward onto one beam while trying to straighten another. Now Garth was scared. Here he was doing the biggest, most elaborate special effects of his career—certainly the most amazing of any country show ever—and these accidents were happening.

Finally the equipment was all in place and everything was ready for the show. When Jerry Jones, the owner of the stadium and the Dallas Cowboys, came in and took a look at all the equipment—sound, lighting, and camera gear, as well as fog machines—he said, "Garth, what have you done to my stadium?" Then Jones presented country's biggest superstar—and former aspiring athlete—with a silver-plated Dallas Cowboys helmet.

Most of the time that Garth went out on the road, Pam Lewis and Bob Doyle stayed back in Nashville. There was so much to do in the management offices—fielding offers, talking to the press, working in conjunction with the record label's publicity department, accepting the zillions of letters and gifts that arrived at the office for Garth all the time—that it didn't make sense to go out on the road, where they had little to do. Garth was perfectly good at meeting the press himself, and besides, the interviews and the show passes for reviewers and photographers were all taken care of in advance.

But they sure did go to Texas Stadium. "The place looked like some kind of huge modern sculpture," Pam says. "It was an amazingly huge place. They have golf carts to get around. Colleen had her own golf cart and was riding all over the stadium." Now, there's a mom who knows how to have fun!

Thursday night, before Garth and his band went out onstage for their first show, they stopped to do what they always did before they went onstage: hold hands and try to say something funny or inspirational. Tonight they were as nervous as they'd ever been about performing—the accidents had them scared and the audience out there was huge! They held hands even tighter than usual, and no doubt a few silent prayers were made. Then Garth Brooks and Stillwater, the band that loved to be onstage, the band that always delivered on what live music was all about, headed out to give their fans what they'd been waiting for.

The houselights went down and the crowd rose up. Amid a cloud of smoke, Garth Brooks emerged from beneath the stage. The cheers of 65,000 fans showed him he'd scored a touchdown just by being there.

"Hellooooo, Texas!" Garth roared. "We came here to raise some hell and have some fun, so let's get to it!"

Get to it they did. Thursday night, Friday night, and Saturday night, it was one thrill—and one scare—after another. From "Papa Loved Mama" to "That Summer." From "The River" to "Much Too Young" . . . from his own monster hits to the kinds of songs he used to love to play back at Bink's and Willie's in Stillwater—songs like "Keep Your Hands to Yourself" by the Georgia Satellites and Bob Seger's "Night Moves." Garth Brooks turned one of America's greatest football stadiums into one giant party.

When he sang "The Thunder Rolls," the sounds of thunder and flashes of lightning filled the stadium. At one point, it actually rained on the crowd when it was only supposed to rain on the stage. The fans loved it. They loved it, too, when Garth picked up his acoustic guitar and accompanied their own singing of "Unanswered Prayers." That quiet moment—if you can call 65,000 people singing together a quiet moment—was special, just as special as the crowd's thundering applause when Garth sang "American Honky-Tonk Bar Association" and they sang along.

Andy Francis, a music industry consultant who has held a variety of key executive positions with a number of major record labels, was at Garth's Texas Stadium shows. Francis had seen plenty of huge shows in his career—he had worked along with Ira Fraitag on the big David Bowie project and seen Bowie's elaborate, special-effects-filled Sound and Vision tour—yet he called Garth's concert "the best performance of anyone I've ever seen. I've seen Prince, Springsteen, and

Bowie, but Garth controls the audience like no one I've ever seen. The rock guys come and they are presentational, but with Garth it's a mutuality. There is something going on with the people—they are on the stage, he's in the audience. He had the whole place in the palm of his hand."

For "Standing Outside the Fire," a ring of fire was going to surround the stage. But on Friday night, when Garth saw the fire behind him there was no fire in front for him to walk through. He turned to the crew member onstage who was in charge of igniting the flames and said, "Where's the fire?" The guy looked at him and said, "You're standing on the pipe."

"I was so fired up—and so pumped," Garth said later, "that I had forgotten to move back. I look down and I'm standing right on the gas pipe. Thank God he was watching or he would've torched me."

A local choir made up of five hundred Dallas-area students and parents sang their hearts out on "We Shall Be Free," doing Garth proud. What a thrill for all of those folks! It was enough to make kids decide that going to choir practice at school every week could give them a lot more excitement than they'd ever expected.

Every artist loves the hit songs that gave them their fame and fortune. But the price is that you can never do a show without those songs. Don McLean, one of Garth's heroes, knew he could never do a concert anywhere in the world without singing "American Pie." If you went to a Rolling Stones show and they didn't sing "Satisfaction," well, you wouldn't be satisfied. A Bruce Springsteen concert without "Born to Run" is still a major rockfest, but it would definitely be missing something.

Garth says there's one song he's done so many times that he and the band often don't even play it in sound check. And if they ever find themselves grumbling about having to play it yet again, which they hardly ever do, Garth reminds them that this particular concert may be the first and only time some fans get to experience it.

"Blame it all on my roots..." Six little words and the loving fans who were already in a frenzy were now beside themselves—literally. When Garth Brooks and Sillwater started performing "Friends in Low Places," tens of thousands of people took to their feet, putting their arms around their friends and singing along. This response was what made each performance of the song a new and special experience even for the band members, playing it for the umpteenth time.

Garth's number-one hit during September of 1993 was "Ain't Going Down ('Til the Sun Comes Up)." The band started playing it, and the next thing you know, Garth Brooks was flying—flying!—all across the stadium. The wire holding him up was almost too slender to see.

Joe and Shirley Harris were watching the shows from a luxury booth in the stadium. So were Ray and Colleen Brooks. Colleen was terrified. "He started flying," Shirley Harris said. "I could not believe him. It was unreal to see him go onto the top of the audience and disappear into the people." Four grown adults who loved their boy—and knew he was afraid of heights—all felt a whole lot better when the song was done and Garth was safely back down.

Shirley and Joe remember the time Garth played in their old hometown of Roanoke, Virginia, and he jumped up on a ladder that hung down at the back of the stage. "He missed it and fell," Shirley says. "The rope wasn't as tight as it should have been. Garth jumped on it and he fell. It scared us all to death." Joe had been standing by the stage and ran toward Garth, but within seconds Garth got up and continued with the show. All that happened was he'd bruised his hip.

At Texas Stadium, Allen Reynolds spent a lot of time in the truck underneath the stage—in the bowels of the stadium, as he put it—popping out to watch Garth on the monitors. "I was so impressed that a guy could go to one town and fill a football stadium three times, three nights in a row. Garth hadn't done a stadium venue like that before," Reynolds says. "It was typical of him to offer himself a challenge like that where he was having to project and communicate with the back of the stadium. And he did it."

Reynolds says it always scared him when Garth flew during his shows. On the third night of the Texas shows, Reynolds was lobbying for Garth not to fly while the production managers discussed how to proceed following the rain that had fallen all day.

"People were showing up and filling the stadium, even though it was raining up until almost show time," he says. During the discussion, one of Garth's bus drivers was just smiling. Allen recalls the bus driver saying, "It won't rain on him." Allen said, "What do you mean, Jim?" "It never has," the driver told Reynolds, then started relating stories about storms and tornadoes and hurricanes happening near but never at Garth's shows, and about rainstorms that held out until Garth was done. "Sure enough," Reynolds says, "it quit raining about half an hour before show time and resumed raining about ten minutes after the show was over. It did not rain during the show."

Around the time of Garth's Texas Stadium shows, Joe Harris decided to leave Buddy Lee Attractions and go to work for the William Morris Agency.

Sol Saffian believes Joe was too honorable a man to say that one of the reasons he left Buddy Lee was the professional jealousy of other agents who were angry at themselves for not seeing what Joe had seen in Garth.

Garth had made a pact with Joe Harris. Joe had helped him get started, and Garth Brooks would always work with

Joe. But a court injunction filed by Buddy Lee Attractions prevented Joe from taking his acts with him to William Morris. Joe had booked everything Garth had ever done. As far as Garth was concerned, there was no other agent for him. From that moment on, he booked his own shows and tours.

In New York in November, Nassau Coliseum on Long Island became Garth country. In addition to his regular lineup of songs, Garth sang Billy Joel's "New York State of Mind." Backstage, he and Pam Lewis held court for the New York press and for the New York staff of Capitol Records. Looking into Garth's eyes that night, everyone at the party saw a man at the top of his game.

"Mr. Brooks aims for the real," the *New York Times* said. "He has translated the small moment into the big events, which is how things work for most people. . . . His whole act is an effort to erase the distinction between artist and audience. . . . For Mr. Brooks' constituents, taking a break from the extremity of most Hollywood movies, pop music and television, Mr. Brooks was clearly a savior, their man, somebody who sang about their lives."

Playing New York was thrilling for Garth, but his stop in Los Angeles gave him even more to get excited about. Gene Simmons and Paul Stanley of KISS came to L.A. to see Garth's show. Afterward, they came backstage, where they told Garth they could see what he meant by being influenced by them. Paul Stanley said he smiled through the show, because it was a KISS show. "I see it. I see it in your show. I see it in your clothes. I'm flattered." Garth was pretty flattered too.

Garth told two of his biggest heroes that they were responsible for anything they saw in his show that they liked. Stanley felt it was nice that Garth hadn't forgotten or denied his influences after he became successful. Gene Simmons liked the fact that Garth had taken some of the KISS theatrics and mixed them with country soul. He called Garth a "true star" who was taking country "where it's never been before." Wow!

But wait—it gets better! KISS played backup for Garth when he recorded "Hard Luck Woman" as part of the KISS tribute album. "It's fascinating," Gene Simmons said. "You don't think it's Garth—it sounds like Rod Stewart."

Coming back out on the road after six months and having people just as hot to see him as before was, Garth said, "the neatest gift people have ever given me." In November, he got another neat gift—his first horse. It was a pony, a spotted saddlehorse he'd been riding for about a year at some friends' place. His friends asked if he'd like to have the horse and Garth said he'd pay any price, but his friends wanted to give it to him. The horse's name was Crackerjack.

Garth, Sandy, and Taylor went to Owasso, Oklahoma, to visit Sandy's family for Christmas. Garth and his in-laws were out shopping when Garth saw a couple come out of a store with bags of food, a little girl, and a stroller. The couple crossed the street and, in front of a Mennonite church, they reorganized their bags and resumed walking. Garth and his in-laws offered them a ride home after learning that the couple's car had broken down and they didn't have enough money to get it repaired.

Garth returned to their home an hour later and gave them the keys to a new car. The woman looked at him and asked, "Are you Garth Brooks?" Garth told her no, he was just a Garth Brooks fan.

On a Monday morning in April of 1994, Pam Lewis was waiting for her subscription copy of *TV Guide* to arrive. When it did, she and her staff cheered—Garth had made the cover! He had given an interview to the magazine in conjunction with the upcoming telecast of *This Is Garth Brooks, Too* but until the magazine was printed, his publicists didn't know whether he'd get the cover spot.

Before the interview, Garth had asked Pam to try to set up a meeting with President Clinton. Garth wanted to talk to him about world peace. Pam felt this was a noble but unrealistic idea. Later, media pundits and cynical writers would make fun of Garth's desire to use his stardom for a larger purpose. Some accused him of caring more about self-promotion than he did about the world. How did they know how he felt? Is it just easier to ridicule big ideas than to believe that someone actually believes in them?

Events in the world certainly warranted giving peace a chance in April of 1994. Fighting in Rwanda and Burundi was claiming thousands of lives—including those of Belgian peacekeepers sent to the African continent. NATO jets had bombed the Serbs for their advance on Bosnian cities and had continued bombing civilian areas. Palestinians had bombed a commuter bus in Israel and Israelis had bombed Palestinian civilians. Internal strife within the former Soviet states was raising concerns that the breakup of the Soviet Union might have unforeseen consequences for the world.

Garth told *TV Guide* that during his upcoming international concerts, he wanted to reach the world's leaders, to encourage them to establish peace on earth. "We've always been told that music can change the world," he said to *TV Guide*. "Well, let's give it a try."

When *This Is Garth Brooks, Too* aired on NBC on May 6, millions of viewers saw the show that had made entertainment history. It was edited in a fast, MTV kind of style and looked and sounded amazing.

"*Howdy*, pardner, let's mosey on down and interview Garth Brooks." This was the rather strange intro to a TV show in London on which Garth promoted the beginning of his first European tour, a tour that would be the biggest news in country music in 1994. With the theme from Clint Eastwood's western movie *The Good, the Bad and the Ugly* playing in the background, the show took an out-of-date and condescending view of the music that was sweeping the States—and about to sweep Europe.

For a long time, Garth's organization had been toying with the idea of an international tour. Like any artist who is popular in his own country, however, Garth wondered how he would be received overseas. During a dinner Pam Lewis asked Ira Fraitag what he thought about the idea of Garth in Europe. Fraitag had extensive experience touring Europe with many acts, including David Bowie and Don McLean. Fraitag told Lewis that he felt the ideal place for Garth to play first in Europe would be Ireland, where he would have instant recognition.

The reason? Ireland has always been a country where the traditon of the singer/songwriter—the troubador—is held in high esteem. The very roots of country music are in fact Irish, Scottish, and English folk songs and melodies. Irish and English fans have always been passionate about country music and its artists. When Don McLean, despite his huge talent, had a tough time filling concert halls in the United States, he could hop on a plane and play for 30,000 people in one show in places like Cork, Ireland, or play five nights at the RDS Arena in Dublin.

Fraitag told Pam that to play any other European country before playing England and Ireland might unnerve Garth, since the rest of Europe was not so familiar with American country music. In fact, Fraitag told Pam, he felt that playing Ireland and England first would give Garth added confidence to play in countries such as Spain, Germany, and France, where fan acceptance might not be as great as he had become accustomed to.

Well, the Irish people were so thrilled to have Garth Brooks come to play that the loudspeakers in Dublin Airport filled the air with Garth Brooks music on the spring day in 1994 when he arrived. Throughout his stay, pubs across the country held Garth Brooks nights. And when he went out on-stage and started playing, he was amazed that the people already knew his songs.

"I wasn't sure how the Irish would react. I was amazed," Garth said. His first show was at The Point, a structure, formerly called a "railroad roundhouse," where trains could be turned around. "They seemed to know all the songs and could recite the lyrics. Actually country music and Irish music are surprisingly similar, especially in the use of the fiddle."

"Unbelievable," the reviewer for the *Irish Independent* wrote. "Never but never has there been a concert like this in Ireland. Not from U2, Bob Dylan, or Springsteen."

It was the same thing in Birmingham, England, where crowds went wild. And at London's Wembley Arena, between thirty and forty people fainted from a combination of heat and excitement. Garth then went to Switzerland, the Netherlands, Norway, and Sweden, where he made instant country music fans out of all who heard him.

Garth and Sandy's second daughter, August Anna, was born on May 3, 1994.

Also in that month, a radio station in Fresno, California, purchased another station and turned it into K-Garth: all Garth, all the time.

Garth spent the rest of the spring and summer rehearsing and preparing for the second—and biggest—leg of his world tour.

The first stop was Auckland, New Zealand, a twenty-hour plane ride from Nashville. The city had no hall big enough for the likes of Garth Brooks, so the concert was held in a huge tent. Within five minutes of stepping onto the stage, Garth created the feeling of a revival meeting in that tent. He was the preacher spreading the gospel of country music and the audience was a congregation of twenty thousand frenzied fans, hanging on every word and note. Steam was rising from the crowd. Although it was a cool spring night in the Southern Hemisphere, Garth created a show as sizzling as the Fourth of July in Oklahoma. It's safe to say no one in New Zealand had ever seen anything like it—which is probably why his new disciples wouldn't let him off the stage until he'd done three encores. Garth was having as much fun as the fans, and no one wanted it to end.

The world-class excitement that had started in April in Ireland was continuing in New Zealand. And that excitement continued in Australia. In Brisbane, Sydney, Adelaide, Melbourne, and Perth, Garth was on all the front pages and was among the lead stories on the evening news. From Down Under Garth went to Spain, Germany, France, and then back to the United Kingdom, dazzling audiences of people who witnessed the sheer entertainment power of Garth's brand of country music.

News of Garth conquering the world was everywhere. Following his lead—and the establishment of Country Music Television in Europe—country stars such as Vince Gill, Reba McEntire, Trisha Yearwood, George Strait, and Clint Black also brought their music to Europe. Garth had kicked the door wide open, and Europeans now realized that here was a form of American music they needed to pay attention to.

With all of the emphasis on his international touring, Garth played only one concert in the United States in

1994—a benefit held in Los Angeles during the World Cup at the famed Hollywood Bowl in July. It was a benefit for One Voice, a city-based group that helps low-income families with physical, employment, and educational needs. The 18,000 fans assembled in the Bowl saw a rare acoustic set in which Garth brought his most intimate treatment to such favorites as "The Dance," "Unanswered Prayers," and "If Tomorrow Never Comes." He played a portion of the concert with the Hollywood Bowl Orchestra. And saluting some of his musical heroes, Garth sang the Elton John and Bernie Taupin composition "Candle in the Wind" and James Taylor's "Sweet Baby James." At the end of the show, it must have felt like the old days back in Stillwater: Garth performed Don McLean's "American Pie"—just as he'd done all over the world.

An estimated $1 million went to One Voice from one of the greatest voices in American music.

At the corner of Fairfax Avenue and Twenty-fourth Avenue South in Nashville, the two-story, redbrick Ronald McDonald House blends in nicely with the other homes. Its well-tended lawn and trees give a sense of normalcy to parents whose lives are anything but normal when their children are in the hospital.

Garth had been very impressed when he toured Ronald McDonald House over Christmas of 1993 and visited with the parents who stayed there while their children were being treated at one of Nashville's many children's hospitals. Now, on a September morning in 1994, he was back, telling the nation on *CBS This Morning* about his new project with McDonald's. A CD called *Garth Brooks Collection: Garth's Favorites* was being sold at McDonald's restaurants nationwide, along with collections by Elton John and Tina Turner. EMI, the parent company of Capitol Records, had set up the promotion. Garth asked EMI to make it a charity event and donate one dollar to Ronald McDonald House for each album sold. By October he had raised more than $1 million for the wonderful house on Fairfax Avenue, and all the wonderful Ronald McDonald Houses around the country.

*B*y the middle of 1994, sales of country music recordings had doubled since 1989 when Garth released his first album. Garth had sold an amazing 35 million albums and charted sixteen number-one singles. In June 1994, Garth wondered during an interview with *Playboy* magazine, "Three years ago, would you have thought that the largest-selling artist in the nineties would be going bald and have an eating problem and be doing fiddle and steel-guitar music?"

In the five years since 1989, Garth Brooks had released five amazing albums, changing everything about the business of country music with his huge sales. In December of 1994, instead of adding another new collection of songs to his body of work, he decided to look back. It was a great time to introduce the folks who didn't know him to the songs that had made him such a huge star. *Garth Brooks/The Hits* would be available for a limited time so that the new fans it drew might then go back and check out his earlier albums and the great songs on them that hadn't been released as singles.

The year ended with two parties held in the same week for Garth Brooks. His record label celebrated the fact that the Recording Industry Association of America had certified sales of 11 million for *No Fences*. And backstage at the Grand Ole Opry, they celebrated *Ropin' the Wind*'s hitting 10 million in sales. The Opry was the perfect place for that party because, Garth said, "this is the pinnacle of what I do. Nothing has ever touched being a member of the Grand Ole Opry."

Joe and Shirley Harris were at the party at the Grand Ole Opry. They never missed a show when Garth played there. Shirley says it was always amazing to her that so many artists would show up at the Opry surrounded by their managers, publicists, and sometimes even bodyguards, but Garth would just mingle with his fans, taking pictures with them, signing autographs. "He was a people person," she said, "and no one ever tried to harm him in any way."

Garth said he would spend all of 1995 at home with his wife and daughters Taylor Mayne Pearl and August Anna, then begin a world tour in Atlanta in March '96. He planned to do a lot of music in the next few years. "After that," he said, "we're going to have to take a serious look at staying home." By 1997, Garth said, Taylor would be in kindergarten. "The soccer games, the theater, whatever she wants to get into, Dad's going to have to be there for that," he said.

At the Twenty-second Annual American Music Awards in January, Garth walked onto the stage to accept his award for Favorite Male Country Artist (he beat out Alan Jackson and Vince Gill). Wearing a dark brown suede jacket, he looked with joy at the cheering fans in the Shrine Auditorium. "Thank you," he said. "It's been almost a year since we've toured here in the States. We've got another year to go until we come back. I don't know if I'm gonna make it—I miss you guys a lot."

Dick Clark, who has produced the AMA show since its inception in 1974, says he admires Garth tremendously, not just for his talent but for the way he has handled becoming so huge while still retaining dignity and charm. "He's smart and he doesn't lord it over anybody," Dick says. "There's a real good lesson to be learned there."

Later that month, Garth and his organization began planning his next tour, which would begin more than a year later. Kelly Brooks told *Amusement Business* magazine that Garth wanted to show consideration for other touring acts who often didn't want to go into a city right after Garth had been there. And because they knew they would be asking venues for up to six straight dates, they would start booking early, sixteen to eighteen months out.

The show was going to be even more spectacular than Garth's previous live shows, if that was possible. The details were just beginning to be worked out, but one thing was certain: Garth was going to continue to keep his ticket prices low. He felt that made concertgoers happy from the moment they entered the hall. If they thought the lights and stage alone were worth the price of admission, they'd be in a good mood and the party atmosphere would get going right from the start.

Garth and Sandy discussed the upcoming long road trip and how it could work with the kids. They agreed it was good for their marriage and family to keep traveling together.

"I can't do one without the other, and I want it all," Garth said. "I want my musical life, which I enjoy, and as soon as I step off that stage I want that family life."

How much did Garth love his job? "A bad day in the music business beats working for a living any day," he said. He made the comparison to sex and pizza: When they're great they're great, and when they're bad, they're still pretty good.

Getting ready to go out again, Garth reminded his band that the best part of the business is the ninety minutes on-stage, and that during that time there was nothing they could do about any of their problems and nothing he could do about the politics of the music business, so they should all just go and enjoy themselves to the max during the show. He said that when the business got in the way and the music got pushed back, you were in trouble. "You got to fight to make sure the music stays up front," he said.

In February, *No Fences* achieved sales of 13 million copies, making it the all-time best-selling album in country music history.

Garth Goes to Washington: On March 15, Garth joined 350 cultural leaders, musicians, actors, and artists—including Christopher Reeve, Tony Randall, and Kenny G—for Arts Advocacy Day, a lobbying trip sponsored by the nonprofit American Council for the Arts. The entertainers were there to protest the fact that House of Representatives subcommittees had recently voted to cut $5 million from the 1995 budgets of the National Endowment for the Arts and the National Endowment for the Humanities, and $47 million from the Corporation for Public Broadcasting.

Garth went to the office of House Speaker Newt Gingrich, a leading critic of federal spending on the arts, wearing jeans and boots and his hat. "Where I come from, we talk about what's right or wrong," Garth said, "not liberal or conservative, Democratic or Republican." He said that supporting the arts was the right thing for Congress to do. Garth told Gingrich that small towns tended to benefit from spending on the arts as much as, if not more than, big cities. After meeting with Garth, when asked his position on funding the arts, Gingrich said, "Don't know yet."

Texas senator Phil Gramm said, "I like Garth Brooks's music, and if he wants to give me advice about country music, I'll take it. But not about spending taxpayers' dollars."

The House voted a few days later not to make such deep cuts in the arts budgets.

In April, Jimmy Bowen retired from his post as president of Capitol Records Nashville. Bowen had been diagnosed with cancer some months earlier and decided it was time to leave.

(Later, Bowen wrote a book about his life in the music business called *Rough Mix,* in which he talks about some of the conflicts he had with Garth Brooks.) Scott Hendricks, a respected record producer, would become president. At the same time, Garth's management company, Doyle/Lewis, which had been with Garth since the beginning, split up.

With the changes in his label and management structure, Garth began spending a lot of time taking care of business issues. Ultimately, Garth formed a new management company, GB Management, and hired back some of the Doyle/Lewis employees. By the summer, he was free to get back to the music.

In June of 1995, Taya Branton graduated from Pavilion Central High School in Wyoming, New York. When she heard that a senior prom song would be chosen for her class, she jumped into action. "A whole bunch of us made a huge effort to get 'The Dance' as the senior prom song," she said. "We copied down the lyrics and gave them to people, and three or four of us campaigned. We talked to people, played the song constantly, and made people listen to Garth's stuff."

Their campaign worked. At the Pavilion Central High School prom, when the prom queen and king and prince and princess entered the hall, it was Garth Brooks's "The Dance" that was playing, and it played all through the night.

Later that summer, Ty England's first solo album came out, titled, appropriately enough, *Ty England.* Ty had left Garth's band after the '94 world tour to try to make it on his own. Now he had a hit single called "Should've Asked Her Faster" and was back in Oklahoma City to sign autographs and meet fans. Ty had made the same pact with his brother that Garth made with his: When one of them got a shot at something big in the music business, the other would get one too. Now Ty's brother Greg was his road manager.

Garth was getting ready to turn in his next album, going through all the usual last-minute details. Turning in an album or any other piece of work and knowing that there's no more time to fix or fuss with it is hard for any artist. It was even harder for Garth. He was trying to finally get some sleep before turning the record in when he got a call from a neighbor that three horses were in her yard and they looked like his. So instead of getting some sleep, he spent the next few hours rounding up his horses.

Fresh Horses was the name of the Garth Brooks album that came out in November of 1995. "I've been pouring my guts out on my album," Garth said. "I've worked hard—this one hurt."

The first song on *Fresh Horses* was called "The Old Stuff." Garth wrote it with Bryan Kennedy and Dan Roberts. The story of a big star looking back to the days "when the old stuff was new," it celebrates all those long rides in a rented van (before the big tour buses), playing in clubs like The Barn in Sanford, Florida, and Cowboys in Dallas (before Texas Stadium). Back when the old stuff was new, the rise to the top was one big party for Garth and Stillwater.

Garth invited Joe Harris over to his house to play the song for him. Tears came to Joe's eyes when he heard the line "Uncle Joe, you know we owe it all to you."

The first single, "She's Every Woman," cowritten with Victoria Shaw, entered the chart at number thirteen.

The album had a variety of musical styles and feelings, from Aerosmith's "The Fever" to Celtic folk music. "The Fever," originally written by Steven Tyler and Joe Perry, was rewritten by Garth and Bryan Kennedy in an effort to customize the words and music for some friends who were in the rodeo. When Garth met Tyler at an Aerosmith concert, they talked about the song. "Steven knew what we did. It flattered us. I didn't feel like a stranger," said Garth. The song didn't get a great reception from fans, so radio didn't play it much. Garth said he had to make his records for the records' sake and thanked radio for at least playing "The Fever" and letting the fans decide.

The song "Ireland," which Garth wrote with Stephanie Davis and Jenny Yates, is a tribute to the love he received from the Irish people when he went there in 1994. By now, half of the population of Ireland owned a Garth Brooks album and a fourth had seen him live.

"It's Midnight Cinderella" is a song Garth wrote with Kim Williams and Kent Blazy, the story of a guy who tells a girl he's going to make her forget the Prince Charming who broke her heart. Garth wrote "The Beaches of Cheyenne" with Dan Roberts and Bryan Kennedy; it is a haunting tale of the wife of a rodeo rider whose spirit haunts the beach where she ran into the ocean after she learned of his death. By this time, songwriter Kent Blazy had had at least one song on each of Garth's albums. "Cowboys and Angels," which he wrote with Garth and Kim Williams, is about how God decides a cowboy needs some help with life and sends him an angel to love him.

One review of *Fresh Horses* pointed out that Garth had sold more albums since 1989 than Michael Jackson had sold since 1972. By this time, *The Hits* had sold eight million copies. Now everyone wanted to prove Garth could move those numbers with *Fresh Horses*. It was the first Garth Brooks album to be sold with Scott Hendricks at the helm of Capitol Nashville.

The *Los Angeles Times* said that on *Fresh Horses* Garth "comes up with some winners" and that the album "asserts an inhibition and individuality that is rare these days in the flood of mediocre and anonymous Nashville acts." Jack Hurst of the *Chicago Tribune* called *Fresh Horses* "quintessential Brooks: a fistful of fast, loud and daring songs whose thunder is interspersed by serious, heavy ballads."

Fresh Horses hit the stores the same week as *The Beatles Anthology 1*, and sold 480,000 copies the first week, the highest first-week total for a single-disc album since the preceding December, when Garth's *The Hits* had sold 520,000 copies during its first week in release. The *Beatles Anthology* sold an amazing 855,000 copies. Garth would have liked to have beaten that figure, but as Charles Koppelman, chairman and CEO of EMI-Capitol North America, told Garth when he called to congratulate him, "You've got to remember that there were four of them and there's just one of you."

About a month after the release of *Fresh Horses,* Garth appeared at the Grand Ole Opry, where he was introduced by Porter Wagoner, one of the staples of the Opry stage. Garth sang "Beaches of Cheyenne" for his first public appearance in almost a year.

While onstage, Garth told the crowd he wanted to introduce them to someone. "She's my best friend and my wife," he said just before Sandy came out, smiling and waving to all the lucky folks in the audience that night. Then Garth said he wanted to dedicate his next song to Sandy, his two girls, and the third one on the way. It was the first announcement in public that Sandy was pregnant again. After the show, he signed autographs until well past one A.M.

CHAPTER SIX

THE NIGHTMARE

*E*very January, there are conventions in various parts of the country where agents, promoters, and talent buyers get together to talk about the upcoming summer season and which acts will be hot. Booking all of the county and state fairs was only one of the exhausting activities at the Northeastern Convention of Fair Buyers in Syracuse, New York, and Joe Harris was working himself hard in the service of his acts.

By this time, he had left the William Morris Agency and, after a brief stint running his own agency, had taken a position at Agency for the Performing Arts.

Joe drove home from the fair in upstate New York through terrible snowstorms. There was so much snow in Virginia that he had to stop and stay there with relatives for two days before continuing on to Nashville. When he finally made it home, he went to his chair in the living room to rest. A little while later, his daughter had to phone Garth Brooks with the terrible news. Joe Harris had died.

"When Joe passed away, Garth was at my side," Shirley says. "He and Sandy came right over to the house. I said, 'Garth, I don't know what I'm going to do. I've lost a part of my life.' He said, 'Shirley, don't you worry about anything. I had a pact with Joe that I would take care of you as long as you needed. We made that pact one day when we were talking, and I will.' He said if you ever need anything you call. Garth has been very good to me."

Joe Harris, Jr., remembers that when his father's father had died years earlier, he'd died in his sleep, very peacefully. "My daddy said, 'Son, if I ever have one wish in my life, my wish is to go just like my dad,' and he did. He went just like his father, laid back in his chair, peaceful, no painful look on his face."

Woodlawn Funeral Home and Memorial Park on Thompson Lane is just a few miles away from Music Row. Every seat was filled, the walls were lined with people standing, and the crowd spilled into the halls the day of the memorial service for Joe Harris. Later, Shirley Harris said more than seven hundred people had signed the book at the service. Entertainers and managers, other agents and publicists, fans and friends from all parts of the business were there, many who had traveled from as far away as Los Angeles and New York. The love and respect Joe Harris had inspired in so many people was there in that room to accompany him on his last journey.

Reverend Larry Jones, president and founder of Feed the Children and Joe Harris's good friend, delivered a eulogy and recounted all Joe had done, quietly and modestly and generously, for hungry children. The Moffatts, a group of four young brothers with angelic voices that Joe believed in and was booking into the appropriate shows, sang "When God Made You." The Oak Ridge Boys sang a gospel song.

And Garth Brooks, wearing the same white tuxedo he'd worn when he won his first CMA Award with his agent and friend Joe Harris by his side, sang Joe's favorite song, "The Dance." The music business, and the world, had lost a dear friend.

Another song from *Fresh Horses,* "The Change," written by Tony Arata and Wayne Tester, was released in January '96. Garth had first heard it three weeks after the bombing of the

Oklahoma City federal building in April 1995. The powerful and touching song points out how small our acts of goodness can seem in comparison to the horrors people commit, but holds out the hope that we should try to do good anyway so that the world does not make us bitter and hard. Garth created a video to go with the song that used news footage of the terrible scenes outside the federal building in Oklahoma City following the bombing.

At the American Music Awards in the Shrine Auditorium in Los Angeles in January, Garth sang "The Change" against a backdrop of clips from the video. It was a somber moment in an evening of festivities that included two more AMA awards for Garth: Favorite Male Country Artist and Favorite Country Album (for *The Hits*). He accepted those awards with his usual graciousness and humility.

Later, however, a somber and strange moment occurred. Neil Diamond, a pop star who had just made an album in Nashville, was about to present the evening's last, and most important, award: Favorite Artist of the Year. This award cuts across all categories to celebrate the act that has soared above all others. The nominees were Hootie and the Blowfish, TLC, Green Day, Boys II Men, and Garth Brooks.

Neil Diamond opened the envelope and read the winner's name: "Garth Brooks."

Garth walked slowly to the stage. Later, people would say he looked a little sick to his stomach as he took off his hat and took the trophy from Neil Diamond.

"Thank you very much," he said. "Just so you'll know right off the bat, I cannot accept this award." In an evening of happy speeches by artists thanking everyone from their parents to their publicists, this statement got everyone sitting up a little straighter in their seats. What was Garth doing?

"I can't agree with this," Garth said. "Music is made up of a lot of people, and if we're one artist short, then we all become a lesser music." Saying he meant no disrespect, Garth added that he didn't believe in the concept of an artist of the year. Looking at the trophy, he said, "I'm going to leave it right here," which is exactly what he did.

As he came off the stage, Garth told Dick Clark, "I'm really sorry about this." Garth told the bewildered reporters backstage that he thought Hootie and the Blowfish deserved the award. Their album, *Cracked Rear View,* had been huge with fans and critics throughout 1995. A few days later, the AMA decided that the Favorite Artist trophy would become a "traveling award" that the winner could display publicly, place in the AMA's archives, or just keep for a year. Garth's name would be engraved on it this year and then it would be passed on to the next year's winner.

What was Garth's problem? Why did he think he didn't deserve the award? Well, for one thing, he hadn't been on the stage in the United States in quite a while. He'd spent 1994 touring Europe and Australia and New Zealand and 1995 at home in Nashville recording his latest album. For another thing, that album, *Fresh Horses,* wasn't exactly galloping out of the stores.

Garth signed a two-year deal with Twentieth Century Fox giving the studio the first chance to produce movies based on his material. His own film company in Los Angeles, called Red Strokes Productions, was developing several projects.

As for acting in a movie, as George Strait had done in *Pure Country,* Garth was always being offered cowboy roles and singing roles, but he said he wanted to try something different on screen. He had told Barbara Walters he didn't want to be in a movie if he "couldn't act like Jack Nicholson." He wanted to have the same impact in the movies as he'd had in music.

When the tickets went on sale for the opening date of Garth's multiyear, multicity, multicontinent, multi-amazing world tour, they sold out so fast that four other shows were added—and those sold out in just over two hours. The 16,000-seat Omni Arena in Atlanta was the place where Garth would find out whether he still felt the fire onstage and whether his audience still loved him.

J. D. Haas got the answers to some questions of his own: Did Garth still remember him? Would he let J.D. offer a trip to the opening in Atlanta through his radio contests? Haas gave a proposal to Capitol Records executive Bill Catino, who went to Garth and his brother Kelly—and they approved it! J.D. knew Garth was an exceptionally busy star, and he knew enough about the business to realize that Garth couldn't give all the people he'd met along the way the same attention he had in the beginning. He was thrilled to hear that Garth would let him bring his contest winners to Atlanta.

Garth Brooks became the best-selling solo musical artist of all time in May 1996, with more than 60 million albums sold. He surpasssed one of his heroes, Billy Joel, who said he didn't even know his mark of 57 million had been number one until then. Garth was now second only to the Beatles, who stood at 71 million. This was good news for EMI, which had had both Garth and the Beatles for all of their careers.

The Eagles were tied with Billy Joel for third place with 57 million. Barbra Streisand and Elton John followed with 51.8 and 51.1 million, then Led Zeppelin with 50.2. Elvis, Aerosmith, and Michael Jackson came in at 49.9, 48.2, and 48 million, respectively. Garth Brooks had achieved this milestone in only seven years. (Of course he did—seven is his lucky number.)

Capitol threw a huge party at Sunset Studios in Nashville to celebrate. The theme was—how cool is this?— the sixties!

J. D. Haas was thrilled to be on the guest list. "I got a real neat poster as an invitation—it was psychedelic and said to dress in sixties costume."

The studio was decorated with all kinds of memorabilia, including a Volkswagen bus. There were go-go dancers and celebrity look-alikes, including a John Wayne impersonator and a Marilyn Monroe look-alike who sang "Happy Sixty Million to You." Everyone dressed in their best hippie style, with long hair and tie-dyed shirts.

Garth asked Jim Fogelsong to host the event. Fogelsong was head of Capitol when Garth was signed there, but was gone by December 1989 when Jimmy Bowen came in. It was a really nice thing to do, reminiscent of the time Garth insisted that Lynn Shults pose with him for a picture at his first "number-one party" after Shults was gone from Capitol. Garth received a letter from the governor and a plaque from the mayor. The RIAA created a special plaque for the occasion. Capitol gave Garth a gift he liked so much that he started to cry: a Ford New Holland front-loader tractor. Garth told the guests, "Meaning something to you is all I ever wanted to do."

J.D. waited for a long time while everyone talked to Garth. "Garth was wonderful to me," he said. "He gave me a big hug and we talked about the first Fan Fair. When he gives a hug and a handshake, he looks right in your eyes and he hugs strong as a bear. After all those years, it was worth waiting in line to say thanks."

At Hartsfield Airport in Atlanta, J. D. Haas and his contest winners got a first-class welcome. They went to a special reception at Planet Hollywood and the next morning had breakfast at the Hard Rock Cafe.

The following night they went to the Omni, where they were given, according to J.D., "the best seats in the house."

Garth was unveiling his new stage show for the first time, and the audience was dazzled by the stage even before Garth got on it.

In their seats, the Atlanta audience was wild with anticipation—Garth had been in town four years before and knocked their socks off. What would happen tonight?

As a tribute to Joe Harris, Garth opened the show—and every other show on the tour—with "The Old Stuff."

The show was everything anyone could have hoped for. One reviewer described it as "Madonna meets Hank Williams." Garth probably liked that.

Garth Brooks was back, and Atlanta had him first. The radio contest winners had been invited backstage, where they met Garth and watched him talking to the many foreign journalists he had flown in to see the show. After the way the press had treated him in London, Garth knew he needed to work to educate the international media about country music.

The next day, at the landmark Varsity Diner in Atlanta, it was all they could talk about before getting back on the airplanes and going home with a memory for a lifetime.

Life on the road again was great—but back in Nashville a storm was brewing. Perhaps it was that Garth insisted on doing everything his own way. It could simply have been that once he became the biggest solo artist of all time in record sales, the tide was bound to turn against him. But Garth Brooks was taking some heat.

The backlash against Garth from the music industry took on a life of its own in 1996 and would continue through much of 1997. Music Row couldn't stop talking about him and found him baffling. And the media that had helped build the ordinary guy from Oklahoma into an icon of our times now shifted to the other phase of the predictable cycle: tearing the icon down.

It started when Garth turned down the American Music Award in January, something the industry and the media couldn't understand. Then Garth was criticized for using real footage of the Oklahoma City tragedy in his video for "The Change." He was also blasted for having buried the masters of *The Hits* under his star on the Hollywood Walk of Fame—a largely symbolic move given that the original masters of the songs were still part of the CDs they'd first appeared on but a move that nevertheless resulted in huge sales. He was ridiculed because he continued to talk about "Garth" as a separate entity from himself.

After almost single-handedly transforming the country music industry from a small business into a giant one in the 1990s, Garth was now being criticized for hurting that industry by being so big and such a tough act to follow. Was it his fault that record companies, most of which were now owned by multinational corporations, now considered sales in the hundreds of thousands instead of in the millions inadequate—and were dropping or refusing to sign acts that couldn't deliver those numbers?

Why shouldn't Garth have control of his own career and surround himself with trusted allies? The entertainment business is littered with the broken dreams, empty wallets, and ruined lives of artists who put their careers in the hands of strangers. Why shouldn't he expect to make a lot of money from his work when he was making his record company rich? Why shouldn't he take charge of all the decisions that affected his career and his music and his life? As he told David Frost in an interview, reporters had new people to talk to all the time, record labels had many artists, management companies often had many clients. But he had only one career, and he was going to make sure the decisions that were made about his career were his decisions.

As for talking about "Garth" as a person separate from himself, Garth put it this way. "It's easier for me to talk about Garth than to say 'I.' Garth is supposedly the biggest-selling solo act in the United States. I can't say I am. That feels egotistical to me, and I hate that feeling." He said that Garth is what we see onstage, the lighting rig, the band. "Most of the stuff you see or hear from Garth Brooks is an accumulation of a lot of minds put together, and it is not one guy saying do that, do this. I hired them for their talent, not for their ability to follow instructions.

"Most of all," he said in the most accurate description of the whole phenomenon, "Garth Brooks is the people out there. You gotta admit, the guy would look pretty silly doing all that stuff if no one was reacting. So he's a reaction of the people."

The fans didn't have a problem with Garth. We still loved him and always would because of everything he had given us: the great music, the incredible live performances, and the countless hours he spent meeting us, signing autographs, and remembering us when he met us again.

In the middle of the 1990s, there wasn't an icon like Garth around. Michael Jackson and Madonna had been the targets of the same kind of backbiting, but that had died down and their monster celebrity was also cooling off. Elvis was dead. The Beatles didn't exist anymore. Who were the pundits and critics and cynics going to bash and sneer at? Garth was the biggest target around.

Joe Mansfield, who had known Garth from the beginning of his Nashville career, had seen many artists get carried away when the big royalty checks started coming in. But he said that Garth was the same guy he'd been from the start. "He may have tons of money," Mansfield said, "but he's still down-to-earth."

Allen Reynolds, Garth's longtime producer and friend, told him to go be with his fans. "That's what's real and that's what counts," Allen said. When the going got rough, Garth knew there was one other place besides his home with Sandy to find love and acceptance: with the fans.

So Garth took himself to Fan Fair. He didn't announce he'd be there and didn't even tell his record label he was coming. He simply drove over in his pickup truck and walked in, looking like just another country music singer or fan. But when fans spotted him the crowd around him grew, and he stopped where he was and stood—*for twenty-three hours*—autographing whatever anyone gave him, spending time, being gracious to everyone.

Someone used a cell phone to get pizzas delivered and then, in the spirit of the moment, gave most of the pizza to the kids in line. One woman said, "We're doing a Garth Brooks deed. We're . . . just feeding the children."

Some in the industry were taking shots at him, but there were plenty of fans sticking up for him. "Other than God himself," Garth said, "I can't think of anybody I'd rather have on my side."

Garth returned to Cheyenne, Wyoming, for Cheyenne Frontier Days on July 22. By now, fans in many cities around the country were discovering—or rediscovering—the magic of Garth live.

Allie Colleen Brooks, Garth and Sandy's third daughter, was born on July 28, 1996. By this time, Sandy and Taylor and August had been traveling with Garth for a while. They had a separate bus with a nanny and a home-school teacher. Having the family on the road with him had given Garth everything he wanted all in one place.

At the Good Shepherd United Methodist Church in Madison, Tennessee, on October 26, 1996, Garth and Sandy

Brooks renewed their marriage vows. It's the same church Sandy and Garth used to clean as one of their jobs when they first came to Nashville to see if he could make it in the music business.

Fans really had missed Garth's live shows. By November of 1996 he had sold almost two million tickets, more than any other tour that year, including tours by pop, rock, and R & B artists. Garth told Mark McEwen on *CBS This Morning* that when he and Kelly had started planning this tour, they weren't sure if anyone would come to the shows. Once tickets started selling well, it was a lot more comfortable being out on the road again.

Garth was again asked about his low ticket prices, and he said again that since he and his crew were all making a living, they enjoyed making concertgoers happy to be there instead of angry about having to spend so much money on tickets. Sol Saffian says that Garth's insistence on lower ticket prices over the years was "a brilliant move. He's given back to the people by making it easily affordable to see his shows and to try to eliminate the scalpers."

In early 1997, Garth left for a four-month European tour, which ended in May with three shows in Dublin's Croke Park. One night he and Stillwater went into a pub where they planned to sing a few songs. Three and a half hours later, they were still singing and playing, taking requests from the audience just like in the old days. When they sang "Friends in Low Places," they did twenty choruses!

Colleen Brooks came along to Ireland. How great it must have been to see her son the international country music star and spend time with her three grandchildren who were also in Europe. Because Colleen hails from County Cork, the people there gave her a citation as an honorary citizen.

Garth wore his Mo Betta shirts in Ireland—lots of fun since in 1997 Maury Tate was celebrating ten years of making those wild and wonderful shirts.

Despite its huge numbers the first week it was on sale, *Fresh Horses* was not following the sales pattern of Garth's previous albums. Garth was unhappy. He told *Billboard* he felt that Capitol Nashville, under the presidency of Scott Hendricks, had given up on the album before it had a chance to reach its sales potential. He announced in that same *Billboard* interview that the marketing of his next album would be handled in New York by EMI–Capitol North America Chairman/CEO Charles Koppelman, Executive Vice President Terri Santisi, and Senior Vice President of Marketing Pat Quigley.

In other conversations with reporters, Garth also said something that the music world considered utterly radical but which made more sense than a lot of things artists say when their sales take a dip. Garth began to suggest that if his sales declined—meaning the fans were no longer voting for him with their album-buying dollars—he would let that determine whether he should quit the business.

"If the record and ticket sales don't tell me that I'm stirring things up or changing people's lives, then I think it's time for me to hang it up," he said. This sort of talk sent tremors through the music business, particularly the country music business, where almost 20 percent of the albums sold in the past six years had been his. Garth may have been overly modest when he said his singing and songwriting talents didn't match those of other great pop and country artists. But he was right on the money when he pointed out that his success (and everyone else's, really) was a direct result of the response of the audience. The bottom line was that all along it was the fans who were making Garth Brooks the phenomenal success he was. "When the people are through with me, then it's over." He said maybe that was why he had so much energy onstage: He was trying to make the Garth Brooks phenomenon last.

In April '97 it was announced that Garth Brooks would release a new album, called *Sevens,* on August 7 to tie in with another daring and spectacular Garth Brooks event: a free live concert in New York's Central Park that would be simultaneously broadcast on HBO. The Nashville office would continue to handle some aspects of the release. To increase Garth's comfort level, EMI wanted to send Pat Quigley, senior vice president of marketing in New York, to Nashville to serve as copresident of Capitol Nashville with Scott Hendricks. Hendricks rejected the idea of a copresidency, so Quigley was sent to Nashville as executive vice president and general manager of Capitol Nashville.

But suddenly everything changed. In late May James Fifield, president and CEO of EMI Music, shut down EMI-Capitol Music Group North America. Charles Koppelman and executive vice president Terri Santisi, who had been working on the Central Park concert, were leaving. Garth felt this was disastrous for his career. "My security blanket is gone," he said. Even with Quigley in Nashville, Garth felt uncomfortable, because Quigley was still under Hendricks in the corporate chain of command, and Garth felt Hendricks no longer believed in him as an artist.

By June 1997 Garth felt he had no choice but to delay the release of *Sevens,* meaning it would not be out in time for the Central Park concert. A clause in the contract he had renegotiated in 1992 allowed him to do so. Garth said he had "worked real hard to gain the right" to withhold release of a record if he didn't think things at his label were satisfactory at the time of release. "And in my opinion," he said, "things were definitely not right."

Independence Day found Garth and Stillwater playing in Oklahoma City at the Myriad Convention Center. "It's so good to come home to Oklahoma," he told his hometown crowd. Sure was—Garth and his family had a nice July Fourth barbecue together. Wearing a purple, white, and black Mo Betta shirt, Garth said before the show that he was more nervous playing in Oklahoma City than he could ever be in Central Park.

Garth talked about how the new album, *Sevens,* was done and that he had just gone through a personnel shake-up at his label and would hold the album later than its original August release date. Touring was making him feel better, as was the release on Trisha Yearwood's album *Souvenirs: A Collection of Hits* of a duet he'd done with her, "In Another's Eyes," which got lots of play on radio.

Later in July, when Garth played five sold-out shows at Drillers Park in Tulsa, the Drillers were only too happy to move out of their stadium for him. At one of the shows, a storm was brewing and heading straight to Tulsa. What Garth's bus driver had told Allen Reynolds back at Texas Stadium appeared to be true: The rain held off until Garth finished. Then, just as he sounded his last note, the skies opened up and the rain poured down.

CHAPTER SEVEN

THE MAN

"Who is Garth Brooks?" That was the question being asked in New York, particularly in Manhattan, according to several newspaper accounts in the weeks before Garth's concert in Central Park's North Meadow. Garth would be the first country singer to bring his music to New York's beautiful oasis of green trees and big lawns. Placido Domingo, Simon and Garfunkel, Barbra Streisand, Elton John, and Diana Ross had been there before him and nobody had questioned whether anyone would show up. But the media in New York were not convinced that a native Oklahoman in a cowboy hat and boots could attract an audience in the Big Apple.

Like Garth's Texas Stadium show back in September of 1993, "Garth Live from Central Park" would be one of a kind (and, despite the speculation of the media, a full house). A live broadcast on HBO and a subsequent home video would capture it for posterity.

There is a huge country music audience in New York City. As one fan told a reporter, "country music isn't dead around here, it's just underground." The Pony Express in Staten Island, an airplane-hangar-size club with a 3,000-square-foot dance floor, is jumping every weekend—and many weeknights. The New York Metro Country Music Association, the organization that brought Garth to Forest Park in 1990, is still going strong. SoundScan reported that

1.5 million country albums had been sold in the New York region in the preceding year alone. A new country station, Y-107, went on the air in December 1996 after New York lost its only country music station, WYNY, almost a year earlier.

The audience in Central Park wouldn't be just the residents of Manhattan and the surrounding boroughs. Hundreds of thousands of people were coming by plane, car, chartered bus, and train from all over the country. Hotels all over the city were fully booked. Garth Brooks had played some shows in the Northeast as part of his world tour in 1996, and the word had spread throughout the region that this was no ordinary singing cowboy. Bill Flanagan, a vice president of VH-1 and the former editor of *Musician* magazine, summed it up: "Garth is bigger than country," he said, "just like the Beatles were bigger than British rock and Michael Jackson is bigger than R and B."

The world-famous billboard over Times Square had Garth's picture on it, and a full-page ad in the city's newspapers promoting the Central Park event proclaimed "Music's Biggest Star! America's Favorite Music! New York's Biggest Event!" New York mayor Rudolph Giuliani was certainly happy that Garth was coming to town. At a ceremony in City Hall the mayor presented Garth with a crystal (big) apple and a proclamation naming August 7 Garth Brooks Day. The concert was projected to bring $16 million in economic activity to the city, as well as $600,000 in city taxes.

Asked by the *New York Times* if he thought New Yorkers would like him, Garth answered with this carefully worded statement: "We just do what we do, and if it's something that you like, good for us. If it's something that you don't like, you've heard it and now you can make a choice." C'mon, Garth—you had to know you'd dazzle the fans in Central Park!

The stage being erected in Central Park was 360 feet wide, six stories tall, and covered with 3,000 lights. Allen Reynolds was there as the production crews were setting up and was impressed by the vastness of the field where the audience would assemble. People were coming into the area around the park beginning early in the morning and continuing all day, waiting for the excitement to begin.

"I knew New York liked him," Reynolds said about all the chatter over whether country would play in New York. "I have had the experience all my career of people being so sure of who liked country and who didn't. I'm closer to the fans than the critics are. New York has always been a very big market for Garth Brooks."

New York City police, working from aerial photographs, estimated that there were 250,000 people on the big lawn in Central Park's North Meadow. Garth's audience did not exceed attendance records set by Simon and Garfunkel, James Taylor, or Diana Ross, but they did match the crowd for Barbra Streisand. The biggest audience to watch HBO all year was sitting at home enjoying another, more close-up view of the fun. This is what the quarter million in the park and the millions more at home saw:

The sun was setting on a perfect summer night over the New York skyline. Garth rose up from the stage and, to those standing nearby, looked about as nervous as anyone could look. Wearing a black and blue shirt, black jeans, black boots, and a black hat (black is, after all, the fashion color of choice in New York), he began to sing "Rodeo." When he was done he looked out in total amazement at the crowd that welcomed him as warmly as any had ever done.

"Hello, New York!" he screamed—and proceeded to thank everyone for coming to "the world-famous and very beautiful Central Park." Then he added, "I'm naturally scared to death."

The show that followed was vintage Garth. He sang "Papa Loved Mama," running across the long stage. He sang "The Beaches of Cheyenne" with the amazing fiddle playing of Jimmy Mattingly accompanying him. As darkness began to fall over Manhattan, Garth and his band sang "Two of a Kind Workin' on a Full House" and it became clear that Garth was now comfortable. Why shouldn't he be? He had built himself the ultimate entertainment playground in the park, a field of dreams, and they had come. Thunder rolled and strobe lights flashed for "The Thunder Rolls." The audience waved their hands and sang along to "We Shall Be Free." They sang all by themselves to "Unanswered Prayers," and Garth told them, "It's the greatest gift to entertainers when fans take their songs and sing them right back to 'em."

During "The River," he gave his security staff a nice case of nerves by jumping off the stage and wandering through the crowd, shaking hands, collecting flowers from his fans, and even accepting a kiss from a woman who was overwhelmed by the moment. When he returned to the stage, he took the strap off his guitar and tossed it into the crowd. Then he belted out "That Summer" and, with Jimmy Mattingly wailing on fiddle, Garth and his band and backup singers—Stephanie Davis and Susan Ashton—gathered together at the edge of the stage and sang "Callin' Baton Rouge."

The New York crowd loved his rendition of Billy Joel's "Shameless," and loved it even more when Joel, one of New York's favorite musical icons, himself came out onstage to sing "Ain't Goin' Down ('Til the Sun Comes Up)" with Garth. Garth returned the favor when he and Billy sang "New York State of Mind," with saxophone player extraordinaire Jim Horn showing why he is the sax player of choice for so many top artists.

And so it went—"The Fever," "The Dance," "Friends in Low Places"—with the audience singing every word, including the racy last verse.

"When I came here to New York, I didn't know what to expect," Garth said. "I not only thank God that you came, but you came in New York style." He ran across the stage, hat in hand, waving and thanking the crowd.

But New York wasn't ready to let him off the stage just yet. Their cheers for an encore were rewarded when Garth began singing the song he always liked to close his shows with—"American Pie." Then Garth introduced the writer and creator of that true American classic, Mr. Don McLean.

The people standing on the sides of the stage were treated to the sight of Garth's face in awe and wonder as he watched one of his biggest heroes sing one of his favorite songs right there on the stage on one of the most amazing nights of his life.

HBO went off the air, but Garth wasn't ready to leave. He sang the song that started it all for him, the one he'd written as a young singer with big dreams back in Oklahoma. "Much Too Young (To Feel This Damn Old)," even now, all these years into one of the most spectacular careers in the history of entertainment, still sounded strong and true. "If Tomorrow Never Comes," the first of what would become many number-one hit singles, closed the show—until Garth realized Billy Joel was still there and invited him onstage once again, where the two closed down the night with Joel's "You May Be Right."

Garth brought everything wonderful about a country music concert to the Big Apple. There were very few arrests and injuries, a great feeling of community, and something more: In conjunction with Garth's Central Park date, Feed the Children collected food for kids—more than 160,000 pounds from food companies and 10,000 pounds brought in by the fans—and distributed it to churches, food pantries, and other organizations throughout the city.

"Garth Live from Central Park" was the most viewed program ever on HBO. Five days later, HBO said they planned to rebroadcast the show to all cable subscribers, not just those who subscribed to HBO, at Garth's request. It was the first time HBO had ever done that.

From Central Park, Garth headed out to California, where he dazzled fans in Sacramento, Fresno, and San Jose. Dewayne Blackwell's daughter, Lezlie, lived near Sacramento. She had never seen Garth live, so when she heard he was coming to her town, she called her dad and asked if he could help her get tickets, because, she said, as soon as Garth tickets went on sale they always sold out. Blackwell called Garth's office and was told that complimentary tickets for Sacramento were impossible to get. He was also told, however, that the show would be in Reno on September 4 and 5. When asked how many tickets his daughter wanted, Blackwell said, "Well, one for her and maybe three friends, but we'll take only one if that's all you can do."

"Garth comped her four tickets," Blackwell says, "and then as it got close to the time to go he called me and said, 'Dewayne, we're going to be seeing your daughter and we've got this private jet and there's room, so why don't you and Kathleen come and surprise her?' So we rode with Garth and Trisha in this jet-propelled living room with six recliners and a couch, and my daughter didn't know we were coming. He put us up in the Hyatt and paid for everything."

Garth gave Dewayne and Lezlie dressing-room passes for herself and her friends. "I didn't want her to know we were there, because she had never met Garth," Dewayne says, "and I didn't want us to show up at the same time. I wanted her to have the thrill of meeting Garth Brooks." Lezlie and her friends were back in the dressing room for about twenty or thirty minutes before her mother and father came back. "Garth said, 'You got a couple of people here to see you, Lezlie,' and she just looked up as we came through the door and she started crying," Dewayne says. "It was really neat—she had no idea."

Dewayne watched as his daughter had yet another thrill. "The backstage passes are wristband things, and while she was talking to us, hers came loose and fell on the floor," he says. "Garth walks up and picks it up, and while she was talking, he doesn't interrupt, just hooks that wristband on her. I could see in her eyes this was affecting her immensely."

Trisha Yearwood won Female Vocalist of the Year, her first major CMA Award, at the nationally televised presentation in September. "I don't know what to say," she told the audience, "but this is what I've wanted ever since I saw Reba McEntire stand on this stage more than a decade ago and say that if you have a dream, you can make it up here. I believed you, Miss Reba."

As beloved CMA host Vince Gill presided over the festivities, George Strait took Album of the Year (for *Carrying Your Love with Me*) and Male Vocalist of the Year. Brooks & Dunn won their sixth consecutive Vocal Duo of the Year Award. LeAnn Rimes won the Horizon Award.

Garth Brooks was named Entertainer of the Year, his first CMA since 1993. It was presented by Barbara Mandrell. Garth wasn't there. He had booked a concert for that evening, in Lincoln, Nebraska, preferring to be in the company of his fans than with the Nashville industry he felt misunderstood him.

A few days later, he accepted the award on a live broadcast of TNN's *Today's Country*, hosted by Lorianne Crook and Charlie Chase.

"This stuff is not about money. It's about respect," Garth said. Despite a flurry of meetings following the Central Park concert, by October there was still no resolution in the problems

between Garth and his record label. Even so, everyone had an interest in bringing *Sevens* out in time for Christmas.

On Halloween, Pat Quigley called Garth and introduced himself as the new president of Capitol Nashville. On November 3 it was announced that Scott Hendricks was leaving Capitol Nashville and was in discussions with EMI about starting a new Capitol label called Virgin Nashville. On November 5, it was announced that *Sevens* would be released on November 25.

Fueled by the tour and by the long wait, demand for *Sevens* was high. Five million copies were shipped, including a collectible "first edition" of 777,777 copies. Fans lined up outside stores before sunrise on the day of its release and one week later had bought about 897,000 copies. "The people shouldn't have had to wait," Garth said, "but they did, and I really appreciate that."

"Long Neck Bottle," written by Steve Wariner and Rick Carnes, was the first single from *Sevens*. Garth and Steve sang it as a duet. Garth had been friends with Wariner for a long time and had opened for him when he was first getting started.

Steve Wariner is a native of Noblesville, Indiana, who got his start when he was only seventeen as a bassist and singer in the mid-1970s for country legend Dottie West. He had to complete his last high school credits via a correspondence course from the back of a tour bus. At the age of eighteen, he appeared on the Opry stage with Dottie West and then went on to play with Chet Atkins—whose records he had practiced guitar to while growing up.

In the 1980s, Wariner had ten number-one hits, such songs as "Some Fools Never Learn" and "Life's Highway," and a few hits in the early nineties, including a number-three charter with the Whisperin' Bill Anderson song "The Tips of My Fingers." His album sales were never high, although he had one gold album, *I Am Ready,* on Arista in 1991. He then gave up his record contract but continued writing hit songs for other artists while spending more time with his wife and two sons. With Vince Gill and Ricky Skaggs, he won a 1991 Grammy for Best Country Vocal Collaboration, a song from the Grammy-winning album *The New Nashville Cats,* which also won the CMA 1991 Vocal Event of the Year.

Steve Wariner had more than music in common with Garth Brooks—he also had a great interest in children's charities. In fact, he raised enough money at benefit concerts to build an educational wing for physically and mentally handicapped children at a local high school.

When Garth flew to Los Angeles to tape *The Tonight Show,* he invited Steve Wariner to come out and play "Long Neck Bottle" with him. "I still read my letters," Garth says. "To this day, there's only two names that are always mentioned in those letters. If it's not George Strait, it's Steve Wariner. So George Strait's doing extremely fine. I couldn't believe Steve wasn't out there on the active list." Garth asked Steve if he was interested in signing with Capitol, and a deal soon followed.

By the end of December, it was reported that *Sevens* had sold two million copies in less than a month. By the end of January, *Sevens* had sold 3.7 million copies, an unprecedented performance. It had taken *Fresh Horses* more than two years to sell that many. *Sevens* must have been under quite a few Christmas trees.

On February 9, two days after his thirty-sixth birthday, Garth appeared on *Oprah* while the queen of talk-show hosts was broadcasting from Amarillo, Texas, during her trial with the Cattleman's Association. He pledged on the air to donate his earnings from the sale of *Sevens* during the next week to Oprah's Angel Network. He also said he would donate his profits from *Sevens* each week that sales exceeded 100,000 units.

Fans responded to Garth's generosity by buying even more copies of *Sevens*.

The 1998 leg of Garth's huge tour kicked off at Dallas's Reunion Arena later that month. While in the great state of Texas, Garth also played the Fort Worth Convention Center. After the hugeness of the Texas Stadium shows, these places probably felt more like clubs! Trisha Yearwood was the opening act for all six shows, and together she and Garth performed "In Another's Eyes," for which they had just won a Grammy for Best Country Vocal Collaboration.

"In Another's Eyes," written by Bobby Wood, John Peppard, and Garth Brooks, was one great song, and Garth and Trisha were like the Marvin Gaye and Tammy Terrell of country music, belting it out with that much passion and soul. Their performance of the song on *The Tonight Show with Jay Leno* was so powerful that it became the video for the song, airing on CMT and TNN. With Garth showing up at Trisha's concerts and singing the song with her—and because of Trisha's own enormous talents—her album *Songbook: A Collection of Hits* hit the one million mark in just ten weeks, her fastest seller ever.

Mae Boren Axton, the mother of Hoyt Axton and the composer of Elvis Presley's hit "Heartbreak Hotel," was a beloved resident of Nashville and a good friend to Garth and Sandy Brooks. In February 1998, Garth and Sandy donated $1 million to build a children's area at the Nashville Zoo in her honor. She had died almost a year earlier at the age of eighty-two. "Her great success in the music industry was just a small part of who she was," Sandy said. "Mae loved children and lived her life giving to others."

The Garth Brooks *Special* aired in March, the result of the three nights in Dublin's Croke Park in May of '97. It was Garth's fifth special for NBC since 1992 and the first two-hour show. American television audiences could see what a great response Sandy received from the Irish. The last half hour of the show, Garth performed live from Sony Studios in Culver City, California, playing songs from *Sevens* with guest star Steve Wariner.

By April of 1998, *Sevens* had been number one on the charts for thirteen weeks and was the fastest-selling album of the 1990s. "Long Neck Bottle" was a number-one single, as was "Two Pina Coladas," written by Shawn Camp, Benita Hill, and Sandy Mason. That song took fans straight to Jimmy Buffett territory, where the sea really does heal heartaches. "In Another's Eyes" hit number two on the *Billboard* charts, giving both Garth and Trisha plenty to celebrate. So did "She's Gonna Make It," written by Kent Blazy, Kim Williams, and Garth.

One other single from *Sevens* hit the *Billboard* Top 5. Garth has always had his pick of the best songs, and all of the songs he's chosen have of course reflected a philosophy he believes in. With "The Dance," he told us that love is always worth the pain, and with "The River," he said that daring to dream is the only way to really live. Now, with Gordon Kennedy and Pierce Pettis's "You Move Me," he shared the beautiful truth that "life is only therapy." Make light of it, and take delight in everything, the song says. Follow with the heart.

Taya Branton, who followed her heart from Wyoming, New York, to the University of Rochester where she was a junior majoring in psychology, said, "I think *Sevens* was Garth's best CD to date, and the song 'You Move Me' is one of his all-time greatest." She wasn't alone.

But the record-breaking sales of the album and its Top 5 singles tell only part of the story. You can see why Garth was so proud of this one, why it meant so much to him and why he was willing to battle with his record company to make sure it got to all his fans. The Kent Blazy–Garth Brooks composition "How You Ever Gonna Know" is another great song by two writers at the height of their powers. The inspiring message that you have to put yourself out there and chase your dreams is carried on a great melody that is itself so uplifting. Allen Reynolds and keyboard player Bobby Wood join Garth, creating a choir behind Garth's own lead vocal— and call themselves the Ordinaires, a neat twist on the Jordanaires, who provided the same kind of richness to many of Elvis Presley's songs.

"Do What You Gotta Do" is another anthem about taking responsibility for the fact that "nobody in this world is gonna do it for you." Do you think Garth knew, when he chose this song written by Pat Flynn, that he'd have to live its lyrics before this album could come out? In "Fit for a King," about a homeless man preaching on a street corner, the most successful entertainer of our times is telling us it's not our possessions that make us whole but what we possess in our hearts and souls. It's written by Jim Rushing and Carl Jackson. The man in "I Don't Have to Wonder," written by Shawn Camp and Taylor Dunn, watches from his pickup truck as his old flame rides off from her wedding in a white limousine. It's like a poignant sequel to "Friends in Low Places."

On *Sevens* Garth reveals himself to us in new ways. The songs of inspiration are there, but so are those of introspection, like "When There's No One Around," written by Tim

O'Brien and Darrell Scott, in which the guy who flew across Texas Stadium and took on Manhattan says that he sees inside the big star a man in old clothes as well as an immature little boy.

From the start, Allen Reynolds told Garth to follow his instincts when it came to the music, and, he says, Garth has a great ear. Reynolds also calls Garth "one of my favorite songwriters." Garth's instincts, ear, and songwriting skills, as well as his talent for selecting songs, are totally engaged on *Sevens,* and the result is not only his best album to date but one of the best albums of the decade in any category of music.

After taking America by storm and making the 1990s his own, and then fearing he'd lost it all with the disappointment of *Fresh Horses,* Garth gave us fourteen new songs, gambling twice on his lucky number and winning big. Beginning with *No Fences* and its incredible impact on the country music industry, almost every Garth Brooks album and certainly every Garth Brooks show has been a force, a thunder all its own. The music was great, but the momentum often overshadowed it. With *Sevens,* Garth Brooks gave us the best music of his career and proved himself much more than a phenomenon. He became what he'd dreamed of back in Stillwater, Oklahoma—an artist.

No wonder that at the Academy of Country Music Awards later in the month, Garth received another Entertainer of the Year Award as well as a Special Achievement Award for his impact on the country music industry with his Central Park concert. April was also the month that fans in Houston and San Antonio got to see Garth on his world tour. Garth and his amazing road show also called on Baton Rouge, Louisiana, and Evansville, Indiana, before coming to the next stop on the tour, a location that was near and dear to their hearts.

Unbelievable as it may seem, Garth Brooks had never actually played a major show in Nashville. Oh, of course, when he first got to Music City, he played lots of singer/songwriter showcases, including the now historic one at the Bluebird Café that led to his record deal. But after he hit it big, playing every large arena in America, and many huge venues around the world, he hadn't played his adopted hometown.

All that changed on the evening of May 8, 1998, when Garth played the first of three sold-out shows at the Nashville Arena. The new arena was part of the multimillion-dollar revitalization of the Lower Broadway area of Music City known as "The District"—a project that had been fueled in part by the phenomenal growth in the world of country music, the spurt in sales and interest that had itself been fueled by Garth Brooks. "The District" had suffered for years after the Grand Ole Opry was moved from the Ryman Auditorium out to Opryland, several miles east of downtown. Now, numerous old buildings up and down Second Avenue and Broadway had been transformed into a tourist mecca featuring among its many new restaurants and stores a Hard Rock Cafe, a Planet Hollywood, and the Wildhorse Saloon, where country line-dancing parties were broadcast live into towns and cities across America.

Garth's show in Nashville was the eighty-first stop on his world tour. Beginning in Atlanta in March of '96, Garth by now had played in cities and towns all across America. Now his adopted hometown of Nashville finally had a venue big enough to contain the likes of Garth Brooks, which he noted by telling the crowd, "This city should have built this damn place years ago."

The audience thought so. First they were treated to eight songs by another one of their neighbors, Trisha Yearwood. Her sensational voice and wonderful songs were right at home in the arena.

Some people may have been criticizing him on Music Row, but on Lower Broadway, Garth was winning hearts with every song. He pulled out all of his most dramatic moves, leaping across the stage, smiling straight into the eyes and hearts of the gathered fans, finding right here at home the same kind of love he'd found for years on the road.

Now that Garth was back on top, he decided to release his first boxed set. Titled *The Limited Series,* the retrospective was done with typical Garth style. Each of his first six CDs—*Garth Brooks, No Fences, Ropin' the Wind, The Chase, In Pieces,* and *Fresh Horses*—was included, of course, but on each disc there was one additional new song. "Uptown Down-Home Good Ol' Boy," by Dewayne Blackwell and Earl Bud Lee, on the *Garth Brooks* CD in the boxed set, is the story of a rodeo rider whose injury in the arena means he'll never ride again. He sells his name to a line of westernwear and becomes richer than he'd ever dreamed possible, but never forgets his past or his friends. It's a great follow-up song from the writers of "Friends in Low Places."

A special addition to the *No Fences* CD is "This Ain't Tennessee." Written by James Shaw and Larry Bastian, it is one of the most beautiful songs you'll ever hear. A man who now lives with a woman in a fancy estate with palm trees waving in the ocean air cannot forget the Smoky Mountain breezes and hickory trees of Tennessee—or the woman there whom he still loves. Again, Garth chose a song about choices—how we make them and only later realize what those choices have done to our lives.

Garth himself wrote "Which One of Them," which he included on *Ropin' the Wind.* Aaron Tippin and Mark Collie, singers with their own impressive careers, contributed "Something with a Ring to It" to *The Chase.* Tony Arata, whose song "The Dance" marked one of the biggest turning points in Garth's career, wrote "Anonymous" with Jan Schwabe, and Garth featured that spare tribute to a strong but silent love on *In Pieces*.

About his first boxed set, Garth said, "Sometimes we run so fast we don't see what we've been a part of. Doing *The Limited Series* made me stop and look at the work that's been done. I am so proud and thankful to be a part of it."

The Limited Series debuted at the top of the *Billboard* Country Album chart and the *Billboard* 200, selling 372,000 copies in the first week. At a cost of about $30, that was a staggering accomplishment. It stayed in the number-one spot for four weeks and was knocked off only by another Garth Brooks–related project, the sound track for the movie *Hope Floats*.

"To Make You Feel My Love" is written by Bob Dylan, who recorded it himself on his recent highly acclaimed *Time Out of Mind* CD. It was the big single from the *Hope Floats* sound track, and was the new track on the *Fresh Horses* CD in Garth's boxed set. The video of Garth singing "To Make You Feel My Love," complete with footage from the movie, was used for a trailer in some movie theaters promoting *Hope Floats*. The song gave Garth his first adult contemporary hit and was also the first song by Bob Dylan to appear on the country chart since Johnny Cash and June Carter recorded "It Ain't Me Babe" in 1965.

The *Hope Floats* sound track also includes songs by Trisha Yearwood, Deana Carter, Martina McBride, the Mavericks, Lila McCann, the Rolling Stones, Bryan Adams, and Sheryl Crow. The album stayed on the country album charts for nine weeks, setting a new record for sound tracks. The previous record was held by the sound track for *Urban Cowboy*, released in 1980.

After his work with Garth on "Long Neck Bottle," Steve Wariner's "Nothing but the Taillights," which he cowrote with Clint Black, was a number-one hit for Black. Capitol had given Wariner a new recording contract, and his album *Burnin' the Roadhouse Down* was his first ever to chart in the *Billboard* Top 10. Now Wariner's own single, "Holes in the Floor of Heaven," written with Billy Kirsch, an achingly beautiful song about how those who have passed on can still look down upon us with love and care, was rising on the charts.

At the Nashville Motor Speedway on the second day of Fan Fair, Wariner was the last act on the Capitol Nashville concert lineup. First, Trace Adkins, John Berry, Suzy Boguss, Billy Dean, and Deana Carter gave their all to their fans.

Then Steve Wariner came onstage. As he finished singing the first verse of the title song from his album, "Burnin' the Roadhouse Down," written with Rick Carnes, which was recorded as a duet with Garth, Steve stopped to announce a special guest. Suddenly Garth strolled out onto the stage, finished the song with Steve, and sang some of the hits from *Sevens*.

What a lucky bunch of fans at the fair! So that's who that unmarked tour bus belonged to!

Taya Branton was listening to a country radio station on her way to work. It was the summer before her senior year at the University of Rochester, where she had played for three years on the Rochester Yellow Jackets women's basketball team. For all three of her years there, she had played Garth Brooks and other country music in her dorm room, even though her friends, who liked techno, hip-hop, alternative, and hard rock, didn't share her love of country and found it amusing.

On the radio, Taya heard the news she'd been waiting for for a long time: Garth Brooks was coming to Buffalo in late

September as part of his two-year world tour. "I was so excited, but I knew tickets would sell out instantly, so I was just happy that they celebrated this news by playing his songs on my whole ride to work," she said. "I told everyone that Garth was coming, and made them listen to country stations all day in case they were giving away tickets on the radio."

By September 1998, sales of *Ropin' the Wind* were up to 14 million copies. Sales of the album had hit 13 million in July, when *Garth Brooks* had hit 9 million, *The Chase* 8 million, *In Pieces* 8 million, and *Fresh Horses* 6 million. *No Fences* topped them all at 16 millon in September. No other artist in any form of music has ever topped that, according to the Record Industry Association of America. Taya had every one of those albums. She'd also bought *Sevens* and *The Limited Series*.

Taya went to a basketball camp for a week and, on the first day, broke her foot. That was bad news for her upcoming basketball season at school. But when she came back from the camp, she got some good news: a call from her friend Joe Cone, another Garth fan. "He told me he got tickets from his younger brother's girlfriend's older sister, and asked if I wanted to go. I of course said yes, and we made plans to go see Garth on September 25," Taya says. "The tickets were $19.08 plus 42 cents. He keeps his concert prices low because his fans are the most important thing to him."

At a press conference in Buffalo before his six sold-out shows there, Garth told the assembled reporters that he really could see everyone all the way to the back of the arena, all the more so when his adrenaline was really pumping. He said even if you couldn't see a person's face you could tell by their body language if they were slumping and not enjoying a particular song or if they were sitting straight up in the seat, excited to hear the songs they loved best. He wanted to communicate to the crowd the way the late Freddie Mercury had communicated to him at the Queen concerts Garth had loved as a teenager. He wanted to share his love for the fans, to say, "You have done so much for me, you have given me this life, the roof over my head, and helped me buy a home for my parents."

The first show in Buffalo coincided with the broadcast of the Thirty-second Annual Country Music Association Awards from the Grand Ole Opry in Nashville. George Strait won his fifth Male Vocalist of the Year trophy and Brooks & Dunn won their seventh consecutive award for Vocal Duo of the Year. Patty Loveless and George Jones won Vocal Event of the Year for "You Don't Seem to Miss Me," written by Jim Lauderdale. Trisha Yearwood, who was opening for Garth on this leg of the tour, was standing by in Buffalo as the nominees for Female Vocalist of the Year were read. She won for the second year in a row and said she just couldn't believe it. "It hasn't sunk in yet," she said.

Song of the Year and Single of the Year went to Steve Wariner for "Holes in the Floor of Heaven." How nice. Wariner said he felt "total shock" because of all the competition in those categories. "I have kept every letter that I have gotten about this song," he said, "all the stories people tell of someone they lost in their lives and how the song has been uplifting for them. It's just phenomenal."

When Entertainer of the Year was announced, Garth was standing by via satellite on the Buffalo stage. When he won, he threw his hands in the air as the Buffalo, New York, crowd went wild and threw dozens of flowers onto the stage. He became the first artist in the history of the CMA to win four Entertainer of the Year Awards. He had previously been tied with Alabama with three wins.

Garth was thrilled. "It was the perfect night—Trisha winning Female Vocalist and the two Georges [Jones and Strait] walking away with awards. I'm very proud of Steve Wariner, anything that comes to him was long overdue. But my high-light was the performance," Garth says about the duet he and Trisha sang live on the show via satellite from the concert hall. "Where Your Road Leads," written by Victoria Shaw and Desmond Child, was the title song from Trisha's new album.

It was a perfect night for Taya Branton two nights later, on September 25, when she went to see her first Garth Brooks concert. Although she and her friends obtained a sticker to park in a spot reserved for the handicapped, Taya's parents, Terry and Denis, were not happy about their daugh-ter going to a huge crowded arena on crutches with her foot in a cast. "But nothing would keep me from going," Taya says. "It was my dream. All I'd ever wanted was to see Garth Brooks sing and Michael Jordan play."

Sitting in the arena, Taya Branton saw the 1996 to 1998 Garth Brooks world tour (and world class!) show that had dazzled fans all over America, the fans of all ages, the ones who went to work and those who went to college, the ones who were girls and boys and moms and dads and the ones who were grandmas and grandpas. From the Omni in Atlanta in March of 1996, Garth had begun the journey that would bring him here to Buffalo, New York, tonight, a full year and a half later.

The stage was flat, with all of the monitors underneath it. In the center was a giant capsule that had the drum set in it. It had an American flag decal on it that Garth had received from NASA. And it was able to spin around.

As the lights dimmed, a cloud of smoke filled the stage as a giant light rig, which had been lowered from the ceil-ing, began to rise. Drummer Mike Palmer was encased in a glass pryamid that looked like a giant spacecraft. Then a white grand piano rose up from the stage. A man in a white tuxedo and white cowboy hat was sitting at the piano. The audience was screeching its enjoyment of this amazing entrance. But the best was yet to come. From inside the piano Garth Brooks himself emerged and opened his arms, as if embracing each one of the fans who'd come to see him. The player at the piano had been a fake. Taya and eighteen thousand other fans screamed and applauded their delight. It was spectacular.

"He opened with 'The Old Stuff' from *Fresh Horses,*" Taya says. Just as he'd promised Shirley, Garth was still paying tribute to Joe Harris with this live tour, the tour that had its seeds in all the little clubs and state fairs Joe had booked him into when he was unknown to the world. "Then he did 'Unanswered Prayers,'" Taya says, "and from the opening chord the crowd went crazy. The whole crowd sang it as he held the microphone up. From that he sang his new song, 'To Make You Feel My Love.' Then he stopped and said, 'That's what makes an entertainer feel they have succeeded, that the crowd accepts old and new equally.'"

Taya was as excited as she'd ever been in her life. Her dream of seeing Garth live had come true. She wasn't even thinking about her broken foot.

"He sang 'Papa Loves Mama,' he sang everything. 'Baton Rouge.' He joked with the band and introduced all the band members. One guy had a sign for Jimmy the fiddle player. Garth asked, didn't he know he shouldn't be more popular than the star? People held up signs asking for certain songs. He sang 'Somewhere Other Than the Night' and sang Cat Stevens's 'Wild World.' It was so awesome."

Taya had been a little disappointed that Trisha Yearwood hadn't sung "Walkaway Joe" during her opening set and was elated when she came out to sing it with Garth before they sang "In Another's Eyes."

When Garth sang "Friends in Low Places," Taya said she and her friends, Joe Cone and Tom Ball, and Joe's friend Jared were "going crazy. All four of us were standing up. I put the crutches down and we had our arms around each other. I was trying not to put pressure on the cast, there were so many people pushing. I stood on my one leg and we sang the whole time. Then Garth said, 'I have a concert verse to that. If you guys know it, I don't have to sing it.' The whole audience did the concert ending." When it was time to sit back down, no one was near their original seats.

The big moment came for Taya and Joe and Tom when Garth sang "The Dance." It was their prom song.

Having experienced the thrill of seeing her biggest musical hero perform live, Taya Branton still wanted to see Michael Jordan play. Garth Brooks wanted to sell a million copies of his new album in one day. Big dreams for two ordinary Americans born in the twentieth century, but dreams are what America is all about.

Garth took a shot at his dream on November 17. The largest initial album shipping in the history of the American record business was *Garth Brooks: Double Live*—6.8 *million* copies. Garth said he wanted to sell one million copies the first day to break Pearl Jam's one-day sales record of 900,000. He sure had a shot at it: By this time he had already sold more albums than any other artist in history, 82 million.

He was also just completing the biggest tour in the history of country music. Thirty-two months on the road, performing 347 shows in 99 cities, playing for more than five million people. Even with his low ticket price of about $20, Garth's tour was the top-grossing country tour of all time and perhaps the top-grossing arena tour ever. He was one of three country artists—the others were George Strait and Shania Twain—who were ranked among the top ten U.S. touring acts of the year.

All of the fans who'd seen him were waiting for the album. Now Garth was going to give those who hadn't seen him a little taste of what was in store in *Double Live.* First he appeared on *The Tonight Show with Jay Leno.* Then, on November 17, he did a closed-circuit live concert beamed to all 2,400 Wal-Mart stores in the United States and Canada. The next night he did three consecutive specials for NBC, airing live in three time zones at eight P.M., taking questions from fans via phone and E-mail.

Selling a million albums on November 17 would be made a little more challenging by the fact that new releases from megasuperstars Whitney Houston, Jewel, Mariah Carey, Method Man, and Seal would be hitting the stores on the very same day. The industry was calling it "Super Tuesday," and opinions were pretty much split over whether the big releases would enhance one another's sales prospects or cancel each other out.

And what about the album itself? Well, it contained live performances of twenty-five songs going back to Garth's 1991 Reunion Arena show in Dallas. The location where a particular song's live version came from was not identified— it could have been anywhere; it could have been the show you saw. There were seven different packages, with different photos and liner notes about different live events in Garth's astonishing career, including Texas Stadium, Ireland, and Central Park. Garth said he'd wanted to do different covers for the same CD ever since he saw Cher do that with an album when he was an advertising student at Oklahoma State University.

The whole CD totaled 100 sensational minutes and the price was just over ten bucks. And the music? Well, it was just like being at a Garth Brooks concert. The so-called long versions of "The Thunder Rolls" (with its very serious last verse that finds the wronged woman really pulling that trigger) and "Friends in Low Places" (wherein the party crasher tells his old flame what she can kiss as he's leaving her fancy affair) are here, as are amazing versions of Garth in his best voice singing the songs that have all become American anthems of the 1990s.

Double Live had three new songs—"Tearin' It Up (And Burnin' It Down)," written by Kent Blazy, Kim Williams, and Garth; "Wild As the Wind," a duet with Trisha, written by Pete Wasner and Charles John Quarto; and a ballad written by Pam Wolfe and Benita Hill called "It's Your Song," which Garth dedicated to his parents. "It's Your Song" was also a tribute to his fans—it really *was* our song that made him sing.

By the way, Garth says it was harder than he thought it would be to finish the album. When he and Allen Reynolds were in the studio putting it together, he says, they discovered that in some shows the recording equipment was picking up sounds that weren't coming from him or the band. "You'll get a great cut," Garth said, "and right in the middle of it, there's a 'Welcome to McDonald's, can I take your order, please?' off a wireless unit somewhere down the block."

Fans all over America flocked into every retail outlet where *Garth Brooks: Double Live* was on sale. And guess what? Wal-Mart said that *Double Live* had "the largest single-day music sales in the history of our company." By December 5, the report was in: Garth had sold 1,085,000 copies of *Double Live* in its first week on sale.

In December it was also reported that *The Hits* had surpassed the 10 million mark. Garth now had three albums certified in excess of 10 million: *No Fences, Ropin' the Wind,* and *The Hits.* He is the only solo artist in history to have three albums surpass the 10-million-copy mark.

The Billboard Music Awards, televised live on Fox from Grand Garden Arena at the MGM Grand Hotel on December 7, opened with Garth flying through the air on a harness while singing "Ain't Goin' Down." When he came back down to earth, Garth was flying again—he won awards for Country Artist of the Year, Male Albums Artist of the Year, Country Singles Artist of the Year, and Country Albums Artist of the Year. This brought his Billboard Music Awards total to twenty-four, more than any other artist in history.

But the most exciting moment of the evening for Garth was when his biggest idol, James Taylor, after whom his first daughter was named, was given the Century Award, *Billboard*'s highest honor for distinguished creative achievement.

Garth celebrated the holiday season in style. At the request of Elizabeth Dole, he performed on the holiday television special *The American Red Cross Celebrates Real Life Miracles*. And, with First Lady Hillary Clinton, Garth lit the Rockefeller Center Christmas tree—26,000 lights—as 100,000 people stood in the clear, cold New York night. Millions more watched on TV as they had done since 1951, when the tree lighting was televised for the first time on NBC's *The Kate Smith Show*.

"*This* has been the best year of my life," Garth said, when looking back on 1998.

After his record-shattering tour, Garth was taking at least a year off from live playing. His management company would close its doors and the staff would take some time off. His fan club magazine, *believer*, closed down with the last issue of 1998. "The people in my organization have been running at this pace for ten years," he said. "They deserve a break." During the time off, they'd all still be on salary, he said.

Garth would stay home in Nashville with his family and work on several projects, including a TV movie for Christmas

1999, *The Colors of Christmas,* and a feature film about a singing star, called *The Lamb,* both produced by Red Strokes Productions. Each movie would have a soundtrack that Garth was now working on. Garth said he had set a new goal for himself: selling 100 million copies of his albums by the end of the decade. "I figure if I just take care of the music, everything else will take care of itself," he said.

In January of 1999, at the American Music Awards, Garth presented the Special Award of Merit to Billy Joel after winning his own awards for Favorite Country Artist and Album of the Year for *Sevens.*

A duet album with Trisha Yearwood, long hoped for by both singers and their fans, would probably come out in the year 2000, Garth said, when the two would tour together again. Something to look forward to!

Something Trisha had long looked forward to happened on a Saturday night in February, when she was inducted into the Grand Ole Opry. Garth's longtime friend, backup singer, opening act, and duet partner looked dazzling as she sang her first hit, "She's in Love with the Boy."

Another friend of Garth's had his own good news: Steve Wariner's *Burnin' the Roadhouse Down* had been certifed gold. Wariner had a new album slated for release in May, and the first single was "Two Teardrops," which he wrote with Whispering Bill Anderson. Steve had performed the song at a Nashville party celebrating the gold record, and a bootleg of that performance had found its way to radio. Listeners loved the song so much that country radio started requesting official copies for airplay. Capitol Records rushed the single to them, and it started climbing the charts.

On March 15, the Rock and Roll Hall of Fame in Cleveland, Ohio, inducted Bob Wills, calling him an early influence on rock and roll. When he heard the news, Willie Nelson said, "If anybody in the music business or music history deserves it, he does. His music makes you move and feel good—it *is* rock and roll."

How amazing music is. Bob Wills was the pioneer who brought together the sounds of swing, jazz, Tin Pan Alley, boogie-woogie, and Texas folk music. He synthesized the music of black people, white people, Hispanic people, Polish people—all people—and, in the 1930s, '40s, and '50s, united sophisticated city dwellers and laid-back country folk into one big crowd of music-lovin' fools. Bob Wills inspired Merle Haggard so much that in 1970, Haggard released *A Tribute to the Best Damn Fiddle Player in the World (or My Salute to Bob Wills)*, which hooked George Strait on western swing and country music.

What's even more amazing is that Bob Wills was almost turned away from the Grand Ole Opry because he wanted to bring horns and drums inside, and George Strait was almost turned away from Nashville because he was considered "too country."

Then George Strait's brand of country music turned the KISS- and Queen-loving Garth Brooks into a country singer—who then turned music on its head by mixing traditional country with pedal-to-the-metal rock and roll.

Now Garth was saying he'd like to record an album of George Strait cover songs, favorites of his that had never been released as singles, like "Blame It on Mexico," "She's a Barmaid in the Honky-Tonk Downstairs," and "Overnight Male." Garth also loved the only song George ever wrote himself, "I Can't See Texas from Here." For his part, George Strait said he enjoyed the fact that people like Garth were citing him as an influence on their music. "I think Garth Brooks was the first one who said something to me, and it took me back a little," he says. "I never set out to be an influence on anybody. Once I thought about it—and how I looked up to people like Merle Haggard, George Jones, and Bob Wills and remembered how I felt about those people—then I felt real honored."

In March the RIAA announced it was introducing a new level of certification, the Diamond, for albums that sold 10 million copies or more. Shania Twain was eligible for *The Woman in Me,* Kenny Rogers for his *Greatest Hits,* and Garth Brooks for an amazing three albums.

When the Academy of Country Music announced its nominations, also in March, Garth was nominated for Album of the Year for *Double Live,* Top Male Vocalist of the Year, and, once again, Entertainer of the Year. He and Steve Wariner got a nomination for Vocal Event of the Year for "Burnin' the Roadhouse Down." Steve Wariner was nominated for Single, Song, and Video of the Year for "Holes in the Floor of Heaven." Trisha Yearwood and Martina McBride were nominated for Female Vocalist of the Year.

"I do think you need to try to give back something of what everybody is giving you," Garth said. Certainly he has given a lot, not only to Feed the Children but to many other charitable causes. From the time he had contributed $1,000 of his first $10,000 record deal to keep the Tennessee minister and his family from getting evicted at Christmas, Garth Brooks has been known as one of the most generous people in the entertainment industry. He is a shining example of using one's stardom to make a difference in people's lives.

Up until the time Joe Harris died, he and Garth had been trying to find a building in Nashville for Feed the Children. "It was Joe's dream to find a center to supply the whole southeastern region," Shirley Harris said. Larry Jones was all for it, and almost a year after Joe's death, a huge warehouse building in an industrial section of Nashville became Feed the Children's Nashville headquarters. Shirley became a part-time employee.

"People had been bringing in used clothes and yard-sale clothes, and volunteers would come in and help me iron them," Shirley said. She and Steve Highfill, who heads up Feed the Children's Nashville operation, worked on getting companies to donate new items. A room on the second floor near Shirley's office soon became a "store" called Kids World. Local churches and social service organizations bring in children—whose families have little or no money—to "shop" for free.

"These very needy children never get to go shopping," Shirley said. "They'll never know what it is to walk in a store and pick out their own clothes and toys." Joe Harris, Jr., said, "I wish my daddy had been alive to see all those kids and see their eyes. They were saying, 'You mean we can take this stuff?' The look on their faces, my dad would have eaten this up." When those kids stop in Shirley's office, they see a platinum record plaque inscribed to Joe Harris commemorating the sale of nine million copies of *Ropin' the Wind.* "Every time Garth got one of these platinum plaques for his records, he made sure to give Joe one of them," Shirley said. Everyone who visits the Feed the Children warehouse in Nashville passes a plaque in the lobby that says, "This Building Is Dedicated to the Memory of Joe Harris, Friend of Feed the Children."

One way Garth was making a difference in 1999 was by teaming up with major-league baseball players and corporations to help needy children. In early 1999 he announced his project, "Touch 'Em All: Teammates for Kids," a foundation that earns money for children's charities based on players hitting home runs, stealing bases, or striking out batters. The idea had come from talking with baseball players when he worked out briefly with the San Diego Padres in the spring of '98: for every home run hit, a player will donate $1,000. A corporation or celebrity will match it for a total of $3,000 per homer (strikeouts are $100, stolen bases $200).

Garth joined the San Diego Padres spring training camp in Peoria, Arizona, in the spring of 1999 both to fulfill his lifelong dream of playing major-league baseball and to draw attention to his foundation. Instead of paying him a salary, the Padres contributed $200,000 to the Touch 'Em All Foundation. Garth wore number 77, because 7, his lucky number, was taken.

Well, Garth Brooks gave it his all, first by signing autographs for hours after every game and then by being, according to Padres general manager Kevin Towers, "an inspiration to our players. The passion he had for the game of baseball and the way he went about it," Towers said, "is a great reminder for all of us."

Garth wound up his spring training season 1 for 22, and said, "I just hope they remember how bad I wanted to be good."

Coming in the fall of 1999: a pop album, a prequel sound track to the film *The Lamb*. Produced by Don Was, who is better known in the rock world for his work on albums by the Rolling Stones and many others, the album, called *Garth Brooks in "The Life of Chris Gaines,"* leads off with both a pop and country single. The movie is due sometime in the year 2000 and is about an overzealous female fan and a superstar musician. Although Garth is starring as the title character in a video of one of the singles, he hasn't decided whether he will star in the theatrical movie.

A movie? A pop album? Why not? What's the point of becoming one of the biggest entertainers and the biggest musical artist of your time if you can't try to stretch in new directions?

"*The* common theme that's running through all my songs," says Garth, "is that it's usually about passion—the feel for believing in the small guy and believing in the underdog."

Chasing dreams, striving, refusing to compromise, taking risks, being real, and celebrating life's everyday moments—the things he sings about in his songs are the story of Garth's own life. They explain why Troyal Garth Brooks, of all those 318,090 people born in February 1962 (and of all the millions of others born every year here in the great USA) was able to become one of the biggest stories of America in the twentieth century. He was, after all, not much different from the rest of us. He just decided to live to the max—and dared to do it publicly. The simple truth is that he was willing to work his butt off to get what he wants.

"I don't think anyone has wanted success as much as he did," Pam Lewis said. "He was amazingly driven."

Garth Brooks has achieved staggering album sales, unheard-of concert grosses, unprecedented fame, and the total devotion of millions of fans. He did it by doing what he loves best—getting up on a stage, playing his music, and giving it everything he's got.

"He always wanted it so bad and loved it so much that he got it," J.D. said. "He is the flag bearer for country music. He's the example, a shining star, the number-one representative of country music worldwide." What's even better, J.D. says, is that Garth "is the nicest, most accommodating guy."

It must feel like an awesome responsibility to know that so many millions of people hold you on so high a pedestal. And if Garth doesn't always measure up to the large ideals he seems to represent, well, that just proves he's one of us, with all of the conflicts, contradictions, and fears we struggle with.

Garth has always honored the best in his fans, even while showing us, through some of his songs, the times we fall short. That's part of why we love him, for reflecting who we are, for showing that we're all just here trying our best. His belief in us, in himself, in God, and in America is unwavering.

"I think one reason Garth and my father got along so well," Joe Harris, Jr., said, "is that they looked at the moral aspects of life and looked at the Lord in the same way. They followed the same path."

Garth once told the *Los Angeles Times*, "You want to make a difference. When it's all over, you want to look back and think somehow the world didn't spin quite the same way it did before you were here."

Music will never spin the way it did before Garth Brooks. "Like Jimmie Rodgers and Hank Williams," Ira Fraitag said, "Garth is a pioneer who stretched the boundaries and kicked open doors and then withstood a hail of criticism by industry insiders and know-it-alls. Garth taught them it's what you learn after you know it all that counts."

"I wanted to be an artist the American people could relate to," Garth told *Playboy*. "I wanted to be America's guy."

Well, he is.

"He's a human being, somebody I could see myself living next door to," said Taya Branton. "He seems like a great husband and father. He is genuinely grateful for what he has in life. He doesn't act like a star—he's down to earth and loyal to his fans."

Pop your copy of *Double Live* into the stereo. Remember the show—or imagine you're there. Feel the music, sing the songs, and celebrate this: the 1990s are ending just as they began—with Garth Brooks on top.

"It's a cool ride," Garth says about his journey through America in the last decade of the twentieth century, even though it was bumpy in the middle. "As long as it lasts, I'll keep riding."

Listen carefully to the lyrics of "It's Your Song." How long it lasts is up to us. Garth is the lightning. We are the thunder.

ACKNOWLEDGMENTS

I've got friends in all kinds of places. They give me love and laughter, courage and compassion, great fun and wonderful conversation. If friends are blessings, I've been blessed with more than my share. You all know who you are and I thank you.

Bob Martone—whom my husband has called "Bubba" since they both learned to talk—is good at many things but the best at being a friend. It is my pleasure to dedicate this book to him.

Speaking of husbands, I'm very lucky to have one who is also a friend. Ira Fraitag is smart, funny, patient, and kind—and one of the finest music men in the business. Without him, I could never have written this book. His connections in the music business smoothed what would have been a much more difficult path. His knowledge and insights about music have benefited not only myself but every artist, musician, songwriter, and colleague he's ever worked with.

My family is another source of strength and wisdom for me. My father, Dominick A. Sgammato, and my mother, Mary A. Sgammato, have devoted themselves to being wonderful parents. I hope I've been at least as good a daughter. My sister, Mary Sgammato, is funny, smart, and a great friend, as is her husband, Robert Figueroa. To say I am nuts about my nephew Alex Figueroa doesn't even begin to tell the story.

A special thanks to my other "sister," Ginny Nanni, who loved country music when I was still one of those rock and rollers who wondered why. Now I know why.

All of my aunts, uncles, and cousins (and I'll save lots of ink by not naming them all) exemplify the best traditions of a big family and add even more blessings to my life. I want to particularly thank my aunt and godmother, Theresa Bloch, for taking such good care of our cats, Sam and Dave, during our many music business road trips.

For career guidance, smart advice, tons of knowledge, and more laughs per minute than the law allows, I once again thank the music mavens at Entertainment Management Group—Ira Fraitag, Sol Saffian, and Jerry Cohen.

Three of my dear friends—Laurie Kraman, Claire Griffin, and Ali Sgammato—all said the same thing when I told them how busy I was writing this book: "How can I help?" When I realized they were serious, I put each of them to work on complicated research assignments. They all came through quickly, professionally, and cheerfully, and I can't thank them enough.

Invaluable research assistance was also provided by:

- Judith Mandelbaum, Vice President of Research Services, Burrelle's Information Services
- Lauren Bufferd, Country Music Foundation Library
- the library staff of the Museum of Television and Radio
- Judy Mizell at the Grand Ole Opry
- Mark Apostle and Louise M. Gallup-Roholt at NBC
- Helen Sanders at Carson Productions Group
- Mandy Wilson at the Country Music Association

The wizards at Tekserve in New York City and All Service Computer Rental (especially Bob Motamedi) made it possible for to me complete this book by keeping the computer running.

Ruth Koppel, Rob Schulman, Hubie Synn, and the community at the Integral Yoga Institute kept me running through the writing of this book, as they have done for years.

George Kerrigan, Jimmy Harris, and Elizabeth Freid managed to make my author photo look better than I do. Thanks!

It is the fortunate author who is published at Ballantine Books, and I'd like to thank Cathy Repetti, Betsy Flagler, Gareth Rees, Nancy Sheppard, George Fisher, Stanley Cohen, Ronda Stevens, Gina Centrello, Betsy Elias, Ruth Ross, Alex Klapwald, Eileen Gaffney, and copyeditor extraordinaire Peter Grennen. A special thanks to early supporters of this book, George Bick, Judith Curr, and Linda Grey.

To all the fans and all the songwriters and musicians who make the music: thanks for the fun!

Oh, and one more thing: If you agree with me that Feed the Children is doing some of the most important work of any organization around, why not help them out? The address is: Feed the Children, P.O. Box 36, Oklahoma City, OK 73101.

ABOUT THE AUTHOR

Jo Sgammato, a former book publishing executive, is a journalist who writes about popular culture, music, and health and spiritual issues. She is the *New York Times* bestselling author of *For the Music: The Vince Gill Story, Keepin' It Country: The George Strait Story, Dream Come True: The LeAnn Rimes Story,* and *Country's Greatest Duo: The Brooks & Dunn Story.* A certified Integral Yoga instructor, she also coauthored *The Muscle Memory Method: Easy, All-Day Fitness for a Strong, Firm, Younger Body* with New York fitness expert Marjorie Jaffe. She divides her time between New York and Nashville.